Advance praise for
Michael Bassin's *I Am Not a Spy*

"Michael Bassin has given us an indispensable understanding of why Arab-Israeli peace continues to elude the diplomats, even as he imagines a future Middle East freed of its poisonous obsession with Israel and the Jews."
—Yossi Klein Halevi, Senior fellow, Shalom Hartman Institute

"What makes Michael's book come alive is not the politics of the region but the wonderful variety of people he meets on his journeys."
—L. E. Scheier, YA author

"Written from different vantage points as an American Jewish exchange student and later on as an Israeli soldier, Michael Bassin's journey is fraught by tense and dangerous encounters and numerous scary as well as comical misunderstandings. Nevertheless, this extremely entertaining and well-written memoir gives people plenty of reason to hope for a better future as Bassin shows how people on different sides of a deeply painful conflict can put their biases aside and see each other's common humanity."
—Khaled Abu Toameh, Palestinian Affairs columnist for the *Jerusalem Post*

"Michael Bassin's work is a unique and refreshing story of understanding and misunderstanding in the Middle East. Bassin brings readers straight into the messy, complicated, and contradictory hearts and minds of many types of people in the Middle East. He does so without promoting any particular political agenda, except for genuinely wanting to improve the relationship between Jews and Arabs."
—Josh Block, CEO of The Israel Project

"Bassin undertook the daunting experiment of studying in the Arab world and revealing his Jewish identity. The resulting adventure—predictable, surprising, scary, heartwarming—is both insightful and a vicarious pleasure."
—Dr. Daniel Pipes, President of the Middle East Forum

"*I Am Not a Spy* is a fascinating read for anyone who has an interest in the Middle East, and who cares about getting a deeper understanding of the challenges preventing Jews and Arabs from building bridges. It is fast-paced, sometimes funny, sometimes tragic, but most importantly extremely insightful and eye-opening."

—Danny Ayalon, Israeli Deputy Foreign Minister and
Israeli Ambassador to the United States

"Michael Bassin has succeeded in *I Am Not a Spy* in capturing the surreal nature of much Middle Eastern political discussion—the conspiracies, the prejudices, the long-held grudges. The chapters in particular on the UAE present a fascinating and little reported picture of life in that country, for foreigners and Emiratis alike. A worthy book containing fascinating insights."

—Dr. Jonathan Spyer, Director of the Rubin Center and
author of *The Transforming Fire: The Rise of the Israel-Islamist Conflict*

"Not many Jews dare undertake this experiment on Arab turf. Michael Bassin did, and his experiences are as enlightening as they are enthralling. With endless optimism and a sense of adventure, *I Am Not a Spy* captures the essence of Jews facing Arabs, and to no lesser degree, of Israel in the Middle East."

—Elhanan Miller, Journalist and Palestinian politics researcher at the
Forum for Regional Thinking

"This candid memoir shows the challenges—the pervasive disinformation and enmity—that peacemakers face in the Middle East. However, Michael's travels and interactions acted to counterbalance misconceptions and to change the region for the better. A must-read for those who want a genuine account of public opinion on the streets of the Arab world."

—Ilan Grapel, former American-Israeli political prisoner in Egypt

Dear Paula & Harold,
Thanks for all your support!
— Michael Bassin

I Am Not
a Spy

An American Jew Goes Deep in
the Arab World and Israeli Army

Michael Bassin

WiDo Publishing • Salt Lake City

WiDo Publishing
Salt Lake City, Utah
widopublishing.com

Cover design by Rachel Schneider
Book design by Marny K. Parkin

ISBN: 978-1-937178-88-8

Printed in the United States of America

To Mom and Dad,
for supporting my life decisions even when they scared you to death

Contents

Foreword
by David Horovitz — 9

Chapter 1
"California Dreaming" — 11

Chapter 2
Killing Is All They Know — 23

Chapter 3
A Peace of Paper — 37

Chapter 4
The Egyptian Way — 56

Chapter 5
This Is Not a Mosque — 71

Chapter 6
Starbucks Is Evil — 94

Chapter 7
A House Built of Sand — 107

Chapter 8
America Is a Lie — 124

Chapter 9
A Man of Virtue — 145

Chapter 10
I Caught Osama — 160

Chapter 11
A Strange Jewish Wonderland   184

Chapter 12
The Chocolate of the Jews   205

Chapter 13
Real Men of Hezbollah   219

Chapter 14
The Good Jew   241

Chapter 15
An Arabic-Speaking James Bond   248

Chapter 16
Palestinians Are Your Grandparents   260

Chapter 17
A Patrol of Fear   276

Chapter 18
The Law Isn't Always the Law   294

Chapter 19
A Final Resolution   313

Terms/Glossary   327

Acknowledgments   330

About the Author   332

Foreword

MICHAEL BASSIN IS AN UNUSUALLY COURAGEOUS, CURIOUS and well-intentioned young man. Why so? Because he elected to go study and build friendships in the Arab world. And he just so happens to be Jewish. Oh, and a Zionist to boot, who later goes on to serve as a combat soldier in the Israeli Army.

This open-hearted young man's sojourn as a student in the Middle East, which we might like to think would be straightforward and unremarkable, proves near-impossibly complex. Almost every interaction is fraught and complicated. Misunderstanding is everywhere. Hostility is often nearby. And real, life-threatening danger intrudes on more than one occasion.

While innumerable pundits churn out rivers of words about how to deal with the challenges of the Middle East in general and Islamic extremism in particular, Michael Bassin got on a plane, learned Arabic, and spent some time actually living in the region. His book is candid and eye-opening, often disheartening, occasionally encouraging—an unembroidered insight into the lives, the thinking, the preoccupations and the misconceptions of the young Arabs with whom he studies and hangs out. And what it highlights most of all is how profoundly miseducation can pollute young minds, and how openness, dialogue and interaction are the only antidote. The simple fact of his presence, and the wisdom with which he negotiates the obstacles his presence creates, impacts everyone with whom he comes into contact, and matures Bassin himself as well.

Policymakers should read this emphatically non-wonkish book, and internalize that healing the rifts, and conquering those misconceptions, between the West and the Arab world requires a strategic focus on education. Replicate Michael Bassin's brave foray many times over, bring young Westerners and young Arabs into ongoing, open conduct, start shattering stereotypes, and you might, just might, start to make the world a better, and a safer place.

David Horovitz,
Editor-in-Chief of *The Times of Israel*

Chapter 1
"California Dreaming"

A *RE YOU NUTTIER THAN A FRUITCAKE?*
My father will ask this question if you tell him an idea he thinks is fundamentally ridiculous and devoid of sense to save you from yourself before it's too late. In his mind, if he must ask the fruitcake question, you should stop in your tracks and reconsider your idea immediately. And if you don't, proceed at your own risk and don't operate any heavy machinery.

I couldn't stop asking myself the fruitcake question as I stared out the window on my red-eye flight to Dubai, anxious and unable to sleep. I sat in an empty row, so I had plenty of space to myself. Nevertheless, my eyes would not shut as I thought about what I was doing.

My parents were terrified about my decision to do a university exchange for a semester in Sharjah, just twenty minutes west of Dubai. Sharjah was the third largest of the seven emirates comprising the United Arab Emirates (UAE).

I was a proud pro-Israel American Jew, passionate about the pursuit of peace in the Middle East between Israel and her neighbors. I wanted to interact with people who held different views than me, who could help me understand how Arabs perceived the Arab-Israeli conflict and how, in their eyes, a lasting peace could be achieved. However, my parents' fears were legitimate. It was August 2006 and the Second Lebanon War between Israel and Hezbollah still raged. Israeli soldiers were pushing deeper into southern Lebanon and Hezbollah was still firing thousands of rockets at Israel. Arabs across the Middle East had taken to the streets to protest their governments' refusal to attack Israel and stand up for their Arab brethren.

I had spent a summer studying Arabic in Cairo, where I saw hundreds of protesters in the streets chanting, "The Arab nation will not eat, will not sleep, and will fight until Israel and all its Zionist followers are wiped out." That was me they were chanting about.

My parents would have preferred I'd just gone back for my junior year at George Washington University (GW) instead of the American University of Sharjah (AUS). Which, in their view, was going into enemy territory again.

"I'll be fine!" I told my parents a few days before flying to the UAE. After all, it wasn't like I was registering for classes at the Al Qaeda College for Explosives Engineering. The American University of Sharjah was an English language, American-style university in the UAE, the Beverly Hills of the Arab world. I specifically chose to study in this oil-rich Persian Gulf nation to engage with educated Arabs in moderate, well-off countries. Those were the people I believed I would most relate to and who would most relate to me, as opposed to the poverty-stricken people that make up the majority of the population in poorer Arab countries.

The AUS student body sounded extremely diverse. Only twenty percent of the students were local Emiratis. Another thirty percent were Saudi Arabian, Iranian, or Palestinian.

"With friends like these who needs enemies?" my father asked me cynically. "Saudi Arabia. Iran! Palestinians! I don't think this is the best time for an American Jew like you to be going off to study in an Arab country, especially not after another Arab-Israeli war. What if people over there hold you accountable?"

"Why would anyone hold me accountable?" I snapped back. "I'm not an Israeli soldier. I'm an American."

"It's not a good idea," my mother said, siding with my father.

"Let's compromise," I suggested. "I'll still go. I just won't tell anyone I'm Jewish."

After that, my parents agreed and I began mentally preparing myself to deny the rich religious and cultural heritage that formed an enormous piece of my identity.

But, as I sat on the plane to the UAE, I stared into the monitor, watching the airplane blip approach Dubai International Airport. I went numb with the thought of disavowing my identity to everyone I met during my exchange.

Hiding my Jewish identity seemed cowardly. I wanted to study in the Arab world to connect with Arab moderates and advance the vision of peaceful, prosperous relations between the Arab world, America, and Israel. How could I build lasting bonds with people to whom I'd lied?

Eventually people would find out my true identity. All they'd have to do is see a photo of me on Facebook with a kippah on my head and that would be it. They'd remember me as a liar, a coward, and a Jew—in that order. What a great emissary I'd be.

No, I could not lie about who I was. That would have been nuttier than any fruitcake. If I planned to lie, there was no point in going. But I also realized that if a fatal tragedy befell me while I was gone, my parents would blame themselves for the rest of their lives and I would be remembered as a naive fool.

My plane touched down on the tarmac and I knew I had to decide something or I would drive myself crazy. I decided that I'd only discuss being Jewish when directly asked about it. If no one asked about my religion, no one needed to know. If they did need to know, so help me God.

After exiting the airplane, I walked through the Dubai airport terminal. Fake flying saucers hung from the ceiling, adding to the feel of being on a different planet. Stepping outside into the extreme August heat, even at midnight, was like entering an alien environment to which I'd never totally adjust. I hailed a taxi and, as my Indian Sikh driver put my suitcases in the trunk, I watched some US servicemen laugh at a fellow soldier whose glasses had fogged up in the humidity.

Despite it being the middle of the night, traffic was bumper-to-bumper the entire forty-minute drive to Sharjah. Wide boulevards and skyscrapers made up the Dubai landscape. These were replaced by massive sand dunes and empty roads as we drove out of the city toward Sharjah.

Sharjah was an emirate with a particularly strict Islamic orientation, where swimming at the beach required full body covering and drinking alcohol in public was strictly forbidden.

We reached the entrance to University City, the district housing all of Sharjah's universities. My taxi stopped at a security checkpoint. All of University City was partitioned off with a twelve-foot high fence that trailed off as far as I could see. I felt like I was entering a prison.

A smiling security guard sporting a thick moustache and wearing a neatly pressed black uniform asked me in Arabic for my student ID.

"I am a new student in this university," I belted out in mangled Arabic. "I don't have an ID yet."

The guard grinned.

"I need your ID or you can't come in," he said.

"How can I have a student ID if I've never been here before?" I asked.

"You cannot go inside without an ID."

Caught in a catch-22, I abandoned the Arabic and in English, demanded he call his supervisor to get this straightened out. The guard whipped out his cell phone, made the call, and put the phone on speaker.

"Hallo, hallo," a choppy voice said.

"Yes, hello," I answered. "My name is Michael Bassin and—," the voice cut me off.

"Ah, that is enough. I am expecting a Michael Samuel Jeffrey Carl Bassin. This is you?"

"Yes," I said with a sigh.

Strangely, my semester exchange application to AUS had required me to fill out my full name and my father's and grandfather's names too. I complied, though I didn't know why the school needed to know the name of my dead Grandpa Carl. Later, when I received my student ID, I saw that my father and grandfather's names had officially been added to my full name in accordance with local custom.

Once past the security guard, the taxi driver dropped me off at my dormitory, one of twelve gender-segregated dormitories on campus. At the door, another security guard buzzed me in. Once inside all I saw was white: white walls, white tile floors, and bearded men in white robes. For a moment, I thought the color disappearance was due to the humidity and jet lag, but as I made my way further into the building, I realized the color wasn't returning. Everything was just really white. As I walked passed them, some of the bearded men giggled and whispered in an Arabic dialect I couldn't understand.

A bearded security guard with slicked back hair waved me to his office. As I sat in front of his metal desk, he gave me a packet of paperwork to fill out and explained some rules.

"Curfew is at twelve o'clock," he said. "If you break curfew three times, I will call your parents."

"Just so you know, I don't think my parents would really care about me breaking the curfew," I said. "There's no such thing at universities in the US."

"Well, for your sake, I hope I don't have to test your confidence!" he warned.

I rolled my eyes as I handed him the paperwork I had filled out, and then headed to my room.

Before reaching my room, however, I was distracted by some white robed men loitering in the hall. I had come here to immerse myself in the local culture, and if I was going to fit in and forge bonds, I needed a white robe too. I dropped my bags in my room then stepped into the hallway and tapped a tall, robe-wearing gentleman on the shoulder.

"Excuse me, my name is Michael. Where can I get a robe?" I asked.

Taken a bit off guard by my openness, he introduced himself as Rashid from Abu Dhabi. He then pulled me down the white corridor to his room and called out in Arabic for some of his friends to join us. Nine identically dressed Emiratis piled into his dorm room, squawking and shrieking from the excitement of entertaining a western guest. Their remedial English meant they probably weren't going to initiate a highly intense religious or political conversation that night, much to my relief.

"Michael, you like UAE?" one asked eagerly.

The room went quiet and their curious eyes all fell on me. These Emiratis lived in a country dominated by foreigners, where nearly eighty-five percent of the population carried a non-UAE passport.

I was surprised that my new friends acted like I was the first outsider with whom they'd ever spoken.

"I love the UAE!" I screamed, determined to flatter my hosts. "The UAE is the best. I want to be an Emirati just like you."

The room erupted with cheers and my new friends jumped up and down excitedly. I had no idea what they were so excited about, but I played along. A fat, sweaty Emirati grabbed me by the shoulders and shouted, "You are a piece of my butt!" Seeing my confusion, he explained it was a compliment in Emirati culture.

"I'm a piece of your butt? You're a piece of my butt!" I replied. "That's what I'm talking about."

When our throats grew sore from shrieking, they circled around me and taught me how they greet one another. Two boys stood face-to-face, shook hands, and bumped their noses together.

"Now you try," Rashid urged.

I looked at the fat, sweaty Emirati straight in the eye, banged my nose against his, and proclaimed proudly that he was a piece of my butt. The group continued to cheer and I felt like the sheikh of cross-cultural interaction. Rashid opened his closet door and revealed a wardrobe of ten indistinguishable white robes. He pulled one out of the closet and handed it to me gently.

"This is special white robe for Emirati people," he said. "It is called *kandura*. This you wear on the head is *ghutrah*. It is yours. You are now real Emirati."

I promised my new friends I would wear my *kandura* and *ghutrah* on the first day of classes three days later. I headed off to bed shortly thereafter feeling accepted, secure, and glad to be a part of my new friends' butts.

If my new Emirati friends from my dorm block convinced me I'd entered an alternative universe, the rest of the student body I met in the few days before classes started made me wonder if I was California dreaming.

Though most were observant of Islam on some level and dressed modestly by American standards, they were infatuated with American culture and seemed to know more about what was going on in Hollywood than in Abu Dhabi. No matter where they were from in the

Middle East, their English skills were impeccable and they had spot-on American accents. Many seemed to just want to discuss topics on every American college student's mind: partying, hook-ups, and booze.

An Egyptian girl wearing a hijab described how she wanted an American boyfriend like the main character from *Dawson's Creek* and club-hopping Saudis boasted of how much they could binge drink on an average weekend. While dome-covered buildings, marble-tiled white walkways, and tall thick pillars may have given AUS an Arabian mystique, the KFC, Burger King, and Pizza Hut on campus made me question whether I'd left home at all.

I immediately started to feel like I was back in the US hanging out with the children of first generation immigrants, rather than living in a country right in between Saudi Arabia and Iran. While it wasn't exactly the experience I was expecting, I reveled in how easy it was to make friends and how welcoming and open the student body was.

I bought a cell phone my third day in Sharjah, and while I sat with a group of robed and veiled Arab girls flirting with me, my father called. I put my father on speakerphone so he could hear how wonderful things were going for me, proving that studying in Sharjah had been the right decision. As we talked, one of the girls pulled the phone out of my hand and yelled, "We love Michael! Thank you for sending him to us!"

The night before school started, a Syrian girl invited me to grab dinner at the Mall of the Emirates with a group of a dozen guy friends. We drove to the mall in three high-end luxury sedans, blasting Sean Paul music.

We ate at a Chili's Grill and Bar in the food court then headed back to campus. We reached AUS right before midnight and hung out in the parking lot to kill time until curfew. The guys discussed classes and cars while I stood by quietly, perfectly content, thrilled to be among the people I'd hoped to connect with.

A heavyset Syrian with a short ponytail and goatee suddenly turned to me and asked the question that would change everyone's perception of me for the rest of the semester.

"*Shoo dinak?*" he asked. What's your religion?

I knew the moment would come when my new friends would attempt to get to know me on a more personal level, and few topics were more personal than religion. So, surrounded by those I thought were supportive members of the Michael Bassin fan club, I grabbed the bull by the horns and unleashed the truth.

"*Ana Yehudi,*" I declared. I am a Jew.

Silence filled the parking lot, their wide eyes exposed red veins usually hidden by eyelids. Each person smiled radiantly from ear to ear, but the color of their faces turned as white as the *kandura* I planned on wearing to class the next day. No one said anything for a full ten seconds. The Syrian girl who invited me stared at the pavement. The deafening quiet was eventually broken by the sound of fingers pressing buttons on cell phones. I wondered who they were texting and what they were texting about.

"Where are you from in America?" the pony-tailed Syrian asked me to end the awkwardness.

It was a nice try, but he'd already asked me that question earlier in the evening. He then turned to the others and they began speaking to each other in Arabic, presumably about me. I stood there silently, feeling ignored and suddenly deeply alone. I considered hastily saying goodbye and rushing back to my dorm, but I thought that would be awkward and perhaps offensive.

After about ten minutes, a thin, dark-skinned guy with wavy black hair sprinted towards us from one of the dorm blocks. I didn't know him yet, but his face was plastered with a smile I so badly wanted to trust.

"Are you Michael?" he asked.

I nodded.

"I am Hassan. Our friends here sent me a text message about you. They said I should meet you. I'd like to be your friend. We would all like to be your friends."

I shook hands with Hassan and told him I would like that very much. Hassan then shared that he was a Palestinian who'd lived his whole life until then in Abu Dhabi. He studied mass communications and hoped to work for a digital media company. As he spoke about himself, my nerves calmed and I began feeling more comfortable. After a few more minutes of conversation, everyone said goodnight and left the parking lot.

As I walked back to my dorm alone in the sweltering humidity, I pondered how extreme heat could drive people mad and trick them into seeing and believing impossible things. Distinguishing reality from make-believe is difficult when temperatures soar beyond one hundred and ten degrees and life becomes one heroic effort to escape the devastating heat.

So, I couldn't really be sure of what to think of my interaction with Hassan and his friends. I wanted to believe that despite their clear surprise at hearing that I was a Jew, they saw me as their peer, accepted me, and were genuine about including me in their social circle. But deep inside my gut I had a terrible feeling of dread. Was my intuition trying to tell me something? Or was I feeling insecure due to exhaustion from the heat and the stress of being somewhere unfamiliar?

The next morning before classes began I walked with four Emiratis I'd met my first night over to the Student Center cafeteria, the large building that served as the main campus hangout spot. Strolling around with them, I noticed other students giving me weird glances and looking at me slightly confused, like they couldn't tell if I was real or a mirage.

From the back, I looked just like the other four Emirati boys who walked by my side, all decked out in *kanduras* and *ghutrahs*. There was nothing unusual about Emiratis walking around together in their surprisingly comfortable heat-retardant robes. But, one by one, people circled the five of us to stare at my light-skinned face, look into my exotic green eyes, ogle my earring and eyebrow ring, and gawk upon discovering that I was not your average Emirati, but an imposter.

My Emirati friends giggled nervously from the excessive attention, particularly when the Emirati girls glanced over. People watched in astonishment when my Emirati friends and I bumped noses before we split to attend class.

Waiting in line to order a *halal*-certified Whopper from the campus Burger King, I was tapped on the shoulder by a Palestinian freshman whom I'd met earlier in the week. His name was Mohammad, but I called him Mo for short.

"Hi. Um, I have a question for you," he said nervously.

"Ask me anything," I replied.

"Well there's a story going around campus that . . ."

Mo grew fidgety and uncomfortable.

"That what, Mo?" I asked.

I grabbed my whopper value meal while he stuttered all the way to the table.

"That you're a . . . a."

"A Jew?"

"That's it!"

"It's true."

"How did you get into this country?" he asked in astonishment. "Jews are banned from coming here!"

"That's not true. It doesn't even say I'm Jewish in my passport."

He looked horrified.

"Is it true your Jewish holy books order you to hurt Muslims and cheat them in business?" he asked.

"What? Who told you that?" I shot back defensively.

"We know your books teach you to enslave Muslims and deceive them."

The accusation sounded crazy coming from a person who spoke English with a near spot-on American accent.

"Mo, you're just deceiving yourself."

"They teach us this in the mosque. It says in the Qur'an never to trust the Jews! They are all manipulative and deceiving, and dress as imposters!"

I glanced down at the white robes I wore and thought that, by the looks of things, he had a point.

"Mo, who told you that I'm a Jew in the first place?" I asked.

"My brother," he claimed. "He and his friends say you're dangerous. They're telling people not to talk to you."

"Who is your brother and what does he know about me?"

"My brother is Hassan. He said he met you in the parking lot last night. You made his friends piss their pants when you told them you're a Jew."

Hassan and his friends were behind this? But they told me they were my friends. They seemed so open and welcoming. They loved rap music, partying, fancy cars and, apparently, anti-Semitic conspiracy theories too.

"Why would your brother tell me he wanted to be my friend and then tell people not to talk to me?"

"Because he wanted you to trust him. And because him and his friends are afraid of you."

"Why would they be afraid of me?"

"Because Jews are capable of anything! They lie about everything."

"But it's your brother who lied to me. Doesn't that mean Arabs are capable of anything too?"

"He only lied to you because he thought you were going to lie to him!"

"But I didn't lie to him. I told him I'm a Jew. So, your brother is convinced I'm a liar even though I told him the truth? How does this make any sense?"

"Jews can't be trusted! That's how it makes sense."

"Okay, so I'm a liar, Jews can't be trusted, and your brother told you not to talk to me. So why are you sitting with me right now?"

"Because this is going to be interesting."

"Clearly. I guess I'm going to have to make new friends now that Hassan isn't being very nice to me."

"You won't succeed. Arabs can't be friends with a Jew!"

"What about us? Aren't we friends?"

His eyes glanced down at the floor. He seemed unsure what to say, as if he knew he should have immediately said no, but that some part of him wasn't so sure. Or maybe that was just wishful thinking.

"What about the Emiratis who gave me this *kandura*?" I asked. "They seemed pretty friendly."

"Do they know you're a Jew?"

"No."

"Wait till they find out!" he said threateningly. "Wait till everyone finds out! It's going to be bad for you. This university's not so big. My brother and his friends influence everyone here. You're going to wish you'd kept this a secret."

"You really believe everyone in this whole university is going to hate me because I'm Jewish?"

"Of course. The Jews are the enemy of Arabs everywhere."

I swallowed hard and began to think that maybe I'd made a terrible mistake. Not just in telling Hassan's friends that I was Jewish, but by coming to the UAE at all. Would all these upper class, English-speaking Arabs at AUS truly hate me just for the simple fact that I was Jewish? Would my new Emirati friends who I bumped noses with turn on me so fast? Or would there be more to this story than what Mo predicted?

"Where did you and your brother learn this stuff?" I asked.

"They teach this to us in elementary school!" he said.

"Mo, when I was a kid I went to a Jewish school. There I was taught that Arabs and Jews didn't have to be enemies. I was taught we could live in peace."

"You're lying! Jews don't want peace!"

"I'm not lying!"

"What you are saying is impossible!"

Chapter 2
Killing Is All They Know

Cincinnati, Ohio
2000–2004

IT WASN'T IMPOSSIBLE. IT WAS MY REALITY.

My personal views about the Arab-Israeli conflict were heavily influenced by what I was taught at Yavneh Day School, the nondenominational Jewish school I attended from pre-school through eighth grade. My parents sent me there because they believed a solid Jewish education was the best way to raise someone to be committed to the Jewish people.

We were, after all, Jews who were more committed than most. We kept a strictly kosher kitchen at home and attended Shabbat services at a Conservative synagogue every Saturday morning. But, on Saturday afternoons, my father watched college football on television and my mother gave violin lessons, activities that are prohibited to those whose Shabbat observance is strict. Most of the other students came from backgrounds like mine.

Yavneh had a reputation as the school for children whose families cared about strong Jewish identity, but who were not as observant as the Orthodox. It promoted a pluralistic environment and sought to be as inclusive as possible of people with diverse backgrounds. The school straddled a fine line between being neither too religious nor too secular, and this fit my family's lifestyle and values.

Yavneh was named after the city in Israel where Jews built the first great school of Jewish learning following the Roman destruction of the

Temple in Jerusalem. I'm certain my teachers at Yavneh Day School were very different from the pious men of ancient Israel who taught Jewish texts while on the lookout for Roman persecutors. Our educators were expressive women from modern Israel who applied overpowering perfume and feared nothing and no one. Most of them didn't come with the knowledge base to teach us much about the Jewish religion beyond what was in our textbooks. So, they taught us what they knew the most about: Israel.

Israel. Israel. Israel. My classmates and I began studying Hebrew in kindergarten so that by the third grade, if we had traveled to the Holy Land, we could haggle with Israeli shopkeepers in the holy tongue. We were fed overcooked falafel balls in stale pitas to expose us to Israeli cuisine. Our teachers drilled us on Hebrew songs commemorating the re-creation of the Jewish homeland in the land of Israel.

One of my Judaic studies teachers, an older Israeli woman named Mrs. Rendler, used to lead hours-long Hebrew song sessions immediately before Friday afternoon dismissal. The clock always ticked slowly as bored students counted down the minutes until her relentless singing ceased and we were free for the weekend.

Mrs. Rendler was a Holocaust survivor, the only one on Yavneh's faculty. Her early childhood was spent in Poland, hiding from the Nazis, before she and what remained of her family came as refugees to British-controlled Palestine. No matter how much my classmates and I hated her song sessions, whenever she spoke about her experiences, she had our full attention.

"If there is one thing to be learned from the Holocaust," Mrs. Rendler would say, "it's that no matter what, the world will always see you as a Jew. If there had been an Israel in the 1930s, maybe the Holocaust wouldn't have happened. Having a Jewish state is important because the Jews are a people and every people deserves a country of its own."

Stories about the six million Jews who died in the Holocaust and the anti-Semitism Jews had suffered throughout history ensured that I supported the basic idea of Israel existing as a state for the Jews. Unfortunately, that state was pitted in endless conflict with its neighbors.

At Yavneh, our Israeli teachers taught us a great deal about the objective history of the Arab-Israeli conflict, including the wars fought over Israel's existence. Still, despite the hostile relationship between Israel and the Arab states, my Yavneh teachers continuously emphasized one key theme: Israel wants peace.

Teachers at Yavneh taught that from the Israeli perspective, the conflict between Jews and Arabs in the Middle East was purely political, not personal. If the Arabs requested peace tomorrow, Israel would have it packaged and ready today.

The Oslo peace process between Israel and the Palestinian Authority was in full swing during my formative years at Yavneh in the 1990s. I distinctly remember a pervasive feeling of hope in the Jewish community that Israel's conflict with its Arab neighbors was finally coming to an end. Where I grew up, supporting Israel was synonymous with supporting peace. At no point during my childhood was I ever told loving Israel meant hating Arabs.

Still, ideology and history aside, developing a personal connection with Israel wasn't easy. I didn't have much family in Israel that I knew about. My parents met in Israel at Yad Vashem, the Holocaust museum in Jerusalem, but they immediately relocated their love from the Middle East back to the Midwest.

The only Israelis I grew up around were our teachers at Yavneh, who were pushier and more outspoken than most adults I knew, and the occasional Israeli kid whose family moved to Cincinnati. Most of the Israeli kids were boys who wore awkwardly tight pants, talked with funny accents, and had the rat-tail hairstyle, which was totally not cool. Their names also brought them trouble. Over the years, Dudu Davidovitch, German Kaiser, and Guy Wiener all suffered their share of name calling and teasing. Guy was an especially hyper kid which made him an extremely easy target.

Guy came to Yavneh in the sixth grade. On the first day of school that year, our social studies teacher pointed him out to me and asked me to show him around. I waited for Guy by the door after class. When I saw him, I walked up to him, but he refused to make eye contact with me.

"Do you speak English?" I asked him. Not an unreasonable question, I thought.

"Yes!" he stammered, and ran down the hall and out of sight.

Guy didn't show up to our next class. A janitor found him in the cafeteria banging the keys on a piano, nervously avoiding the realities of adjusting to a new school in a new country.

Guy's first year at Yavneh was tough. Kids picked on him, and when he responded with his fists, as he frequently did, he was punished with suspensions.

Terror attacks and a precarious economic situation pushed his family to leave Israel and come to the US. Being Israeli, Guy found himself very culturally mixed up. He just saw the world through very different eyes than the other Yavneh kids. With time, Guy became more of a fun-loving, free spirit than a recluse prone to anger management problems. But he still bent rules whenever he could and felt unconstrained by American social norms.

Guy and I weren't particularly close friends most of our sixth-grade year until we were paired up as buddies for the day during a school field trip to the Kings Island amusement park in the spring. Waiting in line for a ride, Guy started talking with a couple of eighth grade girls wearing tank-tops from a school across town who were standing behind us.

"Are you going on *this* ride?" Guy asked them. They nodded. "Do you want to go on the ride with *us*?" They did.

We viewed picking up these chicks as a remarkable achievement. The two girls stayed with Guy and me for the rest of the day. Later, while the four of us waited in line to ride a rollercoaster, a clock showed that we had five minutes to get to our school group's meeting point to catch the bus back to Yavneh.

"Relax," Guy urged me. "So, we won't get there on time. They'll wait for us. It'll be okay."

Although Rabbi Ballaban, our six foot four inch extremely intimidating vice principal, had firmly insisted there would be no excuse for being late, Guy's belief that "it'll be okay" convinced me to stay with him and ride the rollercoaster one last time with our older lady friends. But it wasn't okay. After we stepped off the ride, the girls wrote their AOL instant messenger screen names on a napkin, and Guy and I darted towards the meeting point.

The school bus had already left the parking lot and Rabbi Ballaban stood alone in the sun waiting for us, pissed off by our thirty-minute tardiness. We sat silently in the backseat of Rabbi Ballaban's mini-van worrying about what our punishment would be.

Back at Yavneh, Rabbi Ballaban took us to his office, delivered a stern rebuke, and sentenced us to a week's worth of after-school kitchen clean up. The rush of the risk we took at the theme park and the hours we spent cleaning up slop together turned us into solid friends.

Even though Guy became one of my lifelong best friends and was with me in school through the end of high school, he always described his life in Cincinnati as temporary. That he would move back to Israel "any year now" was an indisputable fact, and he remained a fish out of water, never calling Cincinnati home. The Israel of which he spoke sounded like a magical place. He was so certain his place in the world was in Israel. His passion sparked my own curiosity to find out what made him this way.

"Michael, in Israel everything is better," Guy would say. "Kids there go out and have fun whenever they want. People there are friendlier and the girls are prettier. But even more than that," he'd finish, "it's the only place in the world Jews can truly call home."

When Guy and I finally traveled to Israel together on our two-week eighth grade trip with the twelve other students in our class, I began to understand where Guy was coming from. These jam-packed trips for Jewish teenagers are supposed to portray Israel as a Jewish Disneyland, but seeing everyday life there touched me the most. Although visiting the Western Wall in Jerusalem was interesting, and floating in the Dead Sea inspired awe, it was the vibrant Jewish culture in a place where Jews represented the majority that impressed me the most.

My years of learning conversational Hebrew finally seemed relevant. My ability to haggle with Israeli shopkeepers in the improvised and adapted language of my forefathers, coupled with the opportunity to eat some decent falafel, helped me realize that the Jewish state was not just an idea. Israel was a vibrant, successful fact that offered shelter to the world's Jews and presented them with a chance to build a revolutionary new society.

When I graduated from Yavneh, I had developed a strong Jewish identity and a lasting personal connection to Israel.

Guy and most of our other Yavneh friends joined me the next year at Sycamore High, so transitioning to our huge public school from our tiny day school was fairly smooth. I wanted to branch out and make new friends, so I joined the cross-country running team when I found out two of my Yavneh buddies were already doing it.

Right after the first day of school ended, I walked over to the track next to the parking lot to begin my first practice. After a few brisk warm-up laps and twenty minutes of stretching, the coaches told us to partner up for the main afternoon run with someone who ran at the same pace. Pairs of thin teenage boys who already knew each other paired off and left school grounds. My two Yavneh buddies were also nowhere to be found. Scrambling for a partner, I made eye contact with a dark Hispanic-looking boy about my height with buzzed black hair. He pointed at me to grab my attention and offered a complicated handshake as soon as we were in high-five range.

"Yo man. You down to run?" he asked smiling. His slangy speech and minority features hinted that he was probably not a person I would have ever met at Yavneh.

"I'm down," I said, using his hip language to respond. His name was Joe Barkawi and that afternoon, getting to know each other totally distracted us from running with any degree of intensity. We must have jogged or walked half the distance the other freshmen had. It didn't bother me though. I'd made my first real new friend at Sycamore and this excited me more than building up stamina in my legs. Towards the end of our lackluster running effort, I tried asking Joe about his ethnic background.

"So where are you from *originally*?" I asked.

"What do you mean?" he countered.

I felt awkward pressing for details and wondered if posing the question in Spanish would put Latino Joe at ease.

"Like, where are your parents from?"

"Oh, that. I'm from Palestine, but I have Jordanian citizenship. My parents came from Nablus in the West Bank before I was born to study in university. They chose to stay in America afterwards."

That Joe was a Palestinian Arab Muslim and not a Hispanic caught me by surprise. But the idea never occurred to me that my connection to Israel or his Palestinian identity should stand in the way of friendship.

Although Joe knew I had been to Israel earlier that year, we never discussed politics during our afternoon runs throughout the fall. Unlike Guy, Joe never expressed a strong desire to return permanently to the land of his roots. He maintained a connection with his past and even carried a symbolic, but effectively useless Palestinian passport. His life was firmly rooted in America, and he could not realistically envision a state of Palestine providing the same opportunities life in the US could. Besides, we had more important subjects to mull over, such as analyzing which girls to consider asking to the homecoming dance and whether to try out for the school basketball team. We began hanging out on the weekends and soon Guy made our duo a trio.

The three of us bonded over our unique passion for attracting attention through unconventional means. One afternoon on a whim, we bleached our eyebrows bright blonde. The effects blinded our classmates for the next six months. When we visited Kings Island together the next summer, I found a kippah in my car. We made a rule that the kippah must be worn by one of us at all times throughout the day. Joe enthusiastically played the role of the token Jew and even barraged concession stands with requests for kosher food.

Guy's and Joe's parents may have found our dynamic a bit unusual, but they never objected. The three of us always felt welcome at any one of our homes. Unfortunately, only a few short weeks after becoming friends, we couldn't ignore the violence erupting between Israel and the Palestinians.

Palestinian President Yasir Arafat and his negotiating team walked out of American-sponsored final status peace talks with Israel in July 2000. That September, Palestinians launched a violent uprising that saw both Israeli civilians and soldiers become the targets of terrorists. Bombings rocked Israel's cafes, buses, and nightclubs. To prevent Palestinian attacks, the Israelis launched major incursions into Palestinian cities, which resulted in the deaths of Palestinian civilians and combatants as well.

Joe, Guy, and I talked about what was going on, and our discussions left me hopeful, but also confused. While certainly no ardent Zionist, Joe was committed to doing what was best for the Palestinian people. To him, that meant acceptance of a two-state solution and a peace treaty with Israel.

"All I want is a state, man," he said. "A state is all we need. There can be an Israel if there can be a Palestine."

Joe's willingness to put his personal grievances aside and readily condemn terror against Israeli civilians earned my deepest respect.

"Those people blowing themselves up do not represent Islam or Palestine and they don't represent me," he said.

He also never questioned my or Guy's attachment to the land we called Israel and he called Palestine. He understood that denigrating our connection would lead to nothing positive.

Guy also spoke of his desire for peace with the Palestinians since terror was a major reason why his family moved to the US. Still, he resented what he saw as the world's unfair expectation that Israel should constantly give away territory without receiving any additional security.

"We have one teeny tiny country, smaller than the state of New Jersey!" Guy shouted once after we heard news of another suicide bombing in Israel. "The entire world tells us to constantly slice away parts of it and we never get anything in return."

If genuine peace was included in the equation, Guy and I agreed to the establishment of a Palestinian state. We envisioned Israel as a Jewish democracy that supported the basic rights of all its citizens, but held a solid Jewish majority. A state built as a haven for the Jews that enabled the Jewish people to live as a nation seemed incredibly just. But an undemocratic state that served only Jews wasn't worthy of being called Jewish. Despite the Jewish connection to the West Bank and Gaza Strip, these lands and their Arab populations had been imposed on Israel through war and threatened its Jewish majority.

To me, Mrs. Rendler's words that "every people deserves a country of its own" resonated with the Palestinian cause too. Understanding that Israelis and Palestinians embraced separate identities, religions, and languages, I thought the two-state solution was the best option for peace. Guy, Joe, and I could complete Israeli-Palestinian final status negotiations in five seconds. What was the problem with the rest of the world?

Since Jews made up nearly twenty percent of the student body and a vocal, sizable group of Arabs and Muslims also attended Sycamore, the Israeli-Palestinian conflict was also a major topic at school. Joe, Guy, and I saw firsthand that overwhelming passion about what happens between Israelis and Palestinians can boil people's blood and get them to abandon all reason. Few issues evoke such obsession and argument as the conflict about the past, present, and future of the Holy Land.

Sycamore's Hebrew language teacher, an Israeli émigré with red hair named Mrs. Mills, planned events about the Israeli-Palestinian conflicts to encourage students of different viewpoints to discover common ground. These activities became enormously popular, but for all the wrong reasons.

One time, Mrs. Mills invited two "professional moderators" to lead an after-school student discussion about the Israeli-Palestinian conflict. Neither of them was Jewish or Arab/Muslim and both ignored the fact that most of the seventy students in attendance had already picked a side to support. Jewish and Muslim students sat in clan-like groups on opposite sides of the classroom. Only those without direct ties to biblical Abraham mixed in with whomever they pleased, as did Joe and I (Guy was stuck at water polo practice). Right before the moderators addressed the crowd, a few Jewish upperclassmen barged in dressed from head to toe in blue and white, the Israeli national colors, draped in large Israeli flags. They loudly sang cheers in Hebrew, taunting the Arab/Muslim students in attendance.

"Thank you for coming to this dialogue about the Israeli-Palestinian conflict," the female moderator began. "Today, we're only going to hear from people who want to share how the Israeli-Palestinian conflict makes them feel. We are not here to argue facts or versions of history. There is no right or wrong. There are only feelings."

This was doomed from the start and made every pair of Semitic eyes roll. Jon, the only fully observant Jewish student at Sycamore, raised his hand first to express his "feelings."

"I really truly *feel* that the Palestinians are trying to destroy Israel," he said emphatically. "I *feel* that the Palestinians rejected a generous Israeli proposal for peace and are now showing their true colors."

One of the Jewish upperclassmen wearing blue and white clothes and draped in the Israeli flag stood up and shouted, "I'm showing my true colors right here too, baby."

The moderators looked on flabbergasted. Leila, a hijab-wearing girl who was half Palestinian, spoke next.

"Well I *feel*," she said confidently, "that Israel rapes Palestinian women and commits genocide against the Palestinian people."

While she looked proud for saying what she did, her words didn't resonate with the crowd the way she'd probably hoped. The same guy dressed in blue and white shouted at the top of his lungs, "I'm *feeling* a little scared that if this girl gets too excited she might just blow up!"

Some students laughed at the joke and others began arguing points of history at the top of their lungs. A few, Joe and I included, didn't say anything at all. Our moderators proved to be novices at Middle East negotiation.

"That's enough, people!" Mrs. Mills yelled. "This event is over."

I found some of the Jewish students' behavior inappropriate, but I knew I was on their side. I sympathized with Leila because of the laughter generated at her expense, but her allegations of Israeli rape and genocide disgusted me for their venom and complete lack of truth. It has been well documented that few rapes have been committed by Israeli soldiers on Palestinian women throughout the conflict. In addition, during the height of the intifada, Israeli security forces killed no more than two to three Palestinians per day in clashes, the majority of which were armed combatants. This hardly constitutes genocide by any stretch of the imagination.

Since the student discussion proved a failure, Mrs. Mills asked two adults to participate in a debate on the Israeli-Palestinian conflict for the next event. Surely a couple of grownups could show some high school kids what respectful disagreement looked like, right?

Leila's Palestinian father spoke on behalf of the Palestinians and the husband of an Israeli emissary to the Jewish community in Cincinnati represented Israel. They smiled, shook hands, and faced the audience before the debate began. But after only a few questions, their smiles were erased, they clenched their fists, and turned away from the crowd, screaming their points at each other face-to-face.

These two middle-aged, well-educated professionals worked themselves up to such a degree that a real fear existed that their debate might end in violence. The Middle Eastern men moved towards each other aggressively before Mrs. Mills jumped in and physically pushed them apart.

"Well that's enough of that!" she yelled.

The two men decided to answer questions separately and individually, and everyone agreed that public debates aimed at solving the Israeli-Palestinian conflict were doomed for disaster. I heard some people say the two sides would never resolve their differences. But I refused to give up.

I saw Leila often since we'd both joined the staff of Sycamore's student newspaper, *The Leaf*. Leila was a genuinely nice girl and I assumed I could find common ground with her just like I had with Joe. But Leila wasn't Joe and I grew tired of her distorted accusations.

"Michael, can you believe Israeli soldiers shoot Palestinian *children* who carry guns?" she asked once while we worked in the newspaper room one afternoon.

"Little kids with guns?" I asked in response, making sure I understood her correctly. "Like little kids whose parents give them guns?"

"Yes, small children. The Israelis shoot these kids."

"Well, it doesn't take a whole lot to fire a gun. A six-year old can still kill someone with a gun even though he's six. If a soldier kills a kid carrying a gun to protect himself, aren't the parents who gave the kid the gun to blame?"

"Michael, these are children! Most of the time these guns are just toys for the children to play with."

"Why would any parent living in a war zone give a child a toy gun to play with unless they wanted something bad to happen?"

"Children cannot play with toy guns? If you aimed a toy gun at me, does that mean I should kill you?"

"If I was threatening you with a toy gun like an idiot and you thought my gun was real, then you should absolutely kill me."

"I guess this shows people who support Israel and people who support Palestine have very different moral values."

"Yes. According to you, Palestinians prefer death by stupidity!"

"Israelis kill because killing is all they know," she said before barging out of the room.

My conversations with Leila never led to anything productive and I always caught myself staring at the necklace of the map of Palestine she wore, which included all the territory of Israel proper.

The terrorist attacks of September 11th, the American-led wars in Afghanistan and Iraq, and the ongoing violence between Israel and the Palestinians caused a lot of tension between students, provoking them to say lots of stupid things.

When I heard a few Jewish students refer to Arabs as "towel-heads," I felt embarrassed people from my community could stoop so low. Some Muslim students I knew called America and Israel the world's two greatest persecutors of Muslims and berated the US government for its lack of sensitivity for bombing Afghanistan during the holy month of Ramadan in 2001. But when a Palestinian suicide bomber blew himself up at a Passover Seder at a hotel in Israel in March 2002, killing over thirty people, those same Muslim students didn't say a word.

In response to the Passover Seder bombing and other terrorist attacks that month, the Israeli army launched Operation Defensive Shield to destroy the terrorist infrastructure and bring the suicide bombings to a halt.

That April, over one thousand pro-Israel Cincinnatians rallied at an outdoor amphitheater in my neighborhood in support of Israel's right to self-defense and for a peaceful resolution to the violence. I arrived at the rally late and stood by the pro-Palestinian protesters who were separated from pro-Israel activists by police. Many of Sycamore's Jews, including Guy, were scattered throughout the area. I also saw a few of the school's Muslims, like Leila, prominently demonstrating with the other anti-Israel protesters. The noise of the pro-Palestinian activists made it impossible for me to hear any of the speeches. Instead, I just listened to their slogans.

"Two. Four. Six. Eight. Israel is a racist state. One. Three. Five. Nine. Long live Palestine."

"From the river to the sea, Palestine will be free."

"Zionism is racism. Israel is a Nazi state."

Some protesters held signs showing the Israeli flag with a swastika in the middle instead of a Star of David. This infuriated the pro-Israel crowd, me included. I got so worked up, I felt like I might lose control. I was revolted that they could say the descendants of the most horrific systematic slaughter in recorded history were doing the same thing. Other pro-Israel supporters started shouting back and inched dangerously close to the pro-Palestinian protesters.

"Why don't you go home?" a woman next to me yelled at them.

"Nobody invited you! You're disgusting!" a man screamed as he wagged his finger in the face of Leila's father.

Police officers quickly separated the opposing groups and ordered the incitement from both sides to stop. I was glad Joe hadn't been there and didn't align himself with the pro-Palestinian activists. If he had, I wasn't sure our friendship would hold up. Ultimately, the completely over-the-top accusations against Israel pushed me deeper and deeper into the pro-Israel camp. In my attempts to remain neutral, I still criticized Israel plenty, but my criticisms were insignificant compared to the lies spread against it, and I saw Israel's fight as justified and necessary.

As high school wound to a close and Israeli-Palestinian fighting remained a daily reality, Guy, Joe, and I mostly stopped discussing Middle East politics. Nothing seemed like it was changing for the better, so what was the point? Maybe nothing would ever change and we were the only trio of friends in the world comprised of a Palestinian, an Israeli, and an American Jew. We all accepted that Joe was a loyal Palestinian and that Guy and I loved Israel. We finished up high school enjoying ourselves, partying after graduation, and taking our dates to prom together.

But deep down, the belief that Jewish and Arab moderates besides the three of us could come together to establish a peaceful reality for the Middle East never left me. My relationships with Guy and Joe influenced me too much to dissuade me of the possibility. So did the words of a man with decades of experience in leading Middle East peace talks.

While attending a Jewish youth group convention in Washington DC my senior year of high school, Dennis Ross, the former chief negotiator between Israelis and Palestinians under President Clinton, came to speak about the stalled peace process. After the speech, I approached Dr. Ross to glean some wisdom.

"Dr. Ross, what can I do to help bring peace to the Middle East?" I asked him.

"Educate yourself as much as you can," he advised me. "Never doubt your own ability to influence the minds of others. You must get to know the parties on a personal level. Never forget that you don't make peace with your friends."

Discussing the Middle East with the children of immigrants in the US wasn't enough. I had to be in the region to discover how those people thought and felt. Already very familiar with Israel, I determined that I needed to understand the Arab world on an intimate level if I ever hoped to improve relations between Jews and Arabs. So, after completing my sophomore year of college at GW, I took Dr. Ross' advice and left in May 2006 to study abroad in the Arab world for eight months, basing myself first in Cairo and then in Sharjah.

Chapter 3
A Peace of Paper

Egypt and Jordan
May–June 2006

M Y PLANE LANDED IN CAIRO BEFORE SIX IN THE MORNING. THE minute I cleared passport control a stampede of taxi drivers with identical thick black moustaches ambushed me. I scanned the crowd for a sign bearing my name, but I could barely see through the haze of cigarette smoke in the terminal. Two men stepped forward from the mob, grabbed my bags, and tried to usher me to their taxi.

I wanted to yell the Arabic expression for stop but couldn't retrieve the word in time.

"*Lee shufir, lee shufir,*" I insisted. I have a driver, I have a driver. The two wannabe chauffeurs didn't listen, and they headed for the airport exit with my luggage. Just before they exited the terminal, they were blocked by the bulky frame of another mustached Egyptian man who refused to move aside. In his left hand, he held a sign with my name on it and on his right forearm he revealed a black tattoo of the crucifix. It was Jibril who had come to my rescue, like my very own archangel Gabriel.

Jibril was a Coptic Christian who worked as a driver and errand runner for Saint Joseph's Catholic Church in Zamalek, an upscale central Cairo neighborhood on an island in the Nile River. He was picking me up and taking me back to the church on the orders of Father Richard, a Ugandan-born priest who served at Saint Joseph's.

Jewish boys like me don't typically seek out the sanctuary of the Catholic Church, but I was new in Cairo, and Father Richard was my only contact. One of my mother's friends heard I would be studying Arabic at the American University of Cairo (AUC) for the summer. She put me in touch with the Ugandan-born priest, whom she knew through a Catholic charity.

I had corresponded with Father Richard a few weeks before my arrival, telling him that I planned to land in Cairo and travel over to Israel for a couple weeks before my program started. In response, he insisted I spend a day recovering from my flight at Saint Joseph's. He also promised to provide me with free transport to the Israeli border and keep my luggage while I was away.

Conscious of my meager travel budget and greatly impressed by his generosity, I accepted his offer of hospitality.

Riding to the church in Jibril's 1970s-era Fiat, I prayed the real angel Gabriel would protect us in Cairo's traffic mayhem. At six-thirty in the morning, Cairo's two-lane roads had already morphed into congested four-lane highways. Stoplights and traffic police were completely disregarded, and drivers signaled their intent to overtake each other by blasting their horns and shining their high-beams incessantly, if their headlights worked at all.

"*Anta shufir tayib jidan*," I said to Jibril to initiate some conversation. You are a very good driver.

"*Owie*," he moaned loudly. "*Owie!*"

Owie? Did Jibril have a boo-boo?

"In *masri* (Egyptian colloquial Arabic)," he explained, "very is *owie*, not *jidan*. You talk Arabic like a newspaper!"

What Jibril inferred was that I'd been duped by GW's Arabic department. After spending a year studying Modern Standard Arabic (MSA), known as *fushā* (pronounced *foos-ha*), I spoke Arabic like a Shakespearian actor would speak English. Beginners first learn MSA, the formal language of the Qur'an, verbose ceremonial speeches, and antiquated literature, because it's the only version of Arabic that links the Arab world together. Arabic has evolved into a series of national dialects as different from one another as Spanish is from French. That means that while I thought I was improving my speaking skills through oral exercises in class, in fact I was sharpening my ability to recite twelfth-century Arabic poetry with a crappy accent.

I didn't plan to continue like that. I wanted to learn Arabic in order to talk to Arabs. Many Arabs understand some colloquial Egyptian Arabic due to the numerous Egyptian films and television shows broadcast around the region.

Piquing my personal interest in the country was that, once upon a time, Egypt banished its Jewish population and led the Arab effort to destroy Israel. Then, Egypt abruptly changed course, becoming the first Arab country to sign a separate peace with the Jewish state. Egypt seemed like a good place to begin getting to know Arabs.

"I am not an Arab!" Jibril abruptly declared. "If someone calls me an Arab, I spit on him!"

"How are you not an Arab?" I asked confused. "You speak Arabic and live in an Arab country! What are you then?"

Jibril lifted his right arm to my face to give me an up-close view of his crucifix tattoo.

"I am a Copt," he said. His voice became louder with each syllable. "It was my people who ruled Egypt before the Arabs came and forced Islam on this land. Today Egypt is an Arab country. But not a drop of Arab blood runs through my veins. I am an Egyptian, not an Arab."

Once one of the world's most vibrant Christian communities, the position of Egypt's Copts had deteriorated with the rise of Islamism. Since that happened physical assaults and violence against the community often went unpunished and the Egyptian government placed major restrictions on plans to renovate or build new churches.

"Being Christian here is very hard," Jibril said. "Many of us make this tattoo to show we are not going anywhere. The government treats us like we are Jews!"

"How bad is that?" I asked, unsure if I wanted to hear the answer. Jibril looked at me and laughed and never answered my question.

He dropped me off at Saint Joseph's, where Father Richard greeted me with a handshake and a plan.

"The church is sending a mini-bus to the Israeli border to collect a group of visiting bishops," he explained. "Another Copt who works for the church is the driver. His name is Anwar. You depart at midnight."

After taking a brief nap, showering, and eating an early lunch of cheese sandwiches and vegetable porridge with the priests, I went off to explore Cairo alone.

For a few hours, I walked on crumbling sidewalks, dodged the drip of murky water from broken second floor air-conditioners, and inhaled the smoke from exhaust pipes of cars long banned from the roads in western countries. Relaxing on a bench along the banks of the Nile River, I watched passersby throw in bits of trash. A young girl dropped a small candy wrapper into the water. An old man tossed in an empty soda can.

A young man about my age and clothed in black slacks and a gray button-down shirt took a seat next to me. He let out a long sigh as he stared at the river. I presumed he was wondering how the Nile had gotten so filthy.

"The Nile is beautiful," he unexpectedly said in Arabic. "Do you think so?"

"Very beautiful, of course," I lied.

Denial ain't just a river in Egypt, I thought. He introduced himself as Ehmi, a twenty-year-old like me and a youth soccer coach. We quickly realized the limitations of my Arabic and his English. Nevertheless, we persisted using a combination of the two languages and very simple vocabulary.

"How much time you in Egypt?" Ehmi asked in English.

"Six weeks. Tonight, I go away but I will return in a few weeks," I answered.

"Where you go tonight?"

"To Israel." I told the truth to test his response.

Egypt and Israel concluded their peace treaty back in 1979 and shared an open border, which I planned to cross the next morning. Still, the relationship between the countries had often been described as a "cold peace," meaning only that there is an absence of war. Few Israelis traveled to Cairo and even fewer Egyptians made it to Israel. I believed the fruits of peace were three decades overdue and I wanted to see if they were ripe.

With a warm smile on his face, Ehmi put his hand on my left shoulder affectionately.

"Israel is *the* big enemy," Ehmi uttered slowly. "You are very brave to go there."

"I don't need to be brave to go to Israel," I tried to explain. "Israel is not an enemy. Israel and Egypt have *salaam,* peace!"

Ehmi shook his head.

"You are Muslim?" he asked in Arabic.

"No, I am a Jew."

Although the expression on his face stayed the same, his inability to utter any syllable other than "ah" for a minute indicated he might not have expected my answer. After he regained his composure, he somberly said in English, "But Jews hate Egypt. Why you come here?"

"I came to study Arabic. Jews don't hate Egypt!"

"In the school, I learn Israel wants everything from the Nile to Iraq," he said, pointing at the Nile in front of us. "It is true?"

While ongoing debate persists over the exact borders of the land of Israel promised in the Bible, no Jewish or Zionist faction sought to conquer Cairo. Moses led the Israelites out of Egypt and few Jews were looking for reasons to go back.

"No, Ehmi, it is a lie!" I insisted. "I want to be friends with people like you."

"I am believing you," he said, looking at me in the eye. "We are friends."

Ehmi and I spent the rest of the evening together. He offered to pay for the street-side mystery stew sandwiches we ate for dinner, which to my surprise I could eat without an immediate trip to the toilet, and together we mocked the various poses of then-President Hosni Mubarak on billboards.

When we parted, I was happy I'd told the truth about my Jewish identity. Nevertheless, I was bothered that a genuinely friendly, gentle person like Ehmi could harbor so many cliché negative beliefs about Jews and Israel. Like me, he never knew a time when Egypt and Israel were actively at war, yet he viewed Israel as "*the* big enemy."

I arrived back at Saint Joseph's before midnight to find my overnight travel companion, Anwar, already waiting in the mini-bus with my backpack onboard. We managed to head out on time, so he suggested we drop by a *shisha* bar, where people gathered to smoke flavored tobacco, before getting on the road.

Cairo could have easily challenged New York for the title of "the city that never sleeps." The streets were busy twenty-four hours a day and many shops were open throughout the night, including the small, male-only *shisha* bar Anwar and I stepped into that night.

We took two seats at a table with some older Egyptian men, who quickly started chatting me up. They asked me the three introductory questions I would come to expect from nearly every Egyptian I would meet: What's your name? Where are you from? What's your religion?

Though slightly unsure if I should come out as a son of Jacob to so many Arab strangers at once, I figured what the heck. I'm spreading goodwill after all!

Ehmi took the news well, so maybe other Egyptians would too. I thought about how proud and defiant Jibril was about asserting his identity and opinions. Surely Anwar was the same way. If I had any balls, then I should tell the truth too, no matter what.

After answering their questions, the men smiled politely, but waited for someone to say something. A few moments went by until the owner of the bar assured me that "all people are welcome" in his establishment. His other customers nodded their heads in agreement.

Anwar nodded his head too, but in his eyes, I saw distress. He rose from his seat and asked to speak outside. Walking out with his left hand firmly grabbing my shirt collar, I noticed that a cross tattoo was missing from his right arm. Perhaps Anwar wasn't as hell-bent on asserting his identity as Jibril. Once outside, he shoved me against a wall and held me there forcefully.

"Do you want to die in Egypt?" he screamed at me in English. "Never tell anyone you are a Jew! Maybe these men are acting nice because they are in shock! But they hate you, I know they hate you!"

He went silent for a moment, but I was too surprised and scared to say anything back to him.

"You think you are a tourist and that makes you safe?" he asked. "I am a Christian. They don't like Christians. They want us to become Muslim or leave Egypt. But they hate you and your people more. There are many people here who would love to kill you. In this country, they blame Jews for everything. Keep it quiet! Lie! If you don't, people here will think you are a spy. If you tell one more person you are a Jew, I will leave you here!"

Putting a smile back on his face, Anwar dragged me back inside the smoke-infested hangout to say goodbye to the crowd as if everything between us was normal. When we returned to the mini-bus, awkward tension persisted throughout the six-hour journey through the Sinai Peninsula, the enormous chunk of oil-rich territory Israel had returned to Egypt for peace. I pretended to sleep for most of the trip to avoid Anwar's condescending gaze, but my embarrassment at my naiveté and recklessness kept me awake. My soul felt relief only after I crossed the border into Israel, where one of my lifelong friends was expecting me.

After years of talk and solemn vows, Guy finally moved back to Israel permanently in 2005, settling in Haifa to study biomedical engineering at the Technion, one of Israel's most prestigious universities. We didn't see each other often, so we wanted to celebrate our reunion by having a real adventure. Guy could afford only a couple days off from classes and neither of us wanted to pay for a plane ticket, so our destination had to be close by. Lucky for us, a mysterious Arab kingdom was located an hour's drive from Haifa.

"This weekend Amman is on!" Guy howled.

Since I could communicate in basic Arabic and our friend Joe was a citizen, the Hashemite Kingdom of Jordan piqued our interest. Despite having a peace treaty with Israel since1994, few Israelis traveled there, except with organized tour groups with heavy security. Guy wasn't sure how his extended Israeli family would feel about him traveling there independently, so he didn't tell them.

"The only one who knows is my grandma," he said.

We bought tickets online for a bus that traveled directly from Nazareth to Amman on Thursday morning.

We arrived at the bus station in Nazareth just as the driver fired up his engine, and put our backpacks in the luggage compartment at the bottom of the vehicle. A guy who had ridden our bus from Haifa to Nazareth, speaking Arabic on his cell phone the whole trip, accosted us in flawless Hebrew.

"You two are going to Amman? What are you looking for there?"

His eyes were hidden by a pair of thick black sunglasses and the grease in his hair shined in the sunlight.

"Just because," I answered coolly. "You?"

"I'm studying there. I'm trying to get my girlfriend to come visit me, but she's too afraid. She's a Moroccan Jewish girl. That means she knows how to give me trouble if I don't come home often enough. You guys want to go sit for coffee?"

"But what if we miss the bus?" Guy worried.

"The driver knows me," Amir assured us. "I go back and forth with him all the time. He'll wait for us. Trust me."

Arab etiquette requires one to sit and drink coffee if invited to do so. Since Guy and I sought to immerse ourselves in Arab culture, we agreed to sit for one cup. Unfortunately, Amir's relationship with the driver was greatly exaggerated.

The bus left the station before we were even served. Darting out of the coffee shop, we ran after the bus until we were exhausted and out of breath. Normally, it would have been no problem to wait for another bus or travel a different day. But our bags were already in the cargo hold heading to Jordan. We hailed a Skoda taxi cab and Guy and Amir screamed in both Hebrew and Arabic, "Follow that bus."

The taxi driver apparently understood the seriousness of the situation because he pushed the car past ninety miles per hour on the windy two-lane roads. In less than five minutes, we were caught up with the bus. However, the bus driver ignored the honking from our taxi to pull over, as if he refused to halt on purpose.

The bus driver's refusal to stop was a serious affront to our taxi driver's honor, who then boldly declared he'd force the bus off the road "by any means necessary."

"He doesn't know how to stop?" he shouted in thick Arabic-accented Hebrew, the kind that Amir's speech noticeably lacked. "I will teach him to stop!"

The taxi driver swiftly steered the car onto the opposite side of the road and cursed in Arabic. He pulled up directly next to the front of the bus and honked relentlessly. The bus driver looked down on us from his lofty seat, frowned, and sped up to avoid our chase.

"Isn't he supposed to want us to get on the bus?" I yelled.

An oncoming truck forced our driver to move back to the right lane behind the bus. When the truck passed, the driver returned our Skoda to the oncoming traffic lane and pushed the gas pedal as far down as it would go. The engine roared and I feared for my life. We raced past the bus, pulled back into the right lane, and gradually slowed down until we arrived at a complete stop in the middle of the road. We knew our taxi driver had emerged victorious when we saw the bus park on the shoulder and open its door to let Amir, Guy, and me finally board.

"We asked him to stop back at the bus station," a distraught obese woman wearing a purple hijab explained in Hebrew. "But all the driver could talk about was teaching you and your friends a lesson about being on time," she said, pointing her finger at Amir.

"Since when do Arabs ever go anywhere on time?" Amir griped in his own defense.

Guy and I took seats near Amir. It quickly became evident the other passengers saw us as a spectacle for reasons besides our dangerous car chase.

"We never see people like you going to Amman," a pretty young woman wearing a white tank top exclaimed.

"People like you?" I asked confused.

"Jews!" Amir screamed with a grin, answering for her. I looked around and realized it was safe to assume Guy and I were literally the only Jews on the bus. Everyone else was an Israeli Arab traveling to Amman for school or business.

"So, what's Jordan like?" Guy posed to our audience in Hebrew.

"A dry wasteland," Amir said first. "It's boring, conservative, and undeveloped. It's nothing like home. I wish I'd stayed to study in Haifa."

"It's not that bad," the young woman objected. "Amman is a nice city. He's just saying that because it's hard for *us*. The Jordanian Palestinian students give us problems because we are Israeli. They call us traitors because our families didn't leave Palestine in '48."

Many Palestinians that fled or were forced to leave Israel during its war of independence in 1948 now live in surrounding Arab countries, like Jordan. Palestinians make up more than half of Jordan's population and have engaged in violent conflict and power struggles with the ruling Hashemite monarchy. To divert attention from domestic problems and maintain control, Jordan's rulers have fanned anger at Israel and anyone associated with it, including Israel's Arabs.

"It's not only a problem for young people," a bald man sitting a few rows behind us added. "Last year I went on vacation to Aqaba and I was charged three times the price for everything. The same thing happened in Sinai. I asked why and they'd say, 'It's what you get for being a collaborator.' Do they really expect me to move to a refugee camp in Jordan? They don't live in reality."

"Well," I challenged, "if a Palestinian state was created, would you personally consider living in it?"

"I am all for a Palestinian state, but I would never live in one," the bald man said. "I would rather move to Rishon L'Tzion," he quipped, referring to an Israeli city whose name means "first to Zion" in Hebrew.

"But there's peace now between Israel and Jordan," Guy reminded everyone. "Doesn't that mean it's okay for Israelis to go to Jordan?"

"It's okay to go technically," Amir responded. "But is it a good idea? That's the question."

Thinking about that question instantly turned Guy into a stressed-out mess. The bus dropped us off in an empty parking lot on Amman's outskirts. The Arab Israelis scattered and I went off to hunt for a taxi to take Guy and me to the city center to withdraw money and check into a cheap hotel.

Fists clenched and grinding his teeth, Guy sat on top of his backpack protectively as he waited for me and spastically looked around in all directions. Our conversation on the bus made him fear that someone might attack him at any second.

We arrived at the city center and stopped at an ATM next to a restaurant whose entire exterior was covered in pixilated images of kebabs. I hurriedly retrieved a stack of Jordanian dinars from the ATM as Guy paced around nervously and rubbed his hands together. When the ATM rejected Guy's credit card, his anxiety intensified. He tried another two ATMs down the street without any luck. As crowds of curious Jordanian men stared at us from the sidewalk, Guy's rage took over.

"What the fuck is wrong with this country?" he screamed. "I'm from Israel! We have peace! Doesn't anyone here know that? I know what's going on. They're boycotting my credit card since I'm from Israel."

"I'm sure that's not the case," I said to calm him. In reality, I had no idea what the problem was. "Let's go into a bank and see if someone can help."

We stepped inside a branch of the Bank of Jordan and Guy aggressively approached a female bank teller. A picture of a smiling King Abdullah II hung from above.

"The ATM won't give me money! Tell me why," Guy demanded in English.

"I don't know why," the teller said without flinching. "You should ask your bank what the problem is with your card."

"Talk to my bank? Don't you understand? I want to spend money in your country. I want to buy things here. I want to help your economy."

Worried Guy was about to cause an international incident, I dragged him out of the bank and loaned him enough cash to get him through the trip.

It was early in the afternoon when we finally settled in at the Cliff Hotel, a famous backpacker haunt. After putting our bags down, Guy and I immediately walked around our area of the city and started noticing something extremely unexpected.

"These people are insanely friendly!" Guy remarked.

Amid the hustle and bustle of downtown Amman, Jordanians of all ages constantly stopped us to shake our hands and welcome us. A group of outgoing elementary school children in uniforms took us to ride bumper cars with them at a small amusement park. The owner of a hole-in-the-wall restaurant where we ate dinner presented us with a whole lamb's head to honor us as revered guests in his country.

Though the gesture flattered us, we declined the restaurant owner's offer to wrap up the head for us in a doggy bag.

The openness and hospitality we experienced began to assuage Guy's suspicion that danger lurked behind every corner, and he began to relax. Nevertheless, we still avoided divulging Guy's Israeli identity and that we were both Jewish until we thought it was safe. Or, as it turned out to be the case, until someone's candidness or curiosity took hold of us.

Following dinner that first day, my wandering eye noticed a beverage stall called Palestine Juice just down the road. Thinking it would be funny to see an Israeli guy sitting underneath the main sign with a cup of juice in his hand, we ordered drinks and started chatting with Palestine Juice's main squeezer.

"I want you to know how much I love America," the sticky, juice-covered employee announced when I said I was visiting from the US. Placing his pulp-covered right hand over his chest, he added, "And I love President Bush."

"Why?" I asked.

"He is strong, he gets respect, and he is good for the Jews and Israel. This is good for America."

How's that for a squeeze? Although President Bush was a devoted supporter of Israel, I wasn't his biggest fan. I believed much of his Middle East policy was harmful to the interests of the United States and its allies, especially Israel, regardless of his good intentions. At the time, his domestic and global popularity were at an all-time low. For an Arab to describe President Bush as "strong" and "gets respect" seemed like a glaring contradiction. Nevertheless, it was refreshing to meet someone who defied stereotypes.

Our Bush-loving friend went back to mashing fruit, and he didn't have time to explain his words. We paid our bill and got up to leave when a pale man with a peach fuzz mustache wearing a spotless white *jalabiyya* approached towards us.

"*As-salaam aleikum,*" the fairest Arab in the land greeted us.

"*Wa-aleikum as-salaam!*" Guy answered eagerly before turning to me. "That's all I know. I want to talk for once, so tell me what to say."

Since Guy was tired of me dominating all our Arabic conversations, I relinquished my speaking privileges and served as his interpreter.

"I am from Syria," the man in white said in Arabic. "Where are you from?"

I translated the question for Guy and whispered in his ear how to answer. This amused the Syrian, who waited patiently for Guy's response. Due to the thrill of learning a new Arabic phrase and his honest nature, Guy forgot he'd planned not to reveal where he was from until he felt completely ready.

"*Ana min Is-ra-eel,*" Guy proclaimed. I am from Israel.

Apparently, true readiness turns up without a formal announcement. The fact that the man standing before us came from a self-declared enemy state of Israel didn't faze Guy in the least. The same, though, could not be said for our new Syrian friend. As soon as he heard Guy's reply he turned as white as a ghost and his lips quivered. The Syrian let out a grunt and ran off, nearly tripping over his *jalabiyya* in the process. Guy stood there watching the Syrian flee him, his enemy.

"What can I say?" Guy said, perplexed by it all. "I guess people like him are taught to hate for a reason."

That reason became plainly evident the next morning after we attempted to visit Jordan's Martyrs Monument and Military Museum on the outskirts of town. Guy and I wanted to see how Jordan teaches its citizens about its wars with Israel. To our dismay, the museum was closed.

"Yesterday was Jordan's National Day," a uniformed guard explained. "Today no one may enter."

The previous day, May 25, was the day on which Jordanians acknowledge their independence. Jordanians seemed to treat the holiday as an afterthought, rather than celebrate it. People went to work, cars jammed the streets, and museums were certainly open to the public. Guy and I only discovered it was a holiday when fireworks briefly lit up Amman's sky from our hotel balcony last night, the evening of the holiday. Besides that, nothing seemed out of the ordinary. Puzzled by the museum's closure the day after the holiday, we turned around to go find a ride back to central Amman.

Walking through the parking lot we noticed a group of cameramen packing up their gear after a filming.

"Stop, don't shoot!" I teased in English. The men glanced over at us and, playing along with the joke, pointed their cameras in our direction. A tall husky man wearing a gold watch and necklace introduced himself to us with an air of authority as the cameramen's boss and *the* royal film producer of Jordan.

"I make films for the king," he said. "I teach the people to love King Abdullah and show how he protects them."

"Protects them from what?" I asked.

"Enemies," he stated mysteriously. In other words, he was responsible for overseeing the creation of official state propaganda.

"Now I go to my office," the royal filmmaker said. "You will join me, so I may show you our work?"

Guy and I had nothing better to do and we needed a ride anyway, so we hopped into the producer's black Mercedes and joined his entourage. A ten-minute drive later, our host parked right in front of a sleek modern building with a shiny glass exterior. He hastily tossed the keys to his Mercedes at one of his employees. Welcome to the big time.

He and his crew occupied the fourth floor of the building. His personal office took up almost half of the total workspace. It was filled with big screen televisions, advanced photography equipment, and of course, a mahogany desk. After presenting us with tea and coffee, as a true Arab host would, the producer sat us down on two leather swivel chairs, set up a computer monitor in front of us, and played a five-minute clip from his latest movie.

It was called "Jordan Fights Terror."

Foreboding classical music played in the background and static images of bombed-out buildings and injured people appeared like a collage. Scenes then showed of would-be terrorists plotting a major attack and the valiant Jordanian security forces who were about to foil their plans.

Incredibly, the Jordanian authorities save the day. They literally snuck up on the terrorists in their bomb-making lair by walking on their tippy toes and visibly hushing each other to keep quiet. At the end, a handsome photo of King Abdullah II appears along with a message crediting him with keeping Jordan safe.

"Bravo!" Guy and I yelled as we clapped for our host and his film crew.

It wasn't a "good" movie, but it was somewhat entertaining.

"Thank you, thank you," he said proudly as we continued to clap. "America and Jordan are together against terrorism. Our fight is one fight." This man really sees eye-to-eye with us, I thought. "But Israel is the real terrorist. The world must finish her." Guy and I stopped clapping, though the producer kept talking. "My other movies teach this to the people so they know. You also must know."

"No!" Guy and I said in unison.

"Israel does like this to Jordan and Palestine!"

He put his arms around his neck and pretended to gag, as if someone was strangling him.

"You can't blame Israel for all of your country's problems!" I shouted back.

"Israel must end!" he emphatically contended. "Then Jordan will prosper. You must know, you must know!"

His demeanor turned belligerent and Guy and I abruptly left the building. That propagandist had no idea we were Jews or that Guy was from Israel. All he did was graciously host us and show off his work. I knew that, like all authoritarian dictators, Jordan's ruler needed an issue to deflect attention from domestic troubles to preserve a firm grip on power. But it still depressed me that there were government employees whose job it was to deliberately incite citizens to hate a country with which Jordan was at peace.

"A peace of paper," Guy added.

Dejected and exhausted, we arrived back at the Cliff Hotel just after four o'clock in the afternoon. We hoped to take a nap and hopefully engage in some friendly conversation with some open-minded travelers. But sadly, in the Middle East, what you hope for is rarely what you get.

"Wake up, Michael!" Guy urged. "I have a problem."

"What?" I asked half-heartedly.

"I was sitting out in the common area talking to this Japanese guy. Then, this couple, an English lady and a Palestinian guy overheard me say I'm from Israel. They started yelling at me and accusing me of being an accomplice to murder. They started saying all these things about Israel I don't know how to respond to."

"Just tell them you think there should be peace and you didn't come to Jordan to fight about politics," I advised. "If you're not back in five minutes I'll come out."

Guy left the room. After seven minutes, I knew naptime was over. I got out of bed, raced down the hallway towards the common area, and took a seat next to my friend across from a muscular, jovial-looking Palestinian man and his attractive blonde-haired blue-eyed

English wife. They warmly welcomed me to the conversation and, for a moment, my worries were allayed. Maybe this couple and Guy had already moved beyond their differences and were now discussing other matters of international importance. After all, isn't that what moderate worldly young people do?

"Your friend being from Israel is doing my husband and me a great deal of damage," the English woman charged. "We thought we'd enlighten him to the truth about his country."

"He needs to know about all the crimes and massacres against my people his country commits," the Palestinian added in impeccable English. "He'll be lucky if no one attacks him here in Amman."

Though they looked nice and respectable, this couple was clearly anything but.

"The only person under attack is my friend. By you," I snapped. "So stop it."

Overwhelmed by the futility of the conversation, Guy stayed silent. I, on the other hand, was fired up and curious to see where all this would lead.

"My husband has spent his entire life in a refugee camp in Nablus without the most basic necessities," the English woman griped. "This trip to Jordan is his first time abroad. Now, Israel won't let him back into Palestine. So, we're stuck. You know, I used to be on Israel's side of the conflict. But now I know that Israel should be destroyed."

"Whoa, let me try to understand this," I tried to say calmly. "You're telling me taking vacations abroad is a basic human necessity? Just so you know, we have a good friend whose family also lives in Nablus and his family travels all the time. And if your husband has never been outside of Jordan or the West Bank, then why does he speak English almost as well as a native?"

"I studied English," the Palestinian man insisted. "I worked hard so that I could tell the world about the atrocities. I know your Jewish priests or whoever order you to hate and kill Arabs and laugh about it. Israelis love killing Arabs. It is all they ever do!"

"I think you're lying about your life story," I said. "How can you so blindly accuse all Israelis of hating Arabs when my friend specifically chose to vacation in an Arab country? Israel wants peace. But it requires compromise on both sides. We want two states. Do you want two states?"

"Damn two states!" the Palestinian man screamed. The intensity of our argument startled a group of Japanese backpackers sitting on the other side of the room, and they hurried off to an outdoor patio. "I want all of Palestine because it is all ours. We will not stop fighting with our blood and by the sword until every piece of it is liberated."

Evidently, nothing I said would change this man's mind. So, I decided to tell him something he would never forget.

"You're a stupid child!" I scolded. "If you really don't want peace and you just want to destroy Israel, then I hope Israel locks you up in your playpen and that you end up in prison until you die. You will not defeat Israel in war. You can only try to wage peace. If you want to act like an irascible child and whine and shout and cry, then I'm glad Israel treats you as such. You're disgusting." The couple sat stunned and speechless, and Guy and I rose from the couch to leave. "We're done. Leave my friend alone, leave Israel alone, and have a nice day."

Although I was happy, I concluded the conversation on my own terms, all the fighting left me tense and wound up. Guy's feeling that an attack could happen at any moment suddenly grabbed me as well. In need of an outlet for our stress, we got out a frisbee Guy brought along for the trip and we walked to a park to toss it around to blow off steam.

Flinging the frisbee back and forth for a while as we watched the sun go down quickly calmed our nerves and put our minds at ease. Three Jordanian men, one older and two substantially younger, watched us play. Guy lobbed the frisbee in their direction to invite them to join us. For most of the next half hour, Guy and I did little else but chase down the frisbee these men overthrew every single time.

When we finished playing and approached them to formally meet one another, I realized everything I needed to know about these men was written on their foreheads. Above each pair of Jordanian eyes lay a *zebiba*, a cluster of discolored callused skin generated from banging one's forehead against a rough prayer mat. These men were devout Muslims, not exactly the people in Jordan known for being the greatest friends of the Jews.

I cringed at the thought of getting into another fight about religion, politics, or both. Guy and I had no strength for another argument, but we also didn't feel like lying. So, when the men asked us about our religion and where we were from, we told the truth and readied ourselves for a potentially fiery response. Instead, they replied with heart-wrenching questions.

"Why do Jews and the people in Israel hate Jordan?" the older man asked in Arabic.

Regrettably, it seemed propaganda like that created by our Jordanian film producer friend had an effect on people. However, Guy and I were more than happy to set the record straight if it involved no yelling.

"We don't hate Jordan," I stressed in Arabic and in English. "We think other Jews and Israelis don't hate Jordan either. We all want peace."

"And you like Arabs?" one of the younger men asked in English.

"We just played frisbee with you." Guy said. "That means we're friends."

The young man smiled and his *zebiba* shined prominently in the light of the surrounding park lamps.

"If all Jews and Arabs are very good friends, one day I am very happy," he said.

Despite all the misinformation these men harbored about Jews and Israel, it was refreshing they could set politics and religion aside and see the common humanity in the people standing in front of them.

When Guy and I returned to Haifa a couple days later, Guy called his bank as the Jordanian female teller had told him to.

"They saw someone was using my ATM card in Jordan and worried it had been stolen," he said. "The bank even called my grandmother because they couldn't get in touch with me."

"But your grandmother knew you were going to Jordan," I said.

"She thought I meant the Jordan River, not Jordan the country. She had no idea what was going on. None of my family can believe I traveled to a place like Jordan."

Without a doubt, Israel and Jordan had a way to go before their relationship inspired full trust and friendship among their citizens. Like Guy, I also had Israeli relatives who questioned my choice of travel plans.

I stayed in Israel for another week. A few days before returning to Cairo, I visited my mother's cousin Dovid and his wife Frieda at their home in Beitar Illit, a Jewish settlement southeast of Jerusalem. Dovid and Frieda were Haredi, Hebrew for ultra-Orthodox Jews, and lived a life committed to strict Torah law. In their community, owning a television was forbidden and they used the Internet only to check email and surf websites approved by their rabbis. When I dropped by their home to spend an afternoon with them, I tried to say as little as possible about my upcoming summer in Cairo, out of respect. Egypt was not exactly the place to lead an observant Jewish life, and I knew the idea of living there for any period was unfathomable to them.

To my relief, when I told Dovid and Frieda about my impending bus trip to Cairo, they were extraordinarily polite. They even tried to help me get there in accordance with Jewish law.

"You can't take that bus back to Cairo," Frieda said over lunch.

"Why not?" I asked.

"It is written, 'You must not go back that way again' (Deuteronomy 17:16). A Jew must not go back to Egypt the same way he came out. You can't take that bus. You'll have to take a flight."

Flights to Cairo from Tel Aviv cost at least three hundred dollars, whereas a bus ticket was no more than ten bucks at the time. To me, taking the bus back to Cairo was worth risking a disaster of biblical proportions.

"Do what you want," Frieda urged. "But don't say I didn't warn you."

Chapter 4
The Egyptian Way

Egypt
June–July 2006

STRANDED IN THE WILDERNESS OF SINAI ABOUT TO BE engulfed by flames, I really wished I'd just listened to cousin Frieda and paid for the damn flight back to Cairo. But it was too late. I'd disobeyed her interpretation of God's law and angered the Almighty. Now, His fiery wrath was upon me and I feared my imminent demise. I stared into the flames unsure how much longer I had to live. One question occupied my mind: Why did airfare have to be so expensive?

A few hours earlier, just after sunset, my bus left the station for the overnight trip to Cairo from Taba, the coastal Egyptian town next to the Israeli border. Forty minutes into what should have been a seven-hour journey, the bearded Egyptian man sitting in the torn leather-bound seat in front of me was chain-smoking away on his fifth unfiltered cigarette of the trip. I tried to ignore the smoke at first and thought nothing of allowing him a few puffs to relax. But when he lit up a fifth time, I was fed up. I saw his actions as nothing less than an egregious assault on my lungs and the respiratory systems of all seventeen passengers on the bus. Jen, an American woman in her mid-thirties on a year-long trip around the world, sat in the window seat next to me and urged me not to say anything.

"Let an Egyptian yell at him," she advised. "You're not from here. He's not going to listen to you."

But no Egyptian said anything or looked like they were about to say anything. And that meant I had to say something. Besides, who was she to dictate my behavior? She had the window seat with all the fresh air blowing in her face while I developed emphysema.

I tapped the man on the shoulder and politely asked him to stop. He smiled, exposing a mouth full of yellow teeth, rolled his watery eyes, and lightly sprinkled ash near my feet. I pointed up at the clearly visible "No Smoking" sticker on display above the aisle across from us, but the man only nodded his head and carried on. I tried to make my point using more graphic means. I contorted my face and held my hands up to my neck to show the smoke from his cigarettes was making me sick. I coughed, gagged, and pretended to die, slumping down in my seat with my eyes closed half-way and my tongue sticking out. A group of Egyptians sitting nearby erupted in a round of applause. My adversary laughed playfully. Without missing a beat, he popped another cigarette into his mouth and offered some smokes to my audience.

"That was very cute. Now stop," Jen demanded. "Now four people are smoking, not just one."

"Not yet," I replied defiantly. "There's one more thing I can do."

I rose from my seat and valiantly strode down the aisle towards the driver to lodge a formal complaint against the nicotine-addicted lawbreakers. Normally I hated the idea of snitching, but this mission was bigger than just one bus ride across the Sinai. This was a crusade on behalf of free-breathing people everywhere.

As I neared the driver, however, I realized he would probably not be the best person to ask for assistance. On the wall above his head was another "No Smoking" sticker. In his left hand, he held an almost totally consumed cigarette. I returned to my seat defeated and sunk my face inside my t-shirt to shield myself from the smoke.

"In Egypt, the only way is the Egyptian way," Jen said. "Egyptians won't accept criticism from any westerner. If you criticize something, it doesn't matter how right you are because they will never listen to you. That man thought you were entertaining, so he humored you. But he was never going to stop smoking. If you say they're doing something wrong, it only insults their pride."

"Why should pride be important if what they're doing is wrong?" I asked, my voice muffled by my t-shirt.

"You wouldn't understand because you're not Egyptian. You can't change them. I've traveled a lot in Egypt and in other Arab countries. When I first came here, I was really determined to teach Egyptian men to treat western women with respect. So, I sat next to them on buses and started up conversations. But now I'm sick of mustached men reaching up my thigh, and that's why I'm sitting next to you."

And so we sat, she near the window, breathing the dry clean desert air, and I with my t-shirt over my face, trying to avoid toxic carcinogens, until just after two in the morning when Jen smacked me in the chest in a state of panic.

"Michael, the smoke!" she shouted. "You have to do something!"

"I know there's smoke," I muttered. "Everyone's been smoking cigarettes."

"No, it's different. Look."

Black smoke coming from the front of the bus flooded the cabin. This wasn't cigarette smoke. This was something much worse. I kept my t-shirt over my nose and mouth and saw almost all the passengers cloaking their faces with garments and attempting to stick their heads out the window. Two devout Muslim women draped in the *niqab*, a black cloth that veils the face, took additional cover by wrapping their heads in blankets. Although the other passengers appeared distressed by the unfortunate state of our oxygen supply, no one pleaded with the driver to pull the bus over.

"Why doesn't the driver stop? What's the problem here?" I frantically shouted in Arabic.

An Egyptian teenager sitting directly behind me holding a blue rag over his face put his arm on my shoulder.

"There is a problem with the bus," he said. "The driver wants to get the bus to Cairo."

"How long will it take to get to Cairo?" I asked.

"Three hours maybe."

"In three hours, we could all be dead."

That was no exaggeration. By driving a bus with a dying engine emitting smoke and other poisonous fumes, the driver was putting everyone at risk of severe smoke inhalation, including himself. I, for one, didn't intend to begin my summer in Egypt in a hospital bed. So, I stood up from my seat once more and struggled to advance towards the driver. A cloud of thick black smoke prevented me from marching more than a few rows up. I was forced to retreat to my seat and content myself with shouting.

"*Waakef al-bees! Waakef al-bees!*" I yelled through my t-shirt while I gasped for breath. Stop the bus! Stop the bus!

With his head hanging out the window and the engine wailing louder than I could scream, the driver couldn't hear me. Jen screamed the order out the window, but the howling wind carried her message in the opposite direction, still further from the driver. If just a few of the other passengers had joined our cause, we would have been able to get the driver's attention easily. However, not one Egyptian spoke up and I sat in my seat depleted of energy.

"They think we're freaking out for no reason," Jen said. "Do these people not know anything about the effects of smoke inhalation? If one Egyptian stepped forward others might listen to him."

Using my broken Arabic to encourage an Egyptian to speak up to save our lungs and our lives was more than I could handle at that point. I began to feel light-headed and dizzy, and my vision blurred. I needed the bus to stop and didn't think it was possible for the situation to get any worse. It did.

"Fire!" Jen screamed. "The engine is on fire!" My fuzzy vision and impaired awareness made the flames look far more powerful and daunting than they probably were. For a few moments, I sat paralyzed staring at the fire a few feet away, convinced the bus was on the verge of exploding into a monstrous inferno. Maybe this was the end. Maybe the Egyptians who refused to aid my efforts to stop the bus were actually servants of the Angel of Death. Maybe I should have just asked my parents to pay for the flight to Cairo to avoid incurring the wrath of God.

Due to shock and oxygen deprivation, I wasn't paying attention when the bus finally came to a halt. Apparently, the driver parked on the side of the road, hopped out of an emergency door located next to the steering wheel, and tossed blankets on the engine hood to put out the fire. I watched passively as a couple of well-intentioned Egyptian men struggled to pry open the emergency exit in the passenger area. When they couldn't budge the handle, able-bodied daring folks, including Jen and me, climbed carefully out the window opening and then jumped down. The elderly and less adventurous waited until the fire was completely out before exiting the bus via the main door.

Miraculously, no one sustained any serious injuries, but the close encounter with death had visibly shaken everyone. Some people recovered from the incident by sitting on the ground in silence. Others prostrated themselves towards Mecca and thanked Allah for sparing their lives. I chose to plant myself on a comfortable mound of sand and bitch to Jen.

I was furious it took a full-blown engine fire to convince our bus driver to stop. If the fire had spread out of control, those unable to jump out the windows would have died pointlessly since the bus lacked a functional emergency exit.

It took six hours for another bus to rescue us from the wilderness of Sinai. While those six hours were certainly more tolerable than the forty years the ancient Israelites were stuck there, unlike me the ancient Israelites didn't have to worry about any more Egyptians fouling up their plans. It was at my fellow Egyptian passengers, after all, that I directed most of my anger. Their refusal to help us distract the driver nearly cost us our lives.

During my discussion with Jen, the Egyptian teenager who I'd briefly spoken to during the fiasco kindly came over to make sure we were all right. As soon as he sat down with us, I grilled him with questions about his take on the incident.

"No Egyptian told the driver to stop. Why?" I asked in Arabic.

"People wanted to say something," he said. "But they couldn't be seen saying it with you."

"Why not? If everyone said something together, the driver might have heard us."

"You are not an Egyptian. If you say an Egyptian is doing something wrong, no Egyptian will stand with you. An Egyptian must always stand with his people."

"Even if it means letting people die?"

"I am sorry. This is the Egyptian way."

Then the Egyptian way sucks, I said to myself. I thought about saying it out loud but what was the point? Nobody would have listened to me anyways.

Thank God, I was about to start my summer at AUC, an American-style English-language university that supposedly functioned as a bastion of liberal thought and free speech in the heart of autocratic Egypt. Since moved to New Cairo, at that time the main campus was located next to Tahrir Square in downtown Cairo, the site of the 2011 political protests that led to the resignation of then-President Mubarak. The AUC campus served as a safe place for its six thousand students to debate and deliberate on the future of Egypt and the entire Arab world. Surely there I would find a tolerant atmosphere that encouraged Egyptian students to engage the outsider's perspective, not ignore it.

Thanks to my transportation mishap, I arrived in Cairo just an hour before the start of a mandatory orientation for international students. Rather than risk being late I immediately headed to the main campus to meet and greet fellow students. Seated in a white fold-out chair in a stone-covered courtyard on the AUC campus with the ninety other summer study abroad students, there was no question about it. I stank. My clothes reeked of smoke from the cigarettes and engine fire, and traces of black soot colored my cheeks. While my appearance made me a conversation piece, I wasn't counting on landing any dates.

"Look at you!" A skinny blonde guy in a pink polo shirt said flamboyantly as he took the seat on my right. "Where in the world have you been? You need someone to clean you up."

His tone and vocal inflection suggested he was gay and his flirtatious attitude hinted that he wondered if I was too. Maybe dressing like a hobo could help me land a date, but apparently not with the gender I preferred. Nevertheless, I excitedly told my new friend about my journey.

"You are so brave!" he cheered. "I can't believe you went to Palestine. I can't wait to go there."

Unsure if he fully understood I'd spent less than one afternoon over the Green Line, I asked him where in Palestine he wanted to go.

"Oh, all over. Ramallah, Jerusalem, even to Tel Aviv and Haifa."

"You know Tel Aviv and Haifa are part of Israel, right?"

"I don't know if I can agree with that," he said, pointing to the Palestine solidarity bracelet he wore on his left wrist. "It's all Palestine, but people just call it by different names. Back in California I'm very active in the group Queers for Palestine. I can't wait to go to Palestine to see everything for myself."

And neither could I. Gays in Palestinian society (and throughout the Arab world) are subjected to severe homophobia and harassment. Many try to flee to Israel to escape very real life-threatening danger. I couldn't fathom why he would so ardently support a society that persecuted people of his sexual orientation. I supported him visiting Israel and the Palestinian territories because it was the only way for him to develop a nuanced view of the Israel-Palestinian conflict. If he continued to disagree with everything I believed in afterwards that was his right. After all, we were entitled to express our opinions on the campus of AUC, weren't we?

After a few introductory speeches, a woman in her mid-sixties and dripping in diamonds ascended the podium to share a special message with us.

"As the representative of AUC's alumni association, I want to welcome all of you to Egypt," she said. "I hope you have a truly wonderful experience here this summer. For this experience to be positive for both you and the people of Egypt, one thing must be clear. Never. Ever. Criticize. Anything. Ever."

Her tone became belligerent and students seated near me looked around at each other confused.

"Egyptians are a very proud people with an ancient history," she continued. "If you have a problem with something that goes on here then the problem is with you. You are closed-minded if you want to criticize us. To make my point clear I want to tell you about a situation we had a few years ago that should serve as a warning to all of you. A few years ago, several American students were getting out of a taxi in front of the main campus entrance. They were angry at their cab driver for the fare he charged them. They felt this poor Egyptian man ripped them off. After he drove away they yelled out, 'Fucking Egyptians!'"

She placed her lips on the microphone and repeated the words with gusto.

"Fucking Egyptians!" she screamed, causing the speakers to emit deafening feedback screech. "This upset a few Egyptian students who saw it happen. They complained to the administration about it. Within a day these Americans had all been deported from Egypt. We can make that happen."

The speaker smirked as she scanned the audience observing the intimidated expressions on the students' faces.

"There's only one more thing I want to tell you. Never ever refer to Egypt as an African country. Egypt is an Arab country in the Middle East and we have nothing in common with the black countries south of us."

Her comment was especially strange since a few months earlier Egypt had won the 2006 African Cup, the continent's premiere soccer tournament.

"Remember," she concluded. "This is Egypt, not America. Be warned. Keep your mouths shut."

A week into the summer session, I learned even professors could get into trouble for not toeing the official Egyptian line. International students enrolled in an Arab history class claimed their American professor had been threatened with dismissal after a lecture he delivered infuriated some Egyptian students. Allegedly, the professor said that during the seventh century Muslim conquest of North Africa, Arab armies forcibly imposed Islam on many local inhabitants. This challenged the traditional Islamic view that not only did residents of newly conquered lands voluntarily convert to Islam, but that they joyously welcomed the invading Arab armies into their countries.

The Egyptian students viewed the professor's comments as an assault on their history, and they wouldn't entertain his arguments for the sake of academic discussion. Regardless of the individual opinions held by AUC's American administrators on the history of the spread of Islam, the university wanted to resolve the issue quickly without generating attention. Students in the class later said the professor publicly retracted his statements to keep his job.

The two summer courses I enrolled in were second year Modern Standard Arabic and beginner's Egyptian colloquial Arabic, topics entirely devoid of historical and political content. I wanted to spend my time focusing on my language skills, rather than getting into trouble for expressing unpopular opinions. But it was difficult to remain silent when, on the way to and from class each day, I was forced to pass a collage of photos of starry-eyed American students wrapped in *keffiyeh*s posing with smiling bearded leaders of Hamas, a group the US government defined as a terrorist organization committed to Israel's destruction.

Apparently, AUC had organized a school-sponsored trip to the West Bank the previous semester, and meeting with all major Palestinian "political groups" was a big part of the agenda. At least half a dozen photos showed Hamas representatives boarding the official AUC tour bus, giving speeches, and shaking hands with and hugging students. Considering the tremendous funding AUC received from official US government sources such as USAID, I found it highly inappropriate the university would encourage meetings with a terrorist group, and put it on public display.

"Don't say anything," said my friend Brendan, a pale-skinned shaggy-haired student from Rutgers with a thick New Jersey accent. "In Egypt, you'll get in trouble for opening your mouth. There's nothing that happens here that you can fix."

So, just as instructed at orientation, I kept my mouth shut. But that became increasingly difficult to do as I began to realize just how badly Egypt needed fixing.

To understand that Egypt didn't function the way it should, you only had to watch the mounds of garbage pile up on the cracked sidewalks or endure university-educated taxi drivers begging to take you places you didn't want to go. You could have said hello to one of the numerous police officers constantly patrolling the streets. Egypt had one of the highest police officer-to-civilian ratios in the world, which enabled the government to prevent dissent and prop up the rule of Hosni Mubarak. Maybe the friendly officer would have asked you for *baksheesh*, a "tip," to help him supplement his meager salary.

"You can't do anything in Egypt without paying *baksheesh*," an over-weight computer science student named Hassan told me over tea in the campus cafeteria one afternoon. "They say it's a tip, but it's really a bribe. If you need government documents, want to take out a loan from the bank, or even get a job you must pay *baksheesh*. People in Egypt cannot survive on their basic salaries. They need an additional boost wherever they can get it."

Egypt became stuck in the club of nations whose standard of living was worse in the twenty-first century than it had been a hundred years earlier. Over the decades, government policies repeatedly failed to improve living standards. Unfettered population growth, a lack of arable land and resources, and massive government corruption forced most Egyptians to live lives of crowded squalor. Lacking immediate prospects for a better future, most people turned back to a traditional source for answers and hope.

"Islam," an Egyptian prostitute insisted. "Islam will help you with any problem."

Scantily clad in a green mini-skirt and a strapless black top, the sex worker's lips were painted the color of salmon and her eyelids were smeared with black makeup. She was the last person in Cairo who I expected to dish out religious advice.

Just after dusk one night, I saw her standing outside the main gate of the chic Marriott Hotel in Zamalek, not far from my dorm building. I was walking on the opposite side of the street after finishing up a quick jog when she grabbed my attention with a whistle.

"Excuse me, sir," she said flirtatiously in accented but fluent English as she strutted towards me. "You are very handsome. You have beautiful eyes. You look very strong. I am drawn to you."

I knew she was just trying to drum up business, but it was flattering to hear her compliments. I couldn't help but grin.

"I see that your cheeks are red from seeing me," she said. "Maybe you are drawn to me too?"

I laughed nervously and claimed my cheeks were flushed red from exercise.

"You're very pretty," I told her. "But I'm not interested."

Unconvinced by my rejection, she placed her hand on my arm, pouted, and spoke enticingly in my ear.

"I'm not so expensive for a western man like you. Let's be together. Tonight, you will be my Pharaoh and I will worship you."

Declining her offer, I took a few steps back from her and began walking away when she steered our encounter in a new direction.

"You are a Muslim?" she asked.

"No. Why?"

"Because you behave like a real Muslim," she said flatteringly. "I can see you are already a strong man. If you become a Muslim, you will be stronger. Islam will help you with any problem. Promise me you will become a Muslim."

"I promise I'll consider it," I assured her.

"Are you sure you don't want to bring me back to your home? We can have a nice time together."

"You want to come home with me, get paid for having sex, and then convert me to Islam?"

The woman squinted her eyes at me seductively for another second, blew a kiss in my direction, and returned to the Marriott's main gate without saying a word. I walked alone and bemused back to my dorm. Islam pervaded Egypt to such a degree even its whores were pressuring me to submit.

"But it hasn't always been like that," Dina, my Arabic professor, clarified during a break from one of her lessons early in the summer semester

Approaching retirement age, Dina claimed to have been a devout Muslim from birth and said she was picked on as a child for wearing the hijab.

"Today ninety percent of women wear the hijab, but when I was young, you were more likely to see an Egyptian girl showing off her goodies in a mini-skirt than dressed appropriately in a hijab," she recalled. "All the young men and women I knew growing up were obsessed with being secular. In those days, it was like the Nile flowed with alcohol."

"How did everything change so fast?" I asked Dina.

"People had a lot of questions secularism could not answer. How did Egypt become so poor? How did we lose so badly to Israel in war? For too long, Egyptians had forgotten their heritage and their faith. Secularism doomed us. People realized quickly the truth came from Islam. If you want to understand Egypt, then you must understand Islam."

Either by the grace of Allah or the AUC housing coordinator, I was blessed with a devout Muslim roommate who was more than happy to guide me to a deeper understanding of his faith. I first met Steve in our seventh floor two-person dorm room after the warm welcome all the international students received at the orientation.

When I stepped through the door with my suitcase and backpack, I found a clean-cut Caucasian-looking man with buzzed brown hair. He wore a tucked-in polo shirt and was meticulously arranging and re-arranging his belongings in various drawers. As we divided up the living space and set ground rules, I noticed that not only did Steve smile constantly, but his every word was said with utmost enthusiasm and positivity.

"You want the drawer on the left? Awesome, man!" he said. "You think we should get dinner later? That's the greatest idea in the world!" He had just the right upbeat, charismatic personality to be an extremely successful missionary. After telling me he came from a small town just outside Houston, I wondered if a Christian missionary was exactly what he was.

"So, being from the Bible Belt, does that mean you're a big fan of JC?" I asked.

"No, no," he laughed. "I'm a Muslim. My father is from Pakistan and I'm a Muslim just like him. My mother's family is Irish Catholic. Are you a Christian?"

"No, I'm not."

"So, you're a Muslim too!" he said gleefully.

"I'm a Jew," I said, bursting his bubble.

"Ah," he sighed mildly disappointed. "That's cool. Just so you know, I get up to pray in the morning, pretty early."

That was no exaggeration. Every day just after dawn, Steve woke up to kneel on the ground and diligently recite Islam's first prayer.

Although he did his best to tiptoe around and pray silently, often his morning ritual woke me up too. I never complained because I wanted to encourage Steve to be as devout as he wished. He was, after all, a relatively new adherent to the faith.

"I was pretty anti-religion for a long time," Steve told me. "I had dreadlocks and blamed religion for all the world's problems. But late in high school, my dad started going to the mosque more often and I decided to join him just to see what it was like. After I started going I liked what I saw and haven't stopped attending mosque since."

Fortunately for Steve, Egypt had more mosques than he knew what to do with. He committed himself to attending communal prayers in a mosque at least once a day, usually in the afternoons after our classes were finished. Two weeks in as roommates, I asked Steve if I could go with him to different mosques to see what it was like.

"Of course!" Steve said exuberantly. "I hope you love it like I love it."

Steve didn't count on me converting to Islam, but I'm pretty sure he was open to the idea. Nevertheless, he wasn't completely sure how the leadership at the different mosques would feel about him bringing a non-Muslim to a prayer service. There was no explicit prohibition against non-Muslims entering a mosque, but there were dissenting opinions on the subject. Since Steve spoke very little Arabic and was nervous about making unusual requests at mosques with varying customs, he thought of a different solution to avoid problems.

"I'll teach you to pray like a Muslim, so everyone just thinks you're a Muslim," he suggested. "That way no one will ask you any questions."

"Alright," I said. "I'm ready to go undercover."

That night, Steve administered a crash course in mosque ritual, most of which was spent in the communal bathroom we shared with other students.

"Before you enter a mosque, you must wash yourself carefully," he said as we stood next to a sink. "Even if you're not a Muslim, you must still purify yourself."

The reality was that the very specific procedure he followed to ritually cleanse his hands, arms, hair, ears, face, nose, and mouth was more than I could master in a single night.

"All I've learned is how to make a mess in the bathroom," I said, frustrated. "And I thought Judaism was obsessed with rules."

"Don't worry. No one will watch you wash anyways, so just do whatever I do. The important thing is to memorize the *Shahada,* the declaration of faith in Islam. It comes up often during prayers. If you just keep repeating it over and over again no one will give you a second glance."

Before heading to bed, Steve carefully showed me how to kneel, bow, and stand during prayer. He patiently listened as I recited the words that, if said sincerely, would have made me a Muslim: *lā 'ilāha 'illallāh, Muhammad rasūlu-llāh.* There is no god but Allah, and Muhammad is the messenger of Allah.

When I first started praying with Steve at different Cairo mosques, I felt like I stood out among the worshippers, who were mostly Egyptian men of various ages. Few women, if any, showed up for services I attended and, when they did, they prayed in the back. Every time I lined up in one of the dozens of parallel rows of men behind the chanting imam, everyone around me recited the afternoon prayers in unison.

I mumbled the *Shahada* repeatedly, as Steve advised, but I made mistakes with everything else. When the worshippers around me bowed, I accidentally kneeled. When they rose to stand, I was still kneeling on the ground. I remembered the motions Steve taught me, but had trouble with the order. Services were conducted surprisingly fast and I found it difficult to keep up. Still, none of the other men in attendance ever seemed bothered by my obvious lack of experience praying in a mosque, and I was never questioned about my reasons for being there.

"It seems everyone assumes you're a Muslim," Steve surmised. "And if you're not, that's between you and God."

I wound up going to the mosque for afternoon services a couple times a week for a few weeks. While other worshippers who prayed in our vicinity usually said a kind word to us before or after prayers, these polite gestures rarely developed into substantial conversations. As soon as prayers were finished, most of the people would dash out of the mosque as quickly as possible to get back to work. Few stuck around to schmooze or listen to any lectures from the imam unless it was a Friday, the Muslim Sabbath.

"It's amazing so many people come to the mosque even when they're exhausted and in the middle of their day," Steve would say. "I've never been to a country before where the people have such incredible faith."

Undoubtedly, faith played a powerful role in Egypt. But faith alone could not provide tangible solutions to Egypt's modern ailments. People needed an outlet for their frustration and something to hold responsible for their nation's fall from grace. Since criticism of the government was forbidden, Egyptians were encouraged to blame their problems on the Arab world's favorite scapegoat.

Chapter 5
This Is Not a Mosque

Egypt
June–July 2006

ISRAEL!" THE DRIVER BURST OUT IN ARABIC. "WITHOUT ISRAEL in the world, Egypt would not have one problem."

Yet again, I was being driven to campus one morning in a taxi after missing the free shuttle bus from the dormitory. Rants by cabbies like this one were becoming all too common and it was easy to see where this unwarranted speech was headed. Usually after lambasting Israel, the extremely passionate driver would criticize the evil monsters responsible for the terrible mayhem the Zionist entity inflicted on poor Egyptians and Arabs everywhere.

"The Jews!" the driver continued. "Know this about the Jews. Among every people in the world, there is good and there is bad, except for the Jews. It is not important if they are in Israel, America, or in Egypt. They are all very bad."

Although Egypt's government permitted the practice of Judaism and enjoyed two billion dollars a year in US military aid for upholding its peace treaty with Israel, it also actively shoved anti-Semitic and anti-Israel propaganda in its citizens' faces from nearly every direction.

Filling the pages of leading government-owned newspapers were countless articles disparaging Israel and in-depth analyses about global Jewish power. On prominent display in the windows of bookshops were hit best sellers *Mein Kampf* and the *Protocols of the Elders of Zion,* an anti-Semitic hoax purporting to describe a Jewish quest for world domination. Even the most popular programs on government-sponsored television demonized Jews.

At the time, Egyptians excitedly anticipated the premiere of the television series *Horseman Without a Horse,* whose producer promised to include scenes depicting Jews upholding the *Protocols* conspiracy.

To a certain extent, efforts to divert the public's attention away from the government were understandable. If Egyptians attributed their problems to a worldwide Jewish conspiracy, pressure was taken off their own leaders to carry out reform. However, for any regime to stick around, a government must not only dispense blame, but highlight past accomplishments. Since stories of such accomplishment in Egypt were quite scarce, the government simply made stuff up.

"It's a shame you will not be here for the October celebrations," my bushy eyebrowed waiter lamented in English at Café Tobasco, an upscale coffee shop in Zamalek, as he presented me with a tall Oreo milkshake one afternoon. He was in the middle of telling me about his political science studies at Cairo University, when he changed topics after hearing I would not be in Egypt in the fall.

"To understand Egypt," he said, "you must see how we celebrate victory."

"And what victory do you celebrate in October?" I asked facetiously.

In fact, I thought I knew exactly what Egyptians celebrated every October: the anniversary of the outbreak of the 1973 war with Israel. It wasn't important to Egyptians that, by the time a ceasefire was declared, Israeli forces had obliterated their army and were marching straight for Cairo. What mattered was that Egypt won an early battle against the supposedly invincible Israeli army by launching a surprise attack and breaking through an Israeli blockade. History books in the West explained that this was enough to restore Egyptian pride and pave the way for Egyptian-Israeli peace.

"In the 1973 war," the waiter answered enthusiastically, "the Egyptian Army defeated Israel and re-conquered the entire Sinai Peninsula."

"What do you mean re-conquered?" I asked belligerently. I didn't mean to be rude but his assertion caught me off guard. "Israel gave Egypt the Sinai Peninsula back in exchange for peace. You know this, don't you?"

"I think I know the history of my country better than you. I study political science at Cairo University. Egypt won back the Sinai in 1973."

"Then what about the peace with Israel?" I snapped. "Why did Egypt make peace if it already had the Sinai?"

"Egypt made peace with Israel to receive money from America."

"This isn't true. Look at any history book and—"

"You do not tell me that my country is a liar!" he cut me off yelling. "Your government is the one that brainwashes, not mine. You cannot speak against Egyptian pride!"

I should have expected a display of unrelenting Egyptian pride since it never failed to arise at inopportune times. Our tense argument drew stares from other customers, so I dropped money on the table and headed for the door.

The extreme mistrust Egyptians felt towards Jews and Israel influenced their preferences in all spheres of life, even sports.

Just a few days after beginning classes at AUC, the 2006 World Cup kicked off in Germany. Although Egypt's national team failed to qualify, Egyptians followed the month-long tournament religiously. Soccer games seemed to air constantly on every television and radio in Cairo. During the first week of competition in the middle of that June, I asked kiosk owners, taxi drivers, security guards, and even a few children peddling toilet paper on the street which teams they supported. Ghana and Germany were constantly identified as Egyptian fan favorites.

Mahmoud, a postcard salesman in his late fifties who worked right outside the Egyptian Museum, filled me in on how Egyptians decided which country to support.

"Ghana is the pride of Africa," he said in Arabic. "We must support them."

"But Egypt isn't in Africa," I objected, testing the belief held by at least one member of AUC's alumni association.

"That is *majnoon*," Mahmoud declared, using the Arabic word for crazy, as he scratched his head. "Egypt won the African Cup. Egypt is Africa."

"I guess you're right," I agreed. "But why do Egyptians like Germany? Why not England, France, or even America?"

"England and France were our colonial occupiers, America makes colonialism in Iraq. With Germany, there is not one problem. Germany is strong. They fight the Jews. Which team do you like?"

I didn't give a hoot about soccer, but Egyptians couldn't fathom how someone could be apathetic about the World Cup. I wanted to show camaraderie with Egyptians, so I picked the team that presumably did not fight the Jews.

"I stand with Ghana," I stated enthusiastically.

"*Al-hamdu lilaah!*" Mahmoud affirmed in approval of my choice. Praise God!

My decision to support Ghana's Black Stars may have caused a serious re-alignment of the cosmos. Ten days into World Cup play, Ghana went from the pride of Africa to the team Egyptians reviled the most.

I caught only the final minute of Ghana's match against the Czech Republic on June 17, 2006, on the big screen television in the common area of our dormitory. Before I saw the score, the outcome was already clear. Seated on the leather couches surrounding the television were mostly Arab students from other countries and a few Egyptian boarders not from Cairo. They seemed frozen in shock and disbelief. Standing next to me was a tense balding Egyptian student with his arms crossed. I patted him on the shoulder and requested an update.

"How much did Ghana lose by?" I asked.

"Lose?" he responded confused. "Ghana won. They beat the Czechs 2–0."

"Then why is everyone so down? Isn't that good?"

"No! No Egyptian will ever support Ghana again. Ghana's team is filled with Zionists."

Puzzled, I focused my eyes on the television screen and watched clips of the game's highlights. After each of the two goals Ghana scored against the Czechs, a Ghanaian player named John Pantsil paraded around the field waving an Israeli flag he somehow concealed in his sock. Scenes of him draping his teammates in the blue and white were caught on live international television by hundreds of millions of viewers. When asked to explain, Pantsil, who played professionally for an Israeli club, stated simply that he loved Israel and wanted to do something to please his Israeli fans. Naturally, Egyptians were pissed.

"When I watched I could not believe it," Mahmoud said. "As an Egyptian and a lover of football, this brings me pain!"

"Why do you think Pantsil did it?" I asked.

"He is a Mossad spy. That is the only possibility."

Egyptian media outlets ran stories saying the same thing, adding that Israeli coaches routinely kidnapped disadvantaged African children with extraordinary soccer talent, forced them into rigorous training camps, and brainwashed them into loving Israel.

"I cannot support Ghana now," Mahmoud said resolutely. "My pride is hurt. Now I support only Germany. The Ghana football team is in the hands of the Jews."

I wanted to yell. I wanted to scream. I wanted to tell Mahmoud how nuts everything he was saying was. No, not everyone in the world who said a good thing about Israel was a Mossad spy. No, the Ghana soccer team was not in the hands of the Jews. And yes, there were many good reasons to support Germany at the World Cup, but admiration for the Nazis was not one of them. But I didn't.

When I returned to Egypt from my trip to Israel and Jordan I tried to be more discreet about my religion and political convictions. I realized the dangers of admitting to being Jewish in environments that were unfamiliar or where I lacked control, such as in taxi cabs or restaurants. Although it pained me not to set the record straight with every Egyptian who made negative comments about Jews, I wasn't proficient enough in Arabic to participate in nuanced discussions. As a general guideline, I avoided revealing my Jewish identity to people who were unable to thoroughly comprehend English unless it was extremely clear they would not become hostile.

I knew of eight other Jewish students studying at AUC that summer. A few identified as Jews only because their Semitic-sounding last names shackled them to their people. But most of them cared quite a bit about being Jewish. Unfortunately, Cairo didn't offer many options to practice Judaism on any meaningful level.

Less than sixty years before, Egypt had been a nation filled with synagogues, kosher butcher shops, and an active community nearly eighty thousand strong. The Jewish community's position deteriorated drastically following World War II and the founding of the state of

Israel. A brand of militant nationalism with Nazi sympathies took over
and Jewish communal sites became the targets of violent attacks.

Egypt's military losses to Israel led its government to seize Jewish
property, expel tens of thousands of Jews, and declare anyone who
remained an enemy of the state. By the end of the 1960s, the forced
exodus of Egyptian Jewry was nearly complete. In 2006, less than one
hundred mostly elderly Jewish women remained in Egypt, along with
one semi-functional synagogue in Cairo called *Sha'ar HaShamayim*,
or "Gate of Heaven" in English.

"Do you want to go this Friday night?" Sarah, a curly-haired Jewish
girl from Ohio State, asked me with a whisper one afternoon in early
July in between classes. She always looked around carefully and lowered her voice when she wanted to talk about something Jewish.

"Definitely," I said. "Will there be Shabbat services?"

"No idea. All I know is the building hasn't moved in a hundred years."

"Is it safe to go?"

"No idea. How about you try finding out?"

So try I did, but my intelligence gathering efforts only led me to
dead end after dead end. I scoured the Internet in search of contacts
from the Egyptian Jewish community with no luck. I did find the name
of one woman who claimed to serve as the community head, but I
couldn't retrieve an email address or a telephone number.

I phoned the Israeli embassy for help, but the representative I spoke
to said he could only provide information in person in the mornings.

"But I have class every morning!" I protested. "All I need to know is
if it's safe to visit the *Sha'ar HaShamayim* Synagogue."

"And I will give you that information after I meet you in person. This
is an issue of security. And don't speak Hebrew over the phone. It will
bring you trouble."

That Friday afternoon, long before sunset, Sarah and I, and Arlana,
another brown-haired Jewish girl from Ohio State, hopped into a taxi
armed with our American passports and the synagogue's address. We
wanted to avoid telling anyone we were on our way to a synagogue, so
I told the taxi driver to take us to Adly Street, where the synagogue
was located, without specifying a street number.

"Adly Street is very long," the driver said in Arabic. "What number is it? Where do you want to go?"

"Just take us to Adly and we'll let you know," I said.

We asked to be dropped off a few blocks away from the synagogue's exact location. That way we thought we'd be able to casually stroll past the building and see if Friday night services were drawing any negative attention from angry Egyptian bystanders.

As soon as the engraved Star of David above the synagogue's entrance came into view, we saw a scene that made us fear the worst and hope for the best. Guarding the synagogue on all sides were dozens of alert Egyptian police officers in black uniforms and bulletproof body armor carrying semi-automatic weapons. They stood behind large metal barricades and barked orders at Egyptian passersby to move back.

"Maybe a lot of people are coming to services and that's why they have so much security?" Arlana offered.

It didn't look that way from afar. Nobody went in or out of the three story tall stone structure. The three of us smiled nervously as we crossed the street. We offered our passports to the serious-looking mustached police officer blocking the steps leading to the synagogue entrance.

"Good evening, officer," I greeted in Arabic. "Is everything okay here tonight?"

The officer's frown disappeared instantly and he let loose a wide smile. Without saying a word, he grabbed my passport from my hand and glanced through the pages. Each time he found traces of an Egyptian visa stamp he stuck his thumb up and said "Egypt good!" in English. After handing my passport back to me, he looked at us like he didn't have a clue what we wanted from him.

"We can enter?" I asked. "We have come for prayer. You know, to pray like in a mosque?"

"Ah, this is not a mosque!" he belted out.

"We know it's not a mosque," Sarah chimed in. "We want to pray *here*," she emphasized, pointing her finger at the sidewalk.

The officer raised one eyebrow and glared at us with a look of bewilderment. He glanced at the ground and frowned, not appearing to understand why anyone would choose to pray in such an uncomfortable spot. Rapidly losing patience with the conversation, I tried stating our intentions more creatively by emulating the flamboyant act of praying. I imagined all the movie scenes of Native American rain dances and, for about ten seconds, I ran in place, raised my arms towards the sky, shook my hands and head, and sang gibberish with a steady rhythm.

"Ah, you want to pray in there!" the officer said. "There is no praying in this building today."

"Why not?" I asked.

"No one is here."

"Well, is there a problem here? Did something bad happen?"

"No, *Al-Hamdu-lilaah.*"

"So if there are no prayers and there is no problem, then why are all the police officers here?"

"We are always here. We always guard this building. It is our duty."

"Will there be prayers here tomorrow?"

"Maybe. Come back at nine in the morning. I will be here."

True to his word, when Sarah, Arlana, and I returned to the synagogue less than thirteen hours later, we found the exact same police officer standing in front of the entrance.

"Why are you still here?" I asked in disbelief.

"I work nineteen hours straight," he testified. "Soon *khalas* (finished).

"Today we may enter the building?"

"Yes, follow me."

As soon as we started climbing the concrete steps behind him, the front door was pushed wide open by an energetic elderly woman wearing a green night gown and a blue rag over her hair. She enthusiastically introduced herself as Esther and physically grabbed each of us, pulling us one at a time inside the synagogue before slamming the door shut. She then rushed us through the dark foyer and into the empty dome-covered sanctuary before stopping abruptly. Sarah, Arlana, and I gazed around at the hundreds of vacant pews and golden Stars of David painted on the light blue walls. Esther stared straight at the three of us for a full half-minute with soft, disbelieving eyes as if she was witnessing a scene from a bygone era.

"You are really Jews?" she asked in Arabic. We nodded our heads in affirmation. "I am also a Jew. I come here *every* Shabbat to open the synagogue for Jewish people. Every Shabbat."

"That's very nice," Arlana said. "Will there be a service today?"

Esther chuckled and shook her head from side to side.

"There are no Jews, so there can be no prayer. A few times a year a rabbi from France comes. But when he does not come, nothing happens here."

"Do you have a family here with you in Cairo?" I asked solemnly.

Esther shook her head once more.

"There were never enough Jewish men to find someone," she said gloomily. "All the men left for Israel or Europe. So I was here all alone."

"Well, did you ever think about leaving too?" I asked, trying to do so gently.

"Egypt is my home!" Esther insisted. "What would I have done in a different place? If I had left, who would take care of the synagogue? I had to stay."

Her years of loneliness had obviously taken their toll and her desperate justification of her life decisions made us uncomfortable. After the conversation lapsed for a few moments, Esther insisted on giving us a tour of the rest of the building. But just as we stepped out of the sanctuary, her pet cat grabbed her attention and she left us to chase after it.

Over the next half hour, three other young North American Jews trickled in, two boys from Canada who were traveling around with backpacks and an American woman living in Cairo, conducting research for her doctorate. We all snatched prayer books, stood in the center of the sanctuary, and performed a forty-five minute highly abridged version of the Shabbat morning service. Although we were only six people in a space built for hundreds of worshippers, we sang the prayers passionately and the echo of our voices filled the room.

Sometime in the middle of our service, Esther returned to the sanctuary and took a seat near the entrance. Arlana immediately walked over to where she sat and invited her to sit closer to us. But Esther declined, preferring to watch us pray from a distance. Perhaps she didn't think she knew the prayers well enough to participate or didn't feel comfortable with the idea of men and women worshipping together. Or, maybe the scene evoked memories of something familiar she'd lost long ago that brought her pain to think about. Whatever the reason was, Esther just stared at us until the conclusion of the service. She looked away only momentarily to hiss at her cat, which scurried around the hardwood floor chasing a little ball.

Walking towards the synagogue's exit after we concluded our service, the synagogue's non-Jewish maintenance man pulled me aside to tell me what he thought about our visit.

"You people are good Jews," he said slowly in Arabic. "Because of you, Esther is very happy. I am a Muslim, but I believe your prayers brought Allah joy."

"Thank you," I replied graciously.

"People in Egypt hate Jews. This is why the police officers stand outside. If they stopped standing there, the people would burn this building and I would have a lot to clean up. But one day, *inshallah* (God willing), Egypt will be a good place for Jews again and many Jews will come here. Be happy in Egypt."

The maintenance man's vision filled me with hope that the anti-Jewish sentiment that consumed Egypt was a temporary ideology perpetuated by the country's ailments. Other nations had successfully discarded their own detestable ideologies, such as Germany with Nazism and Italy with fascism. There was no reason to believe anti-Semitism would grip the Egyptian psyche forever.

"But the hatred of the Jews in Egypt comes straight from the mosque," the Coptic Christian owner of a Luxor hotel told me in English when I stayed there the next weekend. "It is not a hatred coming from politics. It is the imams in the mosques. If the hatred comes from religion, there is nothing to argue."

I made the quick two-day jaunt down south to Luxor and Aswan with Brendan, my pasty pal from New Jersey. After arriving in Luxor early on a Friday morning following an all-night train ride from Cairo, we shopped around for a cheap hotel and ended up landing a spot at a Coptic-owned establishment. Two bucks a night got us a double room with a private bathroom.

"How do these guys make money off this?" Brendan asked me as we dropped our bags off in our room. I didn't know a thing about price wars in Luxor's hotel sector, so we went downstairs to the lobby and asked how business was.

"Business is terrible," the owner said without expression.

Slightly obese and dressed in a white polo shirt with a dark red stain on it, he slumped behind the front desk and looked like a tired soul who'd lost his drive.

"I am a Christian, so everyone refuses to tell tourists about my hotel," he said. "I do not wish to become a Muslim, so no one will do business with me. In the mosque, all the imams do is tell everyone not to do business with Christians and Jews. Everyone says that the Christians and Jews will only cheat them."

"Just so you know, I'm a Jew," I said.

I didn't plan on revealing my identity so soon, or at all, but I thought it might be nice to express solidarity with someone from another discriminated people.

"Never tell any Muslim in Luxor that you are a Jew!" he insisted. "The people here are not afraid to do very bad things."

All of a sudden, in the middle of his sentence, loud speakers on the street outside the hotel blasted a recorded speech in Arabic.

"Do you hear that? Come with me," he said. The owner raced over to the front door and pushed it open a crack. "Come close and listen. This is the Friday sermon from the mosque. Tell me if you hear the imam say the words *Yehud* (Jew) or Israel."

Brendan and I put our ears to the door and listened carefully to the speech. The speaker quality was poor, however, and I couldn't make out the words.

"The imam is saying," he explained, "'Trust no Jew. They know only evil.' I will tell you again and again. Do not tell anyone that you are a Jew except for Christians. You can trust people like me."

As much as I appreciated his concerned words of advice, a part of me wondered if the owner was trying to alarm us for other reasons.

"He probably just said that stuff to get our business," Brendan suggested later that day. "He thinks if we trust him, then we'll get all our friends to stay at his hotel. Maybe what he said is true to an extent, but it also sounded a little crazy. Is someone here going to kill someone else because of what they heard in the mosque?"

We spent most of the weekend rushing between ancient temples, bargaining for transportation, and rejecting the constant solicitations of tireless Egyptian salesmen offering everything from slow-boat cruises down the Nile to illegal prescription drugs. The only physical assault we endured came from the blazing sun. While the skin on my face turned golden brown and my nose and forehead peeled a bit, the sun's scorching rays penetrated Brendan's t-shirts and colored his entire back a painful purple.

Sitting on chairs at the railway station in Aswan waiting to catch our overnight train back to Cairo, Brendan decided his back couldn't take being touched by anything.

"It feels like my skin is bleeding everywhere," he moaned. "I need to walk around."

With a little less than an hour to kill, we strolled through a dusty neighborhood a couple hundred feet past the railroad tracks. Rows of gray concrete apartment blocks lined the unpaved sandy streets and the smell of a leaked septic tank polluted the air. A group of six teenage boys kicked around a deflated soccer ball in an alley lit up by a blinking orange street lamp.

When Brendan and I walked past them, the tallest of the teenagers whistled to grab our attention and kicked the flimsy ball towards us. I promptly booted it to a different boy who passed it on to Brendan. After a few minutes of kicking the ball, the tall teenager who originally invited us to play grabbed it with his hands and gathered everyone around us. Clearly the leader of the pack, he looked about seventeen, called himself Ishmael, and asked that we speak with him only in English.

"I want practice," Ishmael said. "My English is problem."

His less proficient followers stared at him in admiration of his superior language skills.

"We can speak English," Brendan said eagerly. "What do you want to say?"

"What you think of *Bush*?" Ishmael asked curiously, emphasizing the name so his friends would get the gist of the conversation. Brendan and I looked at each other for a second and then issued the standard response we thought most Egyptians wanted to hear.

"Bush is very bad!" we said. "What do *you* think of Bush?" The crowd of boys booed wildly as soon after they heard the American President's name.

"What you think of *Chirac*?" Ishmael asked next. Since neither Brendan nor I had devoted enough time to observing the French political scene to form an opinion, we delivered the same answer as before.

"Chirac is very bad!" we asserted defiantly.

Pleased, the boys booed the French premiere just as vigorously as they'd booed Bush. This was fun, so I switched roles and posed them a question.

"What do you think of *Mubarak*?" I asked.

The question visibly startled them. Everyone stood quietly and waited for someone else to say something first. After a few seconds, Ishmael finally leaned in towards me, put his hand over his mouth, and softly whispered, "Mubarak boo." The other boys immediately followed his lead and booed quietly in unison.

"So-so," a younger boy joked afterwards when they finished. Led by Ishmael, the others smacked the younger boy in the head. Though rarely discussed out loud, discontent with Egypt's ruling regime was becoming more outspoken.

"What you think of *Sharon*?" Ishmael asked as he wiped sweat from his brow.

Although I didn't particularly support or revile the former Israeli Prime Minister, the question caught me by surprise and I froze up. Before I could fumble a response, the teenagers opened fire on us from point blank range. One by one, they aimed imaginary machine guns in our direction and yelled "Dudududududududu!"

"This is like Sharon, you know. He is killer," Ishmael clarified. "Sharon is Jew. What you think of *Jews*?"

"Well," I said, carefully trying not to blow my cover. "There are good Jews and there are bad Jews like there are good Egyptians and bad Egyptians."

"No, this is wrong!" Ishmael said insistently. "Jews are bad. They want kill *everyone*. If you see Jew you must kill him!" Brendan's face went blank and he intentionally stopped talking. I, on the other hand, was disturbed, but wanted to learn more.

"Have you ever met a Jew before?" I asked.

"If I meet Jew I kill him now!" Ishmael promised.

His friends all clapped and cheered their approval.

"Where did you learn so much about the Jews?"

"We learn in mosque. They teach Jews must die."

They were only kids, I thought to myself. Besides, it wasn't as if they were the first Arabs to ever say they hated Jews because they were told to at a mosque. This was the post 9/11 era. Osama bin Laden, Hamas, and other Muslim extremist groups had been demonizing Jews for decades. I just never expected to hear such venomous words from kids who looked and acted so normal. They weren't taught to revile all western culture and spend their days holed up in a cave memorizing ancient Islamic texts. They played soccer, learned English, and were eager to make friends with Americans like Brendan and me. Their normalcy made me worry that religiously inspired hatred was more common in Egypt than I'd realized.

"Muslims like that are a minority," Steve stressed after I told him about the incident while we hung out in our dorm room after the weekend. "I've never heard anyone at any mosque encourage Muslims to hate or kill."

"I believe you," I said. "But there are over a billion Muslims and it is possible imams say different things in different mosques. We're in Egypt, not Texas, and you and I don't speak Arabic well enough to always understand what's being said."

"Michael, I'm sure there are mosques in Egypt where some imams say bad things. Sometimes I'm glad I can't understand Arabic that well yet because I bet I've accidentally been inside a few mosques where things were said that I would disagree with. But all religions have their psychos. Don't think that most mosques in Egypt have imams that teach their people that hating and killing is Islamic. You should go talk to an imam who can explain this stuff better than me. I bet someone could answer your questions down at Al-Azhar."

Steve was referring to the famous Al-Azhar mosque, the first mosque built in Cairo over a thousand years ago and one of the greatest centers of learning in the Islamic world. If anyone could speak for Islam with authority, it was someone with an Al-Azhar background.

"I heard that in the afternoons they have an imam who speaks English and talks to tourists about Islam," Steve told me. "You should go talk to him. If you want, I can go with you."

It was sweet of Steve to offer to come with me, but I preferred to go alone. It wasn't anything personal against him. I just felt like he, or anyone else for that matter, would complicate things. I decided to visit Al-Azhar two days after my conversation with Steve, but not entirely as myself.

My main reason for visiting was to learn about more mainstream Islamic perspectives on Jews and the State of Israel. However, I realized these were sensitive topics with the potential to arouse controversy. I assumed most responsible Islamic scholars would try to avoid discussing anything controversial with a non-Muslim like me. I didn't want to receive any watered-down, sanitized information told specifically to non-Muslim visitors. I wanted to be treated and talked to like a curious Muslim with questions about the faith. So, that's exactly what I decided I'd be.

Lying is wrong, but going undercover was the only way to obtain the most accurate information. To give my mission a chance to succeed, I knew I had to convince the Al-Azhar scholars of my Islamic credentials. That meant I had to put together a believable cover story and alter my appearance to look more like a religious Muslim.

If I managed to find an English-speaking imam, I'd call myself Mikhā'īl, the Arabic equivalent of Michael. If asked, I'd casually explain that, after reading the Qur'an and receiving encouragement from Muslim friends, I converted to Islam two years earlier. I'd steer the conversation towards Jewish topics by saying I yearned to travel to Palestine, but, before going, I wanted to check the Islamic position on supporting Israel's economy with my tourism dollars.

I headed to Al-Azhar immediately following classes in the mid-afternoon, changing into my Muslim costume in a campus bathroom before I left. I removed my eyebrow ring and earring and covered my head with a light green *taqiyah*, a skullcap popular in the Arab world. I made sure to dress modestly by wearing khaki pants and a dark blue, long-sleeved button-down shirt.

My plan went better than I'd hoped. When I entered the mosque's complex and walked through its open, marble-tiled courtyard, I was immediately approached by a gray-bearded middle-aged man wearing a tie and a blue button-down shirt the same shade as mine.

"I like your shirt," he said with a laugh. "I am Sayed. If you have questions about Islam, I am here to answer them."

Instantly likeable and charismatic, he was someone you trusted right away and wanted to listen to, the perfect front man. I fed him my phony story about converting to Islam and my bogus dilemma about supporting the Israeli economy. He ate it up completely and brought me to his office to talk more. Rather than sit behind his desk across from me, he pulled his leather swivel chair around and planted himself right next to where I was seated.

"You are a young man who understands every facet of life is relevant in Islam," Sayed said. "Many Muslim people who are able to go Palestine just go. They do not think it through. These people are servants of their passion, not of Allah."

"I would be grateful to receive your guidance on the issue," I replied respectfully.

"You should absolutely go to Palestine. You are blessed with an American passport and an American name. You can travel to Palestine freely. You can even mix in among the Jews." Better than you know, I said to myself. "But do not go to Palestine to cause problems with the Jews. Many Muslims go to Palestine only to fight the Jews. They get into trouble and then are deported and can never go back. Do not do this. I say to you, Mikhā'īl, go to Palestine. Try to spend money only in Arab areas, but if you must, know that spending money in Jewish areas is a small sacrifice. Go to Palestine not to fight now, but to learn how to fight later."

"So what should do when I'm there?"

"Become familiar with it. Go there more than once even. Learn how it looks. Talk to the Jews and get to know them. But be careful. They are people attracted to evil and lies. They care only for making money at your expense. Never trust a Jew. They are masters of deception."

"Obviously," I agreed, wondering if the ruse I was pulling proved Sayed correct.

"You live in America," he continued. "There, it is not common to speak the truth about Jews. The Jews today practice a heathen religion. The religion they followed in the days of the Prophet is no more. Their holy books have been corrupted by *Shaytan* (Satan). Until the Jews come to Islam, they will be condemned as enemies of Allah and of Muslims everywhere."

"Are there any good Jews?" I asked.

"The good ones become Muslims. The bad ones do not."

"I am very confused. If the Jews are such a condemned people, how did they manage to conquer Palestine and become so powerful?"

"The reason for this is difficult to accept, but simple. Allah gives every person tests and hardships. Fighting the Jews in Palestine is one of the tests Allah gave to every Muslim. I believe it was more than that. I believe it was punishment for our sins. Before Israel was created, many Muslims turned away from Islam and tried to be secular. They wanted to be just like the Europeans who occupied Muslim lands and to do things that are *haram* (forbidden). When Israel was created and defeated the Arab armies in war, people asked, 'How did this happen? How did Allah give Palestine to the world's most reviled people right in the middle of *Dar al-Islam* (the Muslim world)?' People began to realize it was punishment for abandoning their religion. Since then, Islam has experienced a glorious re-birth. Muslims have returned in great numbers and many others have joined too, just like you."

"If Allah intended to give Palestine to the Jews as a punishment for our sins, why are Muslims fighting to take it back? Won't Palestine become Muslim again when Allah decides it's time?"

"Allah decides and acts through his people. We do not know when Palestine will be liberated, but we know that it must be liberated. To give up trying to liberate Palestine is to give up on Islam."

"What about the Muslims who do questionable things to liberate Palestine? I mean the ones who martyr themselves. Sometimes they kill women and children."

"When any person purposely kills himself only to murder others, it is considered the most evil, most despicable way to die. Today we all know there are Muslims who are confused and do terrible things. They strap on bombs and kill in Iraq, in Afghanistan, in America, and also in Egypt. They believe they act according to Allah's will. They do not. They follow *Shaytan*."

"I couldn't agree more," I said, relieved by those few words of moderation.

"But," he carried on. "Palestine is different. Allah used the Jews to teach the Muslims a lesson. But the Jews have gone too far. They commit massacres and unspeakable evil every day. When a Muslim blows himself up in the presence of Jews who occupy Palestine, he is a martyr."

"What about the Jewish children? What must be done to them?"

"Israel is an entirely militarized society. Every man and woman goes to the army. Every child there will go to their army and kill many Muslim children. Go to Palestine. Learn and prepare. If we do not kill their children, they will kill ours."

While I sat there listening to Sayed speak, I kept a straight face by pretending I was in a movie. This wasn't reality, I told myself. This was make-believe and I was an award-winning actor. When Sayed and I finished our conversation, I thanked him for his time, patted him on the back, and even promised to visit again. But once my act was finished and I left Al-Azhar with my mission complete, I hated the reality to which I was forced to return.

I washed my face in the bathroom sink at a restaurant nearby, put my piercings back into place, and abandoned my *taqiyah* on a random table. I walked around in silence for two hours wondering if I should tell Steve about my afternoon adventure. I wanted to say something for sure.

But I knew if I told him, Steve would never speak to me again. He would be furious at me for lying about being a Muslim and abusing everything he taught me about his cherished faith. He might even accuse me of making up what the imam said. Since I lied about being a Muslim, maybe I was lying about everything else too. He might get so angry that he would tell other students or the AUC administration. I would become a pariah, possibly get deported, or worse.

No, I could not tell Steve about my visit to Al-Azhar. And I couldn't tell anyone else out of fear it would get back to him. My friendship with Steve was far too valuable to me to let extremists like Sayed get in the way. But soon after, that's exactly what happened when events a few hundred miles away spilled out of control.

On July 12, 2006, Hezbollah militants launched a raid into Israel from Lebanon, killing three Israeli soldiers and kidnapping two more. Israel's government demanded Hezbollah unconditionally release the captives. When Hezbollah refused, another Arab-Israeli war began.

During the first few days of fighting, Hezbollah aimlessly fired rockets into northern Israel, and the Israeli army bombed Lebanon's infrastructure and enforced a naval and air blockade of the country. Millions of Lebanese and hundreds of thousands of Israelis fled their homes, including my friend Guy, who headed south to Netanya to stay with his grandmother.

Meanwhile, students living in my dormitory in Cairo flooded the common area at all hours to watch the war unfold on television. Many students had intended to vacation in Lebanon after our summer academic session ended. They stared at the television screen in shock as their travel plans unraveled before their eyes. Everyone had an opinion over who was to blame.

"Israel is crazy," one American guy said. "Hezbollah says it will return the Israeli soldiers when Israel releases its fighters from jail. Israel should just release Hezbollah's men, get its soldiers back, and guard its border better in the future."

"No!" a Jewish student replied defiantly. "If Israel releases prisoners, Hezbollah will attack it again. This time Hezbollah will pay. Hezbollah's leaders will be dead by the end of the week."

But after a week, Hezbollah's leaders were still alive and the conflict had escalated. Israel began deploying ground troops inside Lebanese territory to stop Hezbollah's rocket attacks. Thousands of foreigners were evacuated from Lebanon, including dozens of Americans who had been studying for the summer at the American University of Beirut (AUB).

"Israel's attacking college kids just like us!" an African-American girl proclaimed. I stood with a group of students watching a live CNN broadcast of smiling, waving American AUB students excitedly boarding a US naval ship. "All Israel wants is land. All it does is colonize and hurt people. It doesn't care if Americans get killed."

"What are you talking about?" I fired back. "Those Americans are totally unharmed. They're smiling. Israel is allowing them to be evacuated safely. You think Israel's trying to steal land? Israel was attacked by Hezbollah for no reason. It's defending its citizens like any country should."

"You have to admit Israel's actions are slightly disproportionate," another girl added.

"Disproportionate? Who fights a proportionate war?" I asked enraged. "You fight to win. If Hezbollah didn't want a disproportionate fight it shouldn't have attacked. If Mexico fired rockets into Texas, do you think Mexico would exist the next day?"

Sadly, all the talk about the war put a strain on my relationship with Steve. Over the course of the summer, we discussed the Arab-Israeli conflict only sparingly. Occasionally, I'd ask Steve what he thought about the issue, but he always avoided giving me a real answer.

"I don't really know enough about the history to really take a stance," he'd said early on when I first initiated a conversation with him about the topic.

I was never sure if that was the truth, or if he merely wanted to avoid an argument. I never pushed him on it and I always let our conversations veer to other topics. After the war started, though, I sensed a rift. He spent a lot of time discussing the war with other Muslim students with critical attitudes towards Israel and he stopped inviting me to attend mosque with him. Eventually, even basic conversations in the room felt awkward and forced. I knew something was wrong. Finally, one night it all spilled out. Before going to sleep, I tried to start a conversation about our final exam schedules when he changed the subject abruptly.

"I'm not as knowledgeable as I want to be about all the problems between Israel and the Arabs," he said tensely. "But I don't feel the same way as you. It's been really hard this week with all the fighting in Lebanon. It hurts me to see Muslims under attack. I don't blame you for any of it. But I know you support it. I really don't want to get into a discussion about it. I just thought you should know."

I appreciated his honesty, though his words stung. I didn't want any Muslims to suffer any more than I wanted rockets to rain down on my friend Guy in Israel. Nevertheless, I did as he requested and refrained from insisting on a discussion. Before going to sleep, I told him I was glad he expressed how he felt and that I hoped politics and religion would never divide us. Deep down, though, I knew they already had.

As fighting between Israel and Hezbollah entered its second week, Egyptians took to the streets to call on their government to stand up for Lebanon and declare war on Israel. Each day during my lunch break from class, I walked past people who crowded together in Tahrir Square near the AUC campus chanting, "Israel needs a beating. Mubarak must deliver." But Mubarak, like other Arab leaders, refused to enter the fray, and even condemned Hezbollah's actions as harmful to Arab interests. This infuriated Egyptians and many openly criticized the decision while not explicitly mentioning Mubarak's name.

"None of the Arab leaders have any balls," I overheard an Egyptian male student passionately tell a group of Americans in the courtyard of the main campus. "Egypt must rip up the peace treaty and launch a war against Israel now. That is exactly what the opposition would do."

Although it depressed me to think about, I knew that the main opposition movement in Egypt, the Muslim Brotherhood, was even more vehemently anti-Israel than the Mubarak regime. I disliked Mubarak intensely and it pained me to think of him as the lesser of two evils. I feared that if he and his allies fell from power, something worse would take their place. Egypt provided me with no leader or political movement to root for and I anxiously counted down the days until I left.

All I wanted to do my last weekend in Egypt at the end of July was to enjoy myself with friends. I wanted to flee the chaos of Cairo, forget about the protesters of Tahrir Square, and avoid all news updates about the war. Together with Sarah, Arlana, Brendan, and a few others, I made my way over to the pristine desert beaches of the south Sinai coast for a few days of fun in the sun.

After a day in the mega-resort town of Sharm-el-Sheikh, my friends and I wandered over to the city bus station to catch a ride to Dahab, a quieter town two hours north along the coast. While we sat on our backpacks waiting for a bus to pull up, I saw a strikingly clean-shaven Egyptian man carrying a black purse with the Hebrew female name Shlomit sewn on it.

He certainly didn't look like a Shlomit, so I walked up to him to gather some intelligence.

"Excuse me," I said to the man in Arabic. "You have a very nice bag."

"Thank you," he replied warmly.

"What's the writing on your bag?"

"This," he uttered slowly, "is the Hebrew language. It is the language of the Jews."

"Really? Why do you have a bag with Hebrew on it?"

"I am a waiter in a hotel in Taba," he said switching to English. "Many Israeli guests come for holiday. I became good friends with some of them. A woman gave me this bag."

"So you're not Shlomit?" I joked.

The man clapped his hands and laughed.

"I am sorry. My name is Muhammad. You read Hebrew too. But, you are not an Israeli. You are a Jew?"

"I am."

"Ah, I have many Jewish friends too. But I did not always like Jews. I am from Cairo. As a child I learned to hate all Jews very much. I learned in school and in the mosque that the Jews are only bad. They are the enemies of Egypt."

"But, if you learned to hate Jews in the mosque, then why don't you hate Jews now?"

"Because now I am friends with Jews. I know what they teach in the mosque about the Jews is not Islam. It is politics. It is bad what they teach, but I believe it will change."

"Aren't you afraid to carry a bag around with Hebrew on it? Isn't it dangerous?"

"I take this bag every time I go to Cairo. I hope Egyptians will ask me about it. I want to say good things about Jews and Israeli people."

"You're very brave. You're not afraid someone will think you're a Jew with that bag?"

"I am not a Jew. I am a Muslim. But, if someone thinks I am a Jew, it is okay. It is important for Egyptians to meet Jews. In Egypt, you tell the people you are a Jew?"

"It depends."

"I understand. Where do you go after Egypt?"

"I'll travel, visit my family in the US, and then go study in the UAE."

"Ah, they will know you are a Jew there?"

"I don't know if I will tell them."

"I hope you tell the people. In Egypt people are poor. It is easy for them to hate. In the UAE there is lots of money. The people there have education."

"You think?"

"Of course. People in the UAE are sophisticated and worldly. If you tell the people you are a Jew, they will think nothing of it."

Chapter 6
Starbucks Is Evil

Sharjah, UAE
August–September 2006

H
E WAS WRONG. I TOLD PEOPLE IN THE UAE I WAS A JEW AND it was a very big deal. Hassan, his friends, and his brother Mo made sure the story that a Jewish student had enrolled at AUS spread like wildfire, and the university became gripped with Jew-hysteria.

I was showered with constant attention. After the news got out, many of my initial conversations with people who approached me my first week of classes were strange, but fairly harmless.

An Egyptian film student named Muhammad sat down with me at a table in the Student Center to express his fears that Jewish media executives in Hollywood would never give an Arab Muslim like him a chance to succeed in the film industry.

"If your movies are good, then you'll be successful," I reassured him.

"Really? Then please do me one favor," he requested. "I brought this CD along of one of my short films. Will you make sure it gets to Spielberg?"

"Sorry pal, but I don't know Steven Spielberg personally."

"But you're a Jew. You must know him! Just give him the CD for me."

"Not all Jews know each other. I don't know Spielberg. If you leave the CD with me, I'll watch it once and throw it in the trash."

He placed the CD in an envelope on top of my backpack and walked away with a grin, convinced that by knowing a Jew, he might become famous overnight.

Another Muhammad, an aspiring rock musician from Saudi Arabia, reminded me how lucky I was to be a Jew who lived in America. While I was indeed extremely appreciative of American acceptance of its Jewish community, this budding guitarist wished to identify the fortune of power, not tolerance.

"The Jews control everything in America," he said. "You can't say anything bad about Jews in America without getting shot."

"The Jews don't control America," I countered. "People say bad things about Jews and everyone else all the time."

"Oh really? Then why is eighty percent of Congress Jewish? American foreign policy is controlled by the Jews. Condoleezza Rice is even a Jew I think."

"Condoleezza Rice is not a Jew."

Although these accusations surprised me, stereotypes of Jewish media control and political domination exist even among ignorant people in America. But the Arab world took myths of American commercial support for Israel to new heights.

I failed to understand why anyone would drink hot coffee in one hundred degree heat, but the campus Starbucks remained packed with students demanding hot caffeinated beverages at all hours. I sat outside in the one hundred and ten degree heat sipping an ice-cold Pepsi, accompanied by two secular Lebanese girls, Rania and Yasmine, when they started complaining about the detrimental effects of their caffeine addiction.

"I hate that I need Starbucks," Rania said as she smoked a cigarette. "I know it's bad. I can't stop even though I know Starbucks supports Israel."

"How does a coffee corporation support Israel?" I posed puzzled.

"Are you serious?" Yasmine asked dumbfounded. She looked at me like I was a total ignoramus. "Starbucks buys weapons for Israel. Starbucks is evil!"

"Um, okay. Why do you drink the coffee if you think the company behind it is evil?"

"Because I need it. You become addicted to the caffeine and it forces you to support the Jews. That's not all. Pepsi is the same."

"How does Pepsi support the Jews?"

"Duh!" Rania interjected. "Because Pepsi is an acronym. PEPSI: Pinch Every Penny Support Israel."

She was serious. I tried explaining that PepsiCo had refused to sell its soft drinks to Israel for decades until the Arab League boycott had been relaxed. They didn't believe me.

Since their tales of coffee/soda conspiracy were viewed as common knowledge, the college Americana culture that I had witnessed was fast turning out to be a trick of my imagination, like a mirage in the desert.

I met the five other American exchange students in some of my classes, but I was the only Jew. They all seemed friendly enough, except for Jake, an American University student with wavy brown hair who at first seemed to always have an anxious expression on his face. Jake was strangely silent. I tried initiating conversations with him when we first met, but he was cold and distant.

Jake later told me that some AUS students were on the lookout for Jews. The night he checked into his dorm, which was located in a different building from mine, he was pinpointed as Jewish suspect number one, not me.

"When I got here some of the guys invited me to sit with them," Jake said while we hung out in his room after he finally opened up to me. "When I said my name was Jacob, this Sudanese guy named Ibrahim said to me, 'Jake, you seem like a nice guy, but we have to know something. Are you a Jew? We think America's trying to send Jews over here. We've had some other exchange students before. We've had Benjamins and Joshuas and now you're named Jacob. These names all seem very Jew-ish, you know?' I was terrified and tried to explain that I'm just a Catholic from Vermont. I didn't understand what my first name had to do with anything. Isn't Jacob a Christian and Muslim name too? I was acting so strange the first week because I didn't understand why everyone thought I was a Jew. I was scared shitless because I'm not."

No, Jake was not. But that simple fact fell short of being enough to convince even some of our professors that Jake was who he said he was. During my second Arabic lesson with Rima, the private instructor Jake and I had been assigned to, she confessed she had a secret to tell. The privileged middle-aged daughter of a prominent Syrian diplomat, she squinted her eyes and told me the latest campus gossip.

"There is a Jewish student at the university," Rima revealed. "He is making people very nervous. Many students are quite frightened and many faculty members say the administration doesn't know what to do."

"Rima, why is everyone so alarmed by the presence of a Jewish student?" I asked.

"Because there isn't any logical reason for a Jew to come here! What does he want to do, start a war?"

"What if he came here because he wants peace?"

"Oh, that's crazy. There is something else going on here. I think the Jew is Jake. You know Jacob is a very popular name with the Jews. But don't tell him I know this."

This theory gave a whole new meaning to the idea of a name sounding too Jewish.

"Jake's not the Jew. I am," I revealed.

"Ah!" she screamed, jumping up slightly from her seat. She regained her composure and smiled uncomfortably.

"You know, Michael," she said apprehensively, "I wish the Jews and Arabs had good relations. That would be excellent, right? But the USA wants the Arabs and Israel to fight. It helps the Americans stay strong and keeps the Middle East weak. Look what happened to Sadat."

"Anwar Sadat? What about him? He was assassinated by the Egyptian Islamic Jihad."

"No! The CIA killed him to stop him from getting too strong. That is what America does to strong leaders in the Middle East."

I wasn't sure what surprised me more, that this supposedly educated professor believed in anti-American conspiracies or that she automatically associated me with Israel?

As an American student on an exchange from an American university, I was peppered with questions about US culture and foreign policy. Extreme disapproval of the American military presence in Iraq and funny insinuations about the sexual mores of American women were expected. But, as a Jew, I became unbreakably linked to the policies and politics of Israel, despite my lack of Israeli citizenship.

Private conversations attracted dozens of students who pulled up chairs to participate in the dialogues. I was immediately thrust into the role of chief representative for America, Israel, and the Jews all wrapped into one.

"What do you think should happen in Palestine?" was a question posed often.

My diplomatic answer always stayed the same.

"I believe there should be a just, peaceful two-state solution that fulfills the aspirations of both Israelis and Palestinians to national self-determination," I'd say.

"Israel shouldn't be. Period!" retorted a girl with short-black hair during one such group discussion in the cafeteria early on in the semester. "No one wants peace with Israel. Everyone wants Israel gone. That is Arab land. Israel is an illegal country and Jews should go back to where they came from."

"So Jews should all go back to Judea?" I responded.

"Yes. Go back to Judea!"

"You know Judea is a different name for the southern part of the West Bank. It's where the word Jew comes from. You say Israel's an illegal country. Can you name any other country in the world you characterize as illegal?" She sat silently glaring in my direction. "If Arabs don't compromise and recognize that Jews have a tie to the land that Arabs call Palestine and Jews call Israel, no progress will ever be achieved. Both Israel and the Arabs must compromise."

"Israel commits massacres whenever it wants. Look at what Israel did in Lebanon!" she shot back.

"There are many ways to look at the Lebanon war," I answered. "But Hezbollah attacked Israel first. You can't expect Israel not to defend itself when attacked."

But they did. It became clear that almost everyone described any Israeli effort to defend itself as aggressive, criminal, and illegitimate, regardless of the incident. What was sad was that these students lacked the most basic information concerning Israel's position, and it wasn't hard to argue an opposing viewpoint.

I didn't understand how there could be a complete lack of credible information until I learned that the UAE blocked all Israeli websites and other "content being inconsistent with the religious, cultural, political, and moral values of the United Arab Emirates." This was part of the message that popped up when someone attempted to access an "illegal" website.

Due to its wealth and technological sophistication, the UAE government was capable of stifling free speech and restricting access to information in ways that poor dictatorships could only dream about. Even Skype was banned.

These students all believed Israel was bad, but they couldn't descriptively say why beyond canned rhetoric. Still, students showed surprising interest in my unusual point of view. Even if they disagreed passionately with what I said, they still let me speak. However, it was soon brought to my attention that this openness was not necessarily based on curiosity, but out of fear.

"You're a spy," Mo accused me the second week of the semester one day at lunch. "My brother and his friends are telling everyone. They're making everyone afraid of you. They say you are manipulative and a cunning Jew. They're telling people not to get into arguments with you because you're going to brainwash them with your lies. The whole school is watching you closely now."

"Mo, that's crazy," I said literally on the verge of laughing out loud. "If I was a spy why would I tell people I'm Jewish and openly state my opinions? Wouldn't a real spy try to keep a low profile?"

"If you're not a spy, then why did you come here?"

"I told you! I came because I want to learn about Arabs and share perspectives. Isn't that all I'm doing?"

In the minds of Mo, his brother Hassan, and numerous other students, the idea of an exceptionally friendly, open-minded Jew who sought friendship and understanding with Arabs ran completely contrary to the evil, war-mongering Jew they were raised to hate.

As the phenomenon of the Jewish spy of Sharjah picked up steam, the dean responsible for the exchange students, a Lebanese-born American named Dr. Sami, finally intervened and called me into his office for a chat.

"Michael, stop telling people you're Jewish!" Dr. Sami demanded while we sat across his desk from each other in his spacious office.

"These students don't know Jews. They're not taught accurate things about Jews. They blame all their problems on Jews. This school is not ready for a Jewish student."

"Well how can they be ready unless someone like me comes around?" I countered.

"I'm hearing rumors from students and professors that you're a Mossad agent who speaks Arabic fluently. This whole situation has gone crazy."

"They said I speak Arabic fluently?" I asked incredulous.

"These students are not your friends, Michael. Last year, students from the Palestinian Cultural Club put on a play about Palestine. The play demonized Jews. I invited all the club members to my office and I explained to them very carefully that they can say and do whatever they want about Israel. But leave the Jews out of it. You criticize the Jews and you automatically lose. You know how they responded? They asked me, 'Whose side are you on?'"

"Dr. Sami, everyone wants to talk to me. That means I've already started a dialogue. That's exactly when change happens."

"Michael, the students talking to you either fear you because they think you're a secret agent or are mystified by you because other people think you're a secret agent."

He was right. The more students discussed my potential plans of espionage, the more people believed the rumor. The plot only thickened when I finally touched base with my "accomplices" at a sign-up event for student organizations in early September.

All the leather couches and chairs in the main commons of the Student Center were replaced by booths. Leaders of various student organizations aggressively coaxed their unaffiliated peers into signing up for their apolitical, solely culture-oriented clubs.

With political dissent outlawed in the UAE, these groups primarily allowed students to celebrate their contrasting heritages with generous allocations that paid for field trips to restaurants.

As a devoted fan of free food, I signed up for ten clubs in ten minutes. However, I quickly lost my appetite when I saw the Palestinian Cultural Club's booth decorated with dozens of tiny toy suicide bombers connected to each other with wire. They were cute little dolls with rocks in their right hands, dynamite bomb belts attached to their waists, and *keffiyeh*s tied around their soft, fuzzy little heads.

A Tunisian guy with a thick uni-brow rushed up from behind me and shouted excitedly.

"Michael, I have two friends from Jerusalem who want to meet you!" he said.

"What do you mean *from* Jerusalem?" I asked suspiciously.

National identification is synonymous with citizenship in the Middle East, so stating where you're from is never simple. In the UAE, a person's national identity is defined by the citizenship they held, not their place of birth. Only a sliver of the UAE's population carries Emirati passports. Even if someone never stepped foot in their country of citizenship, they were forever tied to that nation.

None of the Palestinians I'd met thus far in Sharjah had ever lived in Israel or Palestinian Authority-controlled territory, or knew anything about daily life in those places.

Waiting for these two Jerusalemites to show up, I became gripped with anxiety, and relaxed by counting the mini-suicide bombers dangling in the distance. I was nervous because I knew that if these two Palestinians were *actually* from Jerusalem, then their perspectives would hold a great deal more weight than mine, and rightly so. They would either support the positive narrative of Israel I'd been taught, or they would confirm that I was merely spouting baseless Zionist propaganda as my detractors wanted to believe.

"*Shalom, achi. Ma nishma*?" a student said to me in Hebrew to get my attention. Hello, my brother. How are you?

My ears understood his language, but my eyes told me I was hallucinating. Shaking my hand and speaking Israeli-accented Hebrew was an European-looking, white skinned, red-bearded Palestinian.

"I am Ahmad from Jerusalem. And this is also Ahmad from Jerusalem," he said pointing to the tan, gel-haired fellow next to him.

I assigned them nicknames to keep them straight. White-skinned Ahmad was Ahmad Jew and permanently gel-haired Ahmad was Ahmad Greasy.

"We knew you were one of us when we heard there was another Jewish spy here," Ahmad Greasy said with a smile.

Was this a trick? Were they trying to get me to admit I was a foreign agent? We were still speaking Hebrew, so maybe no one understood. Or maybe someone did.

"*Walla* (by God), I told Ahmad the first day I saw you that you were one of us," Ahmad Jew claimed. "I said, 'Ahmad, that guy looks like a Jew from Jerusalem.' It was your eyebrow ring."

"What do you mean I'm one of you?" I asked.

"These crazy people are always saying we are Jewish spies too! They don't know how things really are between Jews and Arabs *ba'aretz*," Ahmad Jew said, using the Hebrew word for "in the land."

These two sophomores were the only students in Sharjah that spoke Hebrew and had experience interacting with Jews. If anyone could accurately explain the realities and complexities of being Arabs in Israel, they could.

Both Ahmads entered the UAE on their Jordanian passports, which many West Bank and East Jerusalem Palestinians possess. Ahmad Jew also carried an Israeli passport, since his family applied for and received Israeli citizenship after the 1967 Six Day War.

"Over in Jerusalem, we feel free," Ahmad Jew insisted. "When we first got to Sharjah, all the students made a big fuss about us. They said, 'You are from Jerusalem. You are so brave for living with the evil Israelis!' But we told them life in Jerusalem is amazing. They couldn't believe it when I said there are many good Jewish people and I even have Jewish friends."

"People here think we're spies too," Ahmad Greasy added. "We told them not to believe everything they hear on Al-Jazeera. Michael, you see now we are real Zionists."

They looked at each other and laughed, and I knew I could trust them. I would learn that, though completely Palestinian in their identities and certainly not adherents to any type of Zionist philosophy, these Ahmads loved to shove their Israeli credentials in people's faces. Ahmad Jew always used his Israeli driver's license to gain admission to nightclubs in Dubai and Ahmad Greasy lamented his decision to study in Sharjah instead of at a private college in Herzliya, a beach town north of Tel Aviv named after Zionism's inventor, Theodor Herzl.

"Those girls in Herzliya are unbelievable," Ahmad Greasy would say with a whistle and a snap of his fingers. "How did I end up here?"

They were definitely proud Palestinians, but they seemed to have much greater affinity for Israel than for other Arab countries.

"One time this Lebanese guy was yelling about how the Palestinians are the cause of all the problems in Lebanon," Ahmad Jew once said. "He says, 'I wish all the Palestinians in Lebanon would die. Someone should finish them off.'"

"So what did you say?" I asked.

"I told the Lebanese guy, 'I'm glad Israel destroyed your country this summer and I hope they do it again soon.'"

The Ahmads formed the backbone of my new posse, and Sharjah students grew more confused seeing the three of us spending so much time together. With my three-man covert operations team supposedly in place, some students began waiting for something big to happen.

"My brother and his friends are talking about you a lot again," Mo relayed one day while I relaxed on a couch in the main commons.

By this point it was clear that if anyone was a double agent, it was Mo. While he dished out the latest gossip coming from sectors of the student body I could not penetrate, I also knew he carried my responses back to my enemies. I didn't trust him entirely, but I found our conversations entertaining and I liked that he served as my own personal red telephone.

"Wait a second," I said. "Let me fix my ear piece so my handlers can listen in." Mo's eyes grew large with worry. "Mo, I'm kidding. I won't get you in trouble. I'm not a spy. Don't you believe me?"

"They think you're up to something. It's very convenient those two guys from Jerusalem all of a sudden became your friends."

"The only thing I'm up to is meeting people and surviving long enough for the weather to cool down."

"If you are up to something, you will be caught."

"By who? By Hassan? Does Hassan work in counter intelligence against spies like me?"

"If you are up to something, the CID (Criminal Investigations Department) will catch you. They are the UAE secret police. I bet they're watching you all the time."

During the third week of school, I received a phone call from an unidentified number. A gruff voice ordered me to report at one o'clock that afternoon to an isolated room at the end of a long corridor near the university's administrative offices. I arrived on time, entered a dimly lit office, and took a seat across from a muscular, bearded man wearing a suit sitting behind a large desk.

"Mr. Bassin, you seem to be enjoying yourself here in Sharjah," he said.

"I am very much," I replied.

"I wish I could say I was enjoying myself as much as you. I work in security for the university. That is all you must know. Sources tell me you are a troublemaker. You are causing political disruptions."

"Is this about me wearing the *kandura*?" I asked, feigning ignorance. "It was a present from my Emirati friends. I wear it only to honor Emirati culture."

"No, Mr. Bassin. The *kandura* is the least of the problems I am hearing about you. I am receiving notifications that you are causing incitement, provocation, and displaying signs of political dissent."

"I'm sorry, but I've been in this country for less than two weeks. I don't know anything about the politics of the UAE. I don't think I'm in a position to cause political problems."

"Mr. Bassin, you know very well what I'm talking about. Remember this is not the USA. In Sharjah, the walls have eyes and ears. They are watching you and listening to you to make sure you're not up to anything suspicious. Be warned!"

Days after our meeting, I lost the ability to connect to the local Internet server from my dorm room. These were the days before Wi-Fi when students got online through an Ethernet cord. At first, I thought my Ethernet cord was damaged. I borrowed a replacement cord from Rashid, my tall Emirati friend who lived down the hall, but his cord didn't work either.

"I do not understand," he said after I gave him back his chord. "It works in my room very good. This is very strange." What was stranger yet was that when I plugged my Ethernet cord into my computer in his room, I connected to the web instantly. Rashid looked at me puzzled and said, "Michael, I think you have a big problem."

The next day I approached our building supervisor in his office, a balding Palestinian man with very thick eye glasses and explained the situation. He kindly offered me a cup of tea and urged me to be patient.

"Very soon the Internet will be re-connected, *inshallah* (praise God)," he said.

I trusted his word and waited. But after a few days, the problem was still unresolved, and I had to nudge him about it again.

"I told you already," he said slightly annoyed. "You will have Internet soon, *inshallah.*"

But soon wasn't soon enough for me. A full week after I first noticed my Internet was not connected, I went to his office and asked him to personally come to my room to have a look at my computer jack.

"I will not come to your room," he refused. "This is not my job. I have told you many times. You will have Internet soon, *inshallah!*"

"Sir, you're the building supervisor," I said frustrated. "Doesn't that mean you're responsible for all aspects of the building? When you say it will be fixed *inshallah*, does that mean you're actually planning to fix it or that you're literally waiting for God to personally step in?"

"It will be re-connected when it is time. Why is it so important for you to use the Internet in your room? Why not just go to the library?"

"Every student who lives in this building can connect to the Internet in their room except for me. Shouldn't I be able to do the same? Can't I check email in privacy?"

"Oh, you want privacy?" he asked as he removed his eyeglasses. "I understand. You know, the people who work in security for the university told me to pay special attention to you. They say you are making trouble."

"What does that have to do with me getting Internet in my room?"

"Tell me, where do you come from again?"

"Ohio. Why?"

"No, tell me where you're *really* come from. What are you *really* doing here in Sharjah?"

"What do you mean?"

"Don't play games with me," he said suddenly in Hebrew. "Just tell me the truth."

Shocked by his choice of language, I smiled nervously and pondered carefully what to say in response. I thought about answering back in Hebrew, but immediately decided against it. Practicing Hebrew with Ahmad Jew and Ahmad Greasy from Jerusalem was one thing. They were my friends. But with this man, I didn't feel safe. I sensed he was trying to get me into trouble.

I saw no point in pretending not to recognize the language he spoke since he clearly knew I was Jewish. What I did do, though, was try to remove any suspicion I was secretly an Israeli by downplaying how much Hebrew I knew.

"Wow, you speak Hebrew really well," I said. "Where did you learn all that? I wish I could speak like you."

"Let's just say I learned under very interesting circumstances in Palestine long ago. I am disappointed you won't speak to me in Hebrew. I could use the practice."

"Sorry, but I'm from America, not Israel. Will my Internet ever get fixed?"

"*Inshallah,*" he said with a smirk. "If you are hiding something about yourself, it will be revealed."

"That's nice to know, but I'm not hiding anything."

"Maybe this is the truth. Maybe it is not. Know this. Lying will not help you here. The UAE is a powerful country with many capabilities. If you continue to make problems, you will be stopped. There are many clever ways of making this happen."

Chapter 7
A House Built of Sand

Sharjah, UAE
September 2006

THE SATURDAY NIGHT AFTER THAT EXCHANGE, AN INTRIGUING, beautiful woman conveniently entered my life. I was coming out of the gym late one evening after playing a few games of pickup basketball just as she was about to go inside to work out. The instant I saw her I was smitten. She was tall, had bleached blonde hair, perfectly clear tan skin, and curves in all the right places.

Without thinking twice, I rushed towards the entrance to hold the door open for her. She thanked me even before she walked through the doorway and gave me an alluring smile that made me quiver. I badly wanted to say something to her, but my mind immediately went blank. What does one say to a woman with such commanding beauty that she can leave a man speechless just by looking at him?

"Oops."

A split second later we were both on the ground picking up the pieces of her cell phone she had dropped on the floor.

"Look what you made me do," she said teasingly. "If you hadn't been here blocking my way this wouldn't have happened."

I was happy to help her gather the parts, but I wasn't sure how the fault lay with me. When she passed by me, we had barely brushed up against each other, and I had no idea what made her drop the phone. There was no point in arguing, I decided. She was a gorgeous woman with a ruined phone, and that automatically meant she was right and I was wrong.

"You know, you're going to have to make this up to me," she said.

"How do I do that?" I asked, concerned I might have to shell out cash if her phone was deemed broken beyond repair.

"Don't worry. It'll be good. I'm going inside now, but I'm glad I got to meet you, phone wrecker. Be ready when I find you."

Over the next week, find me she did, almost every single night. Once, she spotted me walking to the gym. Another time she caught me studying in the Student Center. I asked her to give me her cell phone number to make our rendezvous less random, but she told me I would have to wait.

"I'll call this my revenge against you for almost breaking my phone," she joked playfully.

She said she was from Iran and that her name was Shireen. It means "sweet" in Farsi. During our first real conversation, she demanded I call her "Shireen my sweet" whenever we saw each other. She also insisted I say *kheyli khoshgeli,* "you are beautiful" in Farsi, just for added measure. Oddly, whenever we met up, Shireen demanded we hang out only in places where no one else was around.

"I just want us to get to know each other in private," she told me. "We don't need anyone spreading rumors about us spending time together."

Considering how obsessed AUS students were with gossip concerning me, her explanation made sense. But it didn't explain why I never seemed to see her during the school day.

"I'm a design student," she claimed. "I have to work on my portfolio all day. The only time I see anyone is at night. You should feel flattered I'm choosing to spend my nights with you. I'm definitely a girl who's worth getting to know."

Although Shireen was vain for my taste, she was fun to flirt with. Being with her almost made me forget I was in a staunchly conservative Muslim country. While our behavior in public never crossed the line by western standards, by Sharjah's standards we were engaging in some risky business. If a university official knew just how close together we sat or watched us whisper into each other's ears, we both could have been punished by the chancellor any way he saw fit. At AUS, students of the opposite sex couldn't even come within thirty feet of each other's dorm buildings without receiving a stern rebuke from a menacing security guard.

Like most of the Iranian students at AUS, Shireen described herself as ardently secular and spoke often of the wild underground parties in Iran. When the weekend neared, she invited me to a house party in Dubai that one of her Iranian friends was throwing that Friday night.

"You have no choice. You are coming with me," she ordered.

"Yes, ma'am," I submitted. "Could I invite some of the other Americans to come along? There aren't a whole lot of opportunities to party here in Sharjah. I think they'd like to come out with us."

"Hmmm. You can invite them some another time. Only you can come to this party. Consider this you making it up to me for almost breaking my phone. A taxi will be waiting for us in the main parking lot at nine sharp. Don't be late or you'll be in big trouble."

I wasn't sure if being in trouble was a good thing or a bad thing, so I arrived on time just in case. True to her word, a three-row minivan taxi was already waiting for us in the parking lot. But Shireen was nowhere to be found. I passed the first fifteen minutes by making small talk with the Indian driver. My anxiety level rose with each elapsing minute and my desire to maintain the conversation faded.

"Sir, why don't you call the girl on her phone?" the driver suggested.

"Sorry," I wanted to say, "I can't call her because I'm a schmuck who doesn't have her phone number." There I was pacing nervously around the taxi all stressed out over a girl I'd just met the week before and whose phone number I had yet to obtain. Clearly, Shireen had cast a powerful spell over me that erased my ability to think rationally. Every minute she kept me waiting only amplified my yearning to see her.

Shireen finally showed up at a quarter to ten wrapped in a long brown trench coat and high heels. Without saying anything, she rushed into the taxi and took a seat in the last row. I plopped down next to her and she smiled at me seductively. She let the trench coat slip off her shoulders, exposing a short blue dress and a sparkling diamond necklace that hung prominently above her cleavage.

"*Kheyli Khoshgeli*," I said, too momentarily stunned to speak English.

"*Merci*," she said, using the Farsi word for thank you. "Don't tell me this wasn't worth the wait. I'll put the coat in my purse as soon as we get to Dubai. Are you ready for a night to remember?"

"Oh yeah. Where are we going exactly?"

"To a house my friend rents when she has parties."

"Why's she renting a house? Why doesn't she just have the party where she lives?"

"Because then we might get into trouble," she said mischievously. "But don't worry. I won't let anything bad happen to you."

During the twenty-five minute drive, Shireen flirted with me the same as always. But being outside the university gates, she started getting more physically affectionate. She caressed my hand, rubbed my leg, and for a while rested her head on my shoulder. She was so good at putting me at ease that I almost failed to notice all the bizarre comments she made.

"I think it's really funny that you tell people you're a Jew," she said. "You have everyone in Sharjah going nuts. I bet you're having fun with it, but I think you're making it up."

"Ha!" I laughed. "If I were making it up, I'd be totally insane."

"People say that you're a spy."

"I know, but if I were a spy, why would I tell people I was Jewish?"

"I don't know. Maybe you're on a different kind of spy mission. I like thinking you're a spy. I think it's really hot. If you're a spy I want you to tell me. Maybe I can help you with your mission."

"I'll contact headquarters to get it approved," I joked.

"Really?" she asked.

"What do you mean really? Are you being serious?"

"No," she said with hesitation. "I'm just having fun."

The taxi dropped us off in front of a large, white, two-story house on a sandy lot in a residential neighborhood. All lights in the house were switched off and I didn't hear any music coming from inside. If not for the few cars parked on the driveway, I would have thought the place was deserted.

"It's soundproof," Shireen explained. "It's a little bit more expensive to rent, but it means no one will hear what's going on inside."

A slightly older, muscular, dark-skinned man with the hairiest knuckles I'd ever seen led us from the front door to the living room where the party was. Immediately, I was taken aback by just how average the party seemed. Aside from a few softly glowing incense candles, the only light in the room came from a small, cheesy, rotating disco ball hanging from the second floor atrium. A pair of four-foot detachable speakers blasted trance music, but no more than five of the dozen people there were dancing. Shireen wandered off supposedly to find her friend hosting the shindig. The hairy-knuckled muscle man brought me to a table packed with alcoholic beverages and snack foods.

"We're all here to get drunk," he screamed in my ear. "If we don't get drunk this party will suck. Friend, promise you'll get drunk with me tonight. Promise me!"

I generally tried very hard not to make promises I couldn't keep. I was excited to party, but I wasn't going to drink that night, since I was only twenty at the time. The legal drinking age in the emirates where alcohol was legal was twenty-one, as in the US, but the fines and penalties for underage drinking were more severe.

"I promise I'll be here while you get drunk," I said. "I'm not much of a drinker."

"Ah, I understand," he said as he playfully punched me in the arm. "I see how you pick your poison. If you don't like alcohol, we also have some candy just for you."

I smiled and pretended to know what he was talking about, but really I had no idea. He walked away to mingle with some other people and I stayed next to the table searching for candy. I discovered plenty of salty snacks, but there was no candy in sight. What a weird mix-up to make, I thought.

Over the next half hour, I tried socializing with the other partygoers without much success. Most were Iranians who spoke little English or Arabic. The loud music made most of our conversations inaudible anyway. When I felt my phone vibrate and saw my Dad calling me from the US, I used it as an excuse to step outside the house to talk and take a break from the party. When I finished the call, I went back into the living room and found a much livelier scene than the one I'd left.

Everyone in the room was dancing wildly and jumping up and down to a techno song. Two guys and a girl whom I'd spoken to only briefly ran up to me from different directions and hugged me fiercely. After my strong hairy-knuckled friend snuck up on me from behind and lifted me up in the air, I knew something weird was going on. I returned to the snack table to grab some pretzels and ponder the strange turn of events when I noticed a few tiny round pills sitting in a bowl near the table's edge. A shirtless guy with spiky gelled hair grabbed me by the shoulder and leaned in close to tell me something important.

"I don't know you, but I love you," he stated sincerely. "I love you so much. Have a candy. You'll feel amazing!" My heart raced rapidly and I stared at him with raised eyebrows. I finally connected the dots. "Don't worry," he continued. "There's nothing mixed in with it. It's one hundred percent pure Ecstasy."

I wasn't interested in recreational drug use of any kind. But even if I had been, the UAE was by far one of the most dangerous places in the world to experiment. Aside from the obvious dangers of being caught in possession of drugs, having a prohibited substance in my system could lead to years in prison. Plenty of people in Sharjah were keeping close tabs on my words and actions, and it couldn't be known that I attended a drug party in Dubai. I had to leave.

I hurried past the shirtless guy and slipped into a bathroom near the kitchen. I splashed cold water from the sink faucet on my face and sat on the toilet seat cover contemplating how I would break it to Shireen that I was planning to get back to Sharjah with or without her. Leaving a party without my date wasn't exactly the most chivalrous thing I could have done. Still, I'd already made up my mind and thought there was nothing she could say or do to make me change it. After a few minutes, I went to track her down.

I didn't have to go far. In fact, she found me. Someone must have tipped her off that I was in the bathroom because as soon as I stepped out I saw her standing in the kitchen, covered in her trench coat, lurking.

"I've been looking for you everywhere," she said as she inched towards me. "I have a surprise for you."

Before I could say anything, she stopped two feet in front of me and let her trench coat fall to the floor. Her short blue dress was gone. She stood before me wearing nothing but a blue bra, blue panties, and her sparkling diamond necklace. She wrapped her arms around my waist and pulled me in close.

"Make love to me, Michael!" she cried out. "I'm so hot for you! I'm ready to do anything you want."

Of course I considered it. Who in my position wouldn't have? I was a testosterone-charged twenty-year old male with a nearly naked exotic woman actively trying to seduce me. But before my hormones took over, I remembered all the lectures I sat through during my freshman orientation at GW, warning male students against hooking up with intoxicated girls. "If she says it's rape, then it's rape," we were told. The last thing I needed was a charge of rape or sexual assault brought against me by a Muslim girl who studied at AUS.

"Have you had any candy tonight?" I asked casually to determine her mental state.

"Oh yeah, just one pill," she answered, seemingly dazed with her eyes half-closed. "Having sex on E is the best. Let's find a corner in the living room. I need you to touch me."

"Um, you mean where the party is?"

"Yeah, I like when people watch me fool around. It's like a bonding experience."

"Shireen, this isn't going to work for me. I'm really attracted to you, but now isn't a good time for us to be doing this. I'm going back to campus."

"No!" she said defiantly. She took a step back away from me, shot me a baffled scowl, and suddenly appeared sober. "The police will catch you if they see that you have taken drugs. They will throw you in jail. You must stay here with me. Only here it is safe!"

"I haven't done any drugs tonight. I haven't even taken a sip of alcohol."

"Just wait, just wait!" she pleaded. She collapsed in my arms and appeared to return to her touchy-feely stupor. "Be with me. I promise we can go somewhere private. The people here don't have to know everything."

"If we did anything together, I wouldn't want people to know about it period. You know how much trouble I could get into? What happened to you being discreet? This is crazy."

I zipped out of the kitchen and passed through the living room, where I noticed that most other people at the party had removed their clothes too. Some had coupled off and were getting intimate with each other in empty spaces around the room. I opened the front door to leave when Shireen pulled me by the shirt. I pushed her hand away and walked out towards the street to go search for a taxi. She remained where she stood and hid her body behind the door to avoid exposing herself to the whole neighborhood.

"Michael!" she shouted angrily. "Stay! I thought you were cool. I thought you were into this."

"Well, guess what," I said. "I'm not. I don't even know what *this* is. You're acting really weird. One second you're loopy, the next I could swear you were sober. Enjoy your night. I'll see you back on campus."

Peculiarly, sometime never came. After that night, I never saw Shireen ever again. For the first few days after the party, I was more than happy not to bump into her, averting any potential awkwardness. After awhile though, I found it strange. I asked different Iranian students if they knew where she was. None of them had ever heard of her and no one recognized her description. It was as if she just vanished.

"I don't know this girl, but she was definitely trying to get you in trouble," Mehdi, an Iranian guy who played pickup basketball with me the night I first met Shireen, insisted. Well over six feet tall, he towered over me as we sat at lunch in the cafeteria discussing her potential whereabouts that next week. "Sounds like you almost fell into her trap."

"Are you saying she was a spy?" I asked.

"That's exactly what I'm saying. The CID wants you gone, man. You said this girl wanted you to drink, do drugs, and sleep with her? They could have used any one of those things to lock you up or deport you. Why else would a beautiful woman want to sleep with you?" he said with a laugh.

"Very funny. Why does the CID need a reason to get rid of me? Can't they just deport me at any time?"

"They can't just deport you. You're not some Pakistani or Filipino they can treat like shit. You're an American. If you got deported for nothing or put in jail, do you know how bad that would make the UAE look? No university in the West would send another student here ever."

"So, you really think that entire party in Dubai was just a setup to get me into trouble? That would have taken a ton of coordination."

"Just because she was trying to set you up doesn't mean everyone else there was in on it. Getting people like you into trouble probably isn't even her only job. Maybe she is Iranian and a design student somewhere. Maybe some of what she told you about herself was true."

"So spying is a part time job for college students now?"

Mehdi leaned in close to me and whispered.

"Why not? You think it's strange? That's exactly what happens in Iran. The Iranian government pays university students to snitch on those who say things against the regime. Even outside of Iran. Some do it because they support the mullahs. Others because they don't want to be blackmailed themselves."

"So how do you know who you can trust and who you can't?"

"I don't. I don't talk politics with Iranians under any circumstances."

"That's messed up you can't trust your own countrymen."

"It's the same thing here, but on steroids. You think you're the only one who the CID watches? Everyone is being watched. They do everything they can to stop anyone they see as a threat to Emirati power or their precious local culture. What's weird is that most of the people who work for the secret police aren't even Emirati. You know if I, an Iranian Shiite, wanted to go on a date or become friends with an Emirati girl from a powerful Sunni family, they'd stop me in no time."

"How?"

"I'd start getting text messages on my phone from untraceable numbers, warning me to stay away from her. If I refused to listen, anything could happen. Maybe they'd take me in the night and beat me. Here, the punishments are much worse for Muslims who disobey. You should consider yourself lucky to be a Jew. You have more power around here than you know."

"That's a strange thought."

"In this university, there are secret agents who aren't really students at all. You'll never know who they are. It shouldn't surprise you that many people think you're a spy. In the Middle East, spying is the norm. Without spying, there would be no control. It's the only way the Emiratis can keep living the good life."

There was no doubt about it. Thanks to oil wealth, the lifestyle of most Emiratis, commonly known as "locals," was very good indeed. The national government saw to it that its citizens' basic needs were well taken care of from the "cradle to the grave" in ways that people living in social-welfare states in the West could only dream of. UAE citizens were entitled to free healthcare and education through the PhD level. They were granted land and houses at no cost, generous living stipends, and guaranteed access to phenomenal business opportunities. All foreign-operated businesses in the UAE were required to concede an ownership stake of fifty-one percent to a UAE national.

Nearly every Emirati was well taken care of and most could get rich just by signing their names on a few contracts. This left little incentive for Emiratis to spend their days doing what everyone else in the UAE did: work. Emiratis comprised fifteen percent of the population, but held less than one-third of one percent of private sector jobs.

"Before the oil, these people were living in the stone age," explained Dr. Muntassar, my professor for a course on studies in post-1967 Arab intellectual history, as we sat in his office after class one day. He was a curly-haired Egyptian Copt with a prominent gap between his two front teeth.

Formerly a professor in the US and in Canada, he arrived in Sharjah with the hope of inspiring a new generation of Arab intellectuals to bring Arab culture into modernity. Teaching in Sharjah had jaded him considerably. He enjoyed inviting me and the other American students to his office to complain about the lousy work ethic he said would eventually cripple the UAE as a country.

"All of a sudden without doing anything, they received everything," he went on. "All they care about now is playing with their new cell phones or test driving Lamborghinis. They are totally squandering their opportunities to advance their culture. Tell me, you think my class is easy, right? It's a lot different from your classes in the US."

"Well, there's not as much work to do," I conceded. To describe his or any of my other classes at AUS as particularly challenging would have been a flat-out lie. But I tried attributing just how easy the classes were to the fact that most students were not studying in their native language. "You don't assign as many papers to write either," I added.

"It's because I can't. All I do is give multiple choice tests because all these students know how to do is regurgitate facts and numbers. These students, whether they're locals or not, are not being educated to analyze complex ideas or think critically at all. If I gave tests here that I administered in the US, almost all the Emirati students would fail. And they don't care. They don't need jobs. They all just want to race camels."

"Why do all the locals study if they don't need jobs?"

"They have nothing else to do. Many of the Emiratis, particularly the boys, stay at AUS for eight years, not four. They flunk year after year, but they stay because their tuition is paid for by the government. It's very sad, really. The Emiratis are the biggest joke in their own country. They have no idea what is coming if they don't change their mentality."

"What is coming?"

"Listen," he said as he sat down at his desk. "The only potential the UAE has comes from the ground. If the Emiratis don't get smart, they'll either lose control of their country to the foreigners who run it or they will destroy everything. Don't forget that a house built of sand will crumble when the tide comes in. It saddens me because many of the Emiratis are really very nice people."

I thought so too. Paradoxically, the CID may have wanted me gone, but the Emiratis whose power they were charged with protecting seemed to like having me around. Although the UAE government was strongly anti-Israel and government-affiliated newspapers frequently published articles and editorial cartoons depicting Jews negatively, no Emirati ever said an unkind word to me about being Jewish. They seemed like they couldn't have cared less.

From my first night in Sharjah when I met Rashid and company, I was treated to extraordinary hospitality and friendliness from all Emirati students I encountered. Every day during school, dozens of random smiling Emirati guys would approach me to shake my hand, bump noses, and see if I needed anything. While Emirati girls were also welcoming and kind, they were generally more inhibited.

My Emirati friends frequently brought me to shooting ranges, treated me to movies, and took me off-road SUV racing in the nearby sand dunes. Those who resided in Sharjah and neighboring Dubai would drive me to their homes on a whim to ride their pet camels and indulge in lavish five-course-meals prepared by their multiple Southeast Asian house servants. Sometimes I wondered if my hosts viewed my presence as a burden because every time I visited an Emirati's home, all female relatives would totally disappear from sight. The only evidence they were in the house at all was the echoes of their voices traveling between high-ceilinged rooms and hallways.

"We are always happy when you are coming," a Dubai native swore one night. He was a short mustached local named Muhammad bin Raheem, who usually sat next to me in Dr. Muntassar's class. Together with ten male family members, we waited for dinner to be served at a long elegant wooden table in one of the dining rooms in his house. "We have many rooms for eating because, when there are guests, the men and women must be separated. Women must not be seen by men who are not relatives. It is *haram* (forbidden)."

The members of the bin Raheem clan nodded their heads in agreement.

"But you are like a brother to me," Muhammad bin Raheem resumed. "From today, we will call you Michael bin Raheem!" The men at the table erupted in deafening hoots and cheers, banged on their chairs, and patted me on the back. "This means you must come to our other houses to meet all the family."

"Your other houses?" I inquired perplexed. "I thought you lived here."

"I am here with my mother and her other children. But my father has two other wives—twenty-seven children in all. My father has his house and he gave each of his three wives their own houses too."

"So how much time does your father spend at each house?"

"He spends two days with his first wife, two days with the second, and two days with the third."

"And on the seventh day?"

"He rests!"

My visits to my local friends' homes rarely lasted past dinnertime since the place they really wanted to take me was the mall. It wasn't important which mall we went to because we didn't go to shop. We went to play our own little game of "Where's Waldo?"

We would walk around various shops in our crease-free white *kanduras* and see if other shoppers noticed anything strange about us. How would they react when they spotted me, the green-eyed, light-skinned eye-brow-pierced Waldo, strolling around dressed like an Emirati?

Most people, regardless of nationality or ethnicity, picked me out of my crowd of Emirati buddies right away, but almost never said anything. Indian Sikh shopkeepers would stare blankly, local girls might walk by us repeatedly to double check my face, and European tourists would frequently snap pictures of me from far away.

Whenever we caught someone noticing me, the Waldo of our group, I'd call out to the person to get their attention. Then, in the same vein as the 2003 MTV series "Punk'd," all the Emiratis would wave excitedly and yell "Waldo" before turning away with their hands over their faces giggling uncontrollably.

Occasionally, I did manage to pass as a local through and through. During one game of "Where's Waldo?" at the Mall of the Emirates, Muhammad bin Raheem, some other pals, and I were sitting at a table in the food court when a group of six traditionally dressed middle-aged Emirati women approached our table—two of them with their faces completely covered—and stood still right in front of us. Out of respect, my local friends lowered their gazes. I, on the other hand, glanced up at them wondering why they stopped.

"Ya'll see!" a chubby woman in the middle belted out in a thick southern drawl. "I knew he must be someone we know. I just can't remember who his momma is."

"I bet he's Charlene's boy!" a woman whose face I couldn't see enthusiastically yelled. "No wait. Don't tell me, young man. You're Suzie's!"

"You women are Americans?" I asked surprised.

"That's right," the first one said. "I'm wearing red, white, and blue underneath these black robes. Met my local husband at a horse race in Kentucky. He told me he was gonna turn me into an Arabian princess. My lord, you look just like my son, Ibrahim. All you half-American boys are so darn handsome. Did you get that eyebrow ring in America? You really are trying to stir up trouble, aren't you?"

"You have no idea," I replied.

"Now just tell us who your momma is and we'll leave you alone with all your friends," she said.

Before I opened my mouth to explain that I wasn't really an Emirati at all, Muhammad bin Raheem looked up at these women and answered for me.

"My name is Muhammad bin Raheem," he stated in halting English. "This is my brother, Michael bin Jaheem. We do not have the same mother, but we are brothers all the same."

"That was so cute," another woman said. "I guess we'll have to hire a private eye to find out where you come from. Take care, boys."

Honored as I was by this quasi-Emirati status, I often invited other non-local AUS students to join me on my excursions with locals. But aside from the Americans and a few Arabs from other Persian Gulf countries, none of the students ever accepted the invitation. It didn't matter which Emiratis I proposed we hang out with or what activity I suggested we do. The excuse I was given was always the same.

"It's nothing against *you*," they'd say. "I just won't go anywhere with *them*."

Most students refused to interact with Emiratis unless they were forced to do so for a class assignment. More often than not, if a local came up me to say hello while I sat surrounded by non-locals, my group would confront the Emirati with icy glares and uncomfortable silence until he walked away. On a few occasions, some of my friends even rose from their chairs and switched tables just to highlight their unwillingness to give a local the time of day. After the Emirati in question faded from sight, my friends would return and defend their actions.

"They deserve it!" Mo professed one time while we sat at a table at the Student Center. "They're stuck up and think they can do whatever they want. They don't care about anyone but themselves, so why should I care about them?"

"Mo, you can't judge them all like that," I criticized. "You can't treat them like they're not human."

"I don't. Did you hear me say one bad word to that local? I've lived here my whole life. I know I could get into trouble for that. All I did was move seats. That's one thing I am allowed to do. Before you yell at me for not being friendly to the locals, go see for yourself how they treat people. Look at all the foreign workers. Go up to a Pakistani construction worker in the middle of this crazy heat and ask him if he's treated more like a human being or an animal."

Mo had a point. Millions of foreign workers in the UAE did live and work in subhuman conditions and suffered tremendous abuse from their employers. Construction workers, food service staff, and housemaids toiled for a sadistic number of hours each day, virtually ensuring the country stayed up and running. Many of these foreign workers were forbidden to go out in public and were virtually imprisoned in labor camps or inside the houses of the families they served.

A few Emiratis confessed that they'd lost their virginity by raping their housemaids when they hit puberty. One of them, an unsavory obese Emirati with an extremely arrogant attitude, told me with pride how it happened as we feasted on a meal of lamb meat and rice at his home that his maid had prepared and served to us.

"When I was a young boy I had many urges," my host said with a grin. "I wanted to know a woman, but I knew it was *haram*. My older brother told me that in America everybody touches everybody whenever they want. I knew I wanted to do these things too. But I could not do these things with a local girl. She would never marry if the people knew she was not a virgin. So one time I ordered my maid to come to my room. When she came in I was in my bed naked. She turned her head away, but I said to her, 'Come to the bed.' She came to me and I told her to lie on the bed with me. She was much older than me, but I was very strong. I did what I wanted to do and then ordered the maid to leave. I put my *kandura* back on and ran off to tell my brother, 'Look at me. I am like an American!'"

After concluding the story, my host laughed mightily and disregarded the bits of half-chewed lamb meat that sprung from his mouth and landed on his *kandura*. With multiple reasons to feel sick to my stomach, I pushed away my tray of food and momentarily glanced at the maid. She timidly stood in a corner staring at the floor, waiting for a command. When she left the dining room to go wash dishes in the kitchen, I asked him if she was the same maid he'd forced himself on all those years ago.

"No," he answered. "I did not want to see that one again. I told my mother she stole something from me. So, my mother gave her a beating and sent her away."

Though his attitude and actions revolted me, I knew it would be wrong to just assume this was the norm or that all Emiratis were directly responsible for the country's human rights abuses. Plenty of people of other national origins were also guilty of deceiving impoverished workers and mistreating their household staff in the UAE. For AUS students to specifically socially ostracize locals on campus was hypocritical and mean-spirited.

"The students hate the locals because they're jealous of them," Kareem clarified as we walked together to the main library one evening, he to study and me to check email. "Don't let anyone tell you otherwise."

Built like a linebacker, he was a senior who carried an Egyptian passport and served as the President of the university's Islamic Club. Despite being one of the most popular students at AUS, he was exceedingly modest and levelheaded. He was the kind of guy who truly understood the mood on campus and would be able to provide a nuanced assessment of the relationship between locals and foreigners.

"Sure, the locals have this enviable status," I said. "But why do the other students care so much? It's not exactly like they're underprivileged."

"Because the rest of us don't know for how long we'll have that privilege. There is no such thing as a green card or any kind of permanent residency here. Even the rich students of AUS are almost all here on three-year visas that must be renewed."

"People are angry because they have to renew their visas? Is that all?"

"You don't understand. Life here is temporary unless you have some seriously huge connections. Take me, for example. I was born and raised in Abu Dhabi. But it is forbidden for me to say that the UAE is my home. It's always rubbed in my face that this is not my country, not my home, and that I have no rights. All foreigners get are cheap healthcare and no taxes. That's it."

"No taxation without representation is what they say in America," I added.

"Well, here the government says no taxation, so no representation. It's difficult to be at peace if you always have to worry about your visa being re-issued. I'm a wreck right now. I don't know what's going to happen to me."

"Why's that? "

"I'm graduating soon, Michael. My parents are retired. They moved back to Egypt last year. That means after I finish up at AUS I'll have three months to find an employer that will sponsor me for a visa, or I'll be deported to Egypt. I've lived here for twenty-two years and they can kick me out that easily. I appreciate the privilege of living here. So, when all I see around me are locals who don't work, don't study, and just play on their cell phones all day, I get jealous. It's not fair."

"It sounds unfair. But there are plenty of nice locals. Maybe if other people became friends with them it would help change things. Maybe if you came out with me wearing the *kandura* some local would appreciate it and help you get a job."

Kareem stared at me like that was the dumbest suggestion ever.

"If I wore the *kandura,* like you do, the locals would make sure I never set foot in their country again."

"But they love it when foreigners wear the *kandura.* It shows that you respect their culture."

"No, it shows that *you* respect their culture. You're an American. You're here for a semester. When you wear their clothes, they think it's cool. If I wore their clothes, it would be very bad. They'd accuse me of pretending to be one of them. They'd say I assumed I was good enough to be a local. An Arab can't wear those clothes without getting into trouble. Those clothes are a status symbol here. It's different for you. The Emiratis look at you like you're a toy. They're fascinated by you and accept you because you don't pose a threat."

"And what threat do you pose?"

"Look at this country. Everything's run by foreigners. If this country were a democracy, the official language would be Hindi. No company even wants to hire locals. Everyone knows that hiring a local means shelling out a big salary and getting no productivity in return. The locals keep to themselves just as much as the foreigners keep away. They're scared they'll be swallowed up in their own country, so they cling to their culture as a lifeline. They like you because they know you don't want anything from them. You're a real guest, so the locals treat you well. With other Arabs, they couldn't care less."

"I didn't realize I was so special."

"The UAE's a weird place. Most Arabs around here would rather be friends with a Jew than with each other."

Chapter 8
America Is a Lie

Sharjah, UAE
September 2006

"YOU ARE THE DEVIL!" MO TOLD ME AS WE WANDERED AROUND campus one extremely hot evening in early September. "That's what my brother Hassan and his friends are calling you. They can't stand that all these people actually like you! They're telling people to stay away from you even more now. They say it's in every Jew's blood to tempt people towards evil, just like the devil."

"Why should I care?" I asked as I peeled my sweaty t-shirt off my skin, annoyed that Mo was bringing up the nonsense his brother Hassan and his friends were saying about me.

"Because he's getting people angry at you for wearing the *kandura*. He says you're showing how much you hate Arabs by making fun of the locals' clothes."

"Go tell Hassan his theories are cute and that your mom should give him a cookie for having such a creative imagination."

Instead of getting too worked up over what Hassan and his cadre said about me, I tried making fun of them and their accusations. It entertained me to envision Mo relaying our messages back and forth, and I thought it was more fitting than issuing a direct response to those jerks. Hassan and his friends had never been brave enough to say a nasty word to my face. The last thing I wanted to do was validate the charges they made by openly acknowledging them in the first place. I hoped that other students would appreciate on their own just how ridiculous these claims against me were.

"That's not going to happen," Mo said. "My brother is popular. All the people at school who hate you for being a Jew will believe everything he says."

I wasn't sure how many or which people totally detested my very existence, since no one would step forward to tell me so directly. But then again, I didn't really care. As far as I was concerned, I had been doing my best to behave with everyone at AUS like a true *mensch*, which means "a person of integrity and honor" in Yiddish. If there were students so filled with hatred that they harbored anger against a person they barely knew, like me, then that was their problem, not mine. I didn't see a reason to make an effort with people who wanted absolutely nothing to do with me just because I was Jewish. Anyone else in a similar situation would have had the same attitude, or so I believed.

The week Mo told me what his brother and friends were up to, Dr. Muntassar pulled me aside before I left his classroom. He put his hand affectionately on my shoulder and quietly but eagerly insisted I visit him at his office at six that evening.

"There's something I've wanted to share with you for awhile," he said with a foreboding smile.

"What is it?" I asked.

He took a quick look around the room to verify that no one was listening in on our conversation.

"I can't tell you here. It's private and it could be dangerous if people found out. Just come to my office and I'll reveal everything. Please come alone. This is for your pleasure only."

Dr. Muntassar's strange choice of words made me nervous about what it was he wanted to share. He claimed to have been married and divorced twice, but part of me wondered if his mysterious invitation was actually a subtle attempt to hit on me. It was no secret that the UAE frowned on homosexual activity. Getting caught in the act by the authorities meant risking a stiff prison sentence.

When I ultimately showed up at Dr. Muntassar's office that evening I felt more than a tad anxious. I wasn't sure if the sweat that dripped from my brow was from the sizzling heat outside or my nerves. Within a few seconds of my knock, Dr. Muntassar opened up and graciously welcomed me in. He shook my hand long and hard and firmly rubbed my back as I sat down in one of his guest chairs.

"Before I say anything, I want to show you something just to get both of us on the same page," he said as he hovered over me next to my seat. "I hope what you see excites you."

I closed my eyes for a moment and prayed for the exact opposite.

"It's a book written in Hebrew," he stated proudly.

I breathed a sigh of relief, opened my eyes, and saw a novel. It was *My Michael,* a novel by the Israeli author Amos Oz.

"I have about a dozen Hebrew books on the shelves," he said. "Normally, I hide them behind big textbooks, so that less open-minded people don't see them by mistake. Some students would have a fit if they knew."

"Knew what?" I asked.

"That I used to live in Israel."

Dr. Muntassar sat down in the black leather chair at his desk and leaned back just a bit.

"I studied in Jerusalem at the Hebrew University for a year in 1982," he recounted. "I was the first Egyptian student to study in Israel after the peace treaty was finalized. I don't talk about my experiences there very much because I don't want any students or faculty members complaining about me. But I decided to tell you because your situation reminds me of the one I was once faced with."

"How so? This isn't Egypt and don't forget that I'm not Israeli."

Remembering that in Sharjah the walls have ears, I felt the need to emphasize the latter point just in case a third party was eavesdropping on our chat.

"I know," he said. "But you are Jewish, and a lot of people here don't know the difference between Jews and Israelis. I know what it's like to live in a place where you are seen as a representative of your people first and foremost."

"Fair enough," I said. "So what made you want to study in Israel?"

"Throughout my entire childhood Israel and Egypt were at war. Israel was viewed as this nasty goblin that wanted to do nothing but harm to Egypt. When the peace was made, most Egyptians didn't know what to think, including me. I realized that I didn't really know anything about our next-door neighbor. In order to have an opinion, I thought I had to spend time in Israel for myself. It didn't matter if Israelis turned out to be the devils I'd been taught they were or the nicest people on Earth. Either way, I wanted to know them."

"Did your family support you?"

"Only financially," he said with a laugh. "I was lucky to come from a wealthy family. When I told my family I wanted to study in Israel for a year after high school, they thought I was nuts. They said I was just a naïve nineteen year old who didn't have a clue how the world worked. But I begged and pleaded nonstop. My parents decided to humor me by letting me apply. They thought there was no chance that a university in Israel would admit an Egyptian student so soon after the peace was made. When I was notified of my acceptance, my family was shocked, but I was ecstatic. My parents agreed to let me go because they knew it was the only thing I wanted. But they were never happy about it."

"Well, how did you feel when you got to Israel?"

"When I stepped off the airplane in Tel Aviv, all the excitement I'd felt in Egypt immediately turned to fear. I asked myself over and over again if I was crazy. What was I doing in Israel? How would Israelis react when they found out I was Egyptian? Would they be angry with me? Would someone try to hurt me? I didn't know. I was very stressed out. Eventually, I calmed down."

"What, you took a valium or something?" I asked. "What relaxed you?"

"I'll tell you. One of my first nights in Jerusalem, before classes started or I knew anyone, I went out for a long walk alone in the city. After a couple of hours, I got tired and had no idea where I was. So, I got in a taxi and asked the driver to take me back to my dormitory. We traveled in silence for the first five minutes until the driver asked me in broken English where I was from. I hesitated for a second, but then told him I came from Egypt. Immediately, he stopped the car and got out. 'Oh my God,' I thought. 'He's going to hurt me! I should have never come to Israel.'

"Too panicked to move, I sat in the back seat waiting for something bad to happen. Suddenly, just as I feared, the driver opened my passenger door, grabbed me by the arm, and pulled me out of the taxi. Then, he looked at me in the eye, shook my hand and said slowly, 'You. Me. Home. Shabbat.' He was inviting me to his home for a meal! I was relieved he wasn't going to kill me and flattered by his invitation at the same time. That Friday night, I joined him and his family for dinner. Before he conducted the Shabbat blessings, his wife tried to sneak up on me from behind to put a kippah on my head without me knowing. When I realized what she was doing, I took the kippah from her hand and wore it proudly the whole evening. It even turned out the taxi driver and his wife spoke Arabic because they were both Jews born in Yemen. I went back to that family's house many times that year. They really made me feel welcome in Israel. After meeting them, I wasn't afraid anymore."

"Did you make a lot of friends at Hebrew University?"

"I did. In the beginning, I think a lot of people were suspicious of me. I'm sure plenty even thought I was a spy. In fact, the people who really thought I was a spy were often the ones most eager to sit down and talk to me."

"We do have a lot in common. Were any of the students hostile?"

"Sure, but never directly. The ones who didn't like me usually stayed away. There were many Arab students who weren't so fond of me because I was an Arab who specifically chose to study in Israel. They thought that meant I supported all of Israel's policies. There were also very extremist Jews who hated all Arabs, but Egyptians in particular. Those people weren't really thrilled with me either."

"How did you respond to those types?"

"Actually, I tried my best to get to know them. I didn't go to Israel just to meet people who wanted to be friends with me right off the bat. I went to get to know everyone: Right-wingers, left-wingers, Ashkenazis, Sephardis, Arabs, and kibbutzniks. I even went to a museum in Jerusalem run by the followers of Meir Kahane, that rabbi that wanted to kick all the Arabs out of Israel. I knew that people who hated me didn't really have anything against me in particular. They were against what they assumed I stood for because of where I came from. So I saw it as my responsibility to show everyone that what I, an Egyptian Arab, stood for was peace."

"Did it work?"

"Not with everyone. You can't really change someone's mind unless they let you. The truly closed-minded never cared for me much. However, I did learn that most people, even the ones who belonged to the extremist camps, weren't all as closed-minded as they might have seemed. By actively putting myself out there, I was able to shatter a lot of misconceptions."

Hearing how strikingly similar Dr. Muntassar's experiences were to my own got me thinking about the kind of impact I wanted to make at AUS. Hadn't I decided to study in Sharjah specifically to meet and share ideas with Arabs who held radically different views than I did? Had I completely forgotten what Dr. Dennis Ross warned me never to forget that you don't make peace with your friends? If the AUS student body actually saw me as a representative, then maybe the onus was on me to do more to represent.

Dr. Muntassar's remarks prompted me to consider changing my attitude, but it took another disturbing encounter with an attractive woman to compel me to act.

Later on that same week, I was on a roll. Ahmad Jew had challenged me to a few games of bowling in the dark, disco-themed bowling alley on the ground floor of the Student Center. After I defeated him five straight times, he was tired, dejected, and ready to call it quits.

"Go return our bowling shoes to the counter," I told him. "While you're gone, I'll buy you a Coke from the vending machine as a consolation prize for you getting your ass kicked."

I stepped outside the bowling alley into the nearly empty adjacent café and spotted a vending machine about ten feet away. I walked over casually and waited for a girl wearing a yellow hijab standing ahead of me to select a drink. She was tall and had a nice figure, and her hijab perfectly matched the color of her lightweight blouse. I watched her shove a one dirham coin through the slot, push down on the Sprite button, and wait fruitlessly for her drink to fall down the chute.

"Uhhh!" she muttered as she banged her fist on the machine.

"Ate your money, huh? Maybe if you'd bought a Coke, things would have gone better," I teased.

"Maybe," she said with her back to me as she pulled out another dirham from her coin purse. "I'll try again, this time for a Coke."

She carefully peeped into the slot to make sure nothing blocked it inside, dropped in her coin, and pressed the red button plastered with the Coca Cola logo.

"Yeesh!" she blurted out. "It did it again."

"That stinks," I said. "Listen, I need to go find another vending machine because I promised my friend I'd buy him a Coke. If you want I'll buy you one too, so you don't feel like your two dirhams were spent in vain."

My offer made her laugh, and when she turned around to meet me she was smiling radiantly from ear-to-ear. As soon as I got a clearer view of her face, I recognized her as someone I always noticed whenever we passed each other on campus. We'd never spoken before or even made eye contact, and I didn't know her name or anything personal about her.

Sure, part of why she stood out to me was because she was pretty. Her facial features were soft, her skin was smooth, and she applied just enough makeup to give herself a classy, but still all natural look. However, what really struck me about her was how she mixed her faith with fashion. As a devout Muslim, she covered up her whole body except for her face and hands. Nevertheless, she was able to use her modesty to enhance her physical appearance. Every day she wore a different dazzling, color-coordinated outfit that made her look uniquely stylish and even sexy. To me, she seemed like she'd be an interesting person to talk to and I was happy we finally had the chance to properly meet.

The second she fixed her eyes on me though, it became clear that to her, I needed no introduction. She looked at me like she knew me, but not in a friendly, familiar sort of way. She gasped, and stopped smiling as her jaw tensed up. For a few moments, she stared at me with a terrified expression, as if I were the devil Hassan and his friends had painted me as.

"Are you okay?" I asked. "My name is Michael. Do you want to go get a soda with me?"

Instead of responding, she just gasped again, gawked at me in fright, and darted off towards the nearest exit without looking back. Before she completely escaped from sight, Ahmad Jew walked up, patted me on the back, and caught the last segment of the scene.

"Wow," he said. "You are amazing with women. You have to come out with me to the clubs in Jerusalem to show me how you do it."

"Hilarious. What was that? Who was that?"

"That was Samira. She's a Palestinian too, but she grew up in the UAE. She's usually very nice. You probably weren't someone she expected to see."

"Why wouldn't she talk to me?"

"She's scared of you. All the crap those assholes like Hassan say about you has an effect. They hate you. They've even gotten people who don't really hate you to be too afraid to talk to you."

And that was something I had to change. The time had come for me to launch my own PR campaign against the vitriol spread by punks like Hassan. I still didn't care much about changing the minds of those who hated me with a passion. But I did see the importance of reaching out to students just a bit less vehemently opposed to my presence to show them I was not someone they needed to fear. If fewer people were afraid of me, then more people would be interested in talking to me, I thought. As my opening act, I resolved to step forth right into the lions' den.

I walked over to a nearby table covered in fliers, grabbed the one that caught my eye, and held it up to Ahmad Jew's face.

"No," Ahmad Jew said. "You can't be serious."

"I am," I said with a smile. "Tomorrow night the Palestinian Cultural Club (PCC) is putting on their first big event of the school year and I'm going to make an appearance. I've got to show more students I'm not some monster. I have to show them I came to have dialogue."

"I understand how you feel, but believe me. Going to that event is crazy. That club is run by Hassan's crew. What do you think they're going to do if you show up?"

"I don't know. Maybe they'll invite me to be a guest speaker," I joked.

"You really live in a movie," Ahmad Jew said in Hebrew, using a popular Israeli expression.

"Will you come with me?" I asked. "If I go with a Palestinian it'll show my good intentions. We'll bring along Ahmad Greasy too. Imagine what that would mean having AUS Jew and the two Palestinians from Jerusalem show up together."

"No way. Don't bother asking Ahmad either. The people who run that club will just think the three of us are on spy duty or something. We're not the Palestinians you want to go with. Ahmad and I live in

Jerusalem. That means we're not Palestinian enough for that club. If you go to that event, it won't be with us."

Fine, I decided. I didn't need the Ahmads to come along since I could think of one other Palestinian student I was sure would be more than happy to accompany me.

"Of course, I'll go with you," Mo enthusiastically agreed when I phoned him later that night. "Did you really think you had to ask?"

The truth was I didn't. I chose to formally request his company purely to be polite. I knew Mo would jump at the chance to see me through a potentially messy situation. It wasn't because I viewed Mo as a close, trusted friend. He wasn't. But spending time with him was amusing. I never let it slip my mind just how much he deeply distrusted all Jews, including me, and how stubbornly he clung to his suspicion that I was a spy. Despite his brother Hassan's insistence that he stay from me, Mo hung around me because I offered him something few others could: controversy.

Mo was obsessed with controversy and the gossip it generated. And, at the beginning of that semester, nothing was more controversial at AUS than me, the Jew.

Additionally, I could tell that Mo felt a particularly powerful sense of importance being at the center of my tiff with Hassan. By appearing at the PCC event with me, my thinking went, he'd receive his fix of controversy and I'd gain positive visibility as a Jew with a Palestinian friend.

The event took place outdoors after dusk the next day in the spacious, marble-tiled plaza next to the Student Center. Hundreds of people sat in white foldout chairs facing an elevated stage with a podium in the middle draped in an over-sized Palestinian flag. Lights and loudspeakers were scattered around the perimeter and three long tables packed with refreshments for after the main program were stationed behind the seating area. I spotted Mo hunkered down in a chair near the right side of the stage chatting with two Iraqi girls I was already friendly with. I walked over, said hello to the group, and sat in the seat to Mo's right.

"Good thing you're here," Mo said excitedly. "People couldn't believe it when I told them you were coming. There are already some people pointing and looking at you."

"Oh boy!" I replied cynically.

Just a few minutes later, a petite Palestinian girl with black hair and olive-colored skin stood up at the podium, adjusted the microphone, and addressed the crowd. Her voice was shrill and irritating and to the audience's misfortune, she spent the next twenty-five minutes droning on with welcomes, thank-you's, and an obnoxiously detailed analysis of every meeting and event the club held the year before.

"Her name's Haneen," Mo whispered. "She's the only girl on the board and always talks a lot. She gets angry very easily, so everyone just lets her do what she wants."

When Haneen finished her speech and stepped away from the podium, techno music started thumping from the speakers. Two boys on BMX bicycles rode onto the stage and performed tricks while the audience clapped and cheered. I didn't understand what the performance had to do with Palestinian culture, but it was more interesting than the speech, so I didn't complain. Then, in another style reversal, the bicyclists rushed off, traditional Arabic folk songs started playing, and the club's male board members, including Hassan and his pals, ran onto the stage.

For the next ten minutes, they danced the *dabka*, a traditional line dance popular in the Arab world that vaguely reminded me of the *hora*. Their choreography included a lot of hand-holding, handkerchief twirling, and stomping on the ground in various rhythmic patterns. The board members concluded their act by jumping off the stage and landing on their feet in a dramatic pose. Then the music stopped and all the attendees got up from their seats and stampeded the snack tables.

"Was that it?" I asked Mo as we followed the crowd to grab some refreshments. "Is that the end of the program?"

"That was it," Mo confirmed.

"No guest speaker, no questions from the audience, nothing? Just bike-riding and *dabka*?"

"There was a speech too. Whatever. Their programs are always like that. I want some pretzels."

While I hadn't necessarily expected the event to include a lengthy group political discussion, I had hoped that something interesting or provocative would have been said and prompted students to ask me to respond. That would have given me an opportunity to humanize myself and clarify my opinions to those too apprehensive to approach me privately. However, no one seemed especially interested in engaging in any serious conversation, period. Most people preferred to grab their share of sugary and salty treats and race off to the nearest air-conditioned building to escape the humidity.

For a while, I stood with Mo next to one of the tables, munching on pretzels and watching people clear out. I stayed positive by telling myself that by merely showing my face at the event I must have changed at least some minds.

When I said goodnight to Mo and turned away to walk towards my dorm, I saw Samira chatting with a few girls at the next table over. I thought about saying something to her. I thought that maybe we could put our awkward encounter the night before behind us and start out fresh. Seeing me there at that Palestinian event must have shown her that I wasn't the man she assumed I was.

But before I decided whether to move towards her, Samira made her opinion clear. She glanced over and, as soon as our eyes met, she looked away, quickly said goodbye to her friends, and scurried off in a different direction with the same panicked expression as the night before. I was stunned. Even when surrounded by friends, Samira was still too afraid to be anywhere near me. I began to contemplate how many more people at the event felt as she did. I returned to my dorm thinking that my efforts to reach out had totally failed. I felt stupid for showing up in the first place and for believing my presence alone would have the magical effect of changing people's perspectives. If anything, I worried I might have made things worse.

Less than twenty-four hours later I learned this worry carried weight. I was sitting on a leather couch in the main commons with Ahmad Jew and Ahmad Greasy after finishing up classes for the day. Mo came hurrying towards us with a shady smile stuck on his face. That smile was bad. That smile meant trouble. Whenever Mo greeted me with that smile, I knew to expect nothing less than an in-depth update on the most recent slander about me.

"People are talking about you again," he said as he sat down in a chair across from me.

"Shocking!" I said sarcastically. "Spill it."

"People are saying you came to the event to make fun of Palestine," he said. "I heard Haneen was screaming about you to everyone in her dorm building last night. My brother and his friends are saying you made all the Palestinian students look like cowards, especially the board, because no one dared confront you."

"Confront me?" I asked, flabbergasted. "Confront me about what? Nothing happened at that event. I didn't say or do anything to anybody. I just watched *dabka* and ate pretzels." The Ahmads roared with laughter and banged their fists on the table. "You're always so excited by this gossip, Mo," I continued. "Tell me, why aren't people angry at you? You were with me the whole time. Why don't they expect you to stand up to me?"

"I tell them I'm pretending to be friends with you, so that you'll tell me your secrets. If I stood up to you people wouldn't think you're telling me anything."

"But I don't tell you anything! I don't have secrets. I've said it a thousand times. I am not a spy!"

"I warned you not to get involved with that club," Ahmad Jew interrupted as he draped his arm around my shoulder. "You should go back to being a secret spy. Lay low for awhile to keep people confused," he laughed.

"I don't get this place," I said. "I'm an AUS student. I'm allowed to attend whatever campus programs I want. Who cares if a Jew goes to a Palestinian club event? If this were GW, Palestinian students would be bending over backwards to make me feel welcome precisely because I'm a Jew. They'd do anything to convince me why their perspective was right and why the pro-Israel position was wrong."

"No one cares what Palestinian students do in America," Mo replied angrily. "If Palestinians do anything with Jews in America it's because they're forced to. America is not a country to be trusted. America is a very bad place for Arabs."

Of course, not everyone at AUS identified with this sentiment. A Pakistani friend named Zaid loved watching conservative news shows on the Fox News television network and dreamed of one day immigrating to the US. I'd met plenty of other students who recounted in dramatic fashion the disappointment they endured after their student visa applications to the US had been rejected.

"It was the worst day of my life," a Saudi student told me with a sigh. "I still think about how my life would have been at Idaho State."

Still, a lot of students didn't think America was all it was cracked up to be. These students certainly loved American food, entertainment, and fashion, and they tremendously valued receiving an education from an American-accredited institution. But they also believed that America's democratic principles, such as freedom of speech, religious and ethnic tolerance, and a commitment to representative government, were either one big farce or just didn't apply to people like them.

"People like us. Arabs. Muslims. We know about all the crap that happens in America," said Imad, a heavyset, half-Sudanese-half-Turkish girl with dyed blonde hair, to the cheers and applause of five of her friends.

The six of them wanted to smoke cigarettes, so we sat outside the Student Center at an umbrella-shaded picnic table one afternoon. They were part of the punk-rock clique on campus and had very different skin colors and facial features than one another. If I'd laid eyes on them in the US, I would have never suspected any of them were Arab or Muslim even.

"We hear all about the attacks in the streets against Muslims," Imad claimed. "It's dangerous just to wear a hijab in America. I don't wear one myself, but I decided when I was applying to college that I didn't want to go study in a place like that. It wasn't worth risking my safety."

"That's right," Rima, a short, light-skinned Iraqi girl with dyed black hair and black eye makeup, chimed in. "The police in America pick Muslims up off the streets and beat them until they confess to being terrorists. The American government taps the phone of every Muslim in America. Why should we deal with that?"

"Wait a second," I said as I flapped smoke away of my face. "Yes, there was some anti-Muslim sentiment after 9/11, but attacks are few and far in between. America's a great place for anyone regardless of religion or ethnicity. You have to come visit and experience it for yourselves."

"Man, you are brainwashed," Imad said. "You have to stop listening to your government. You can't believe everything that President Bush tells you to believe."

"Excuse me," I said. "In the US we have something called freedom of speech. That means anyone can and will say whatever they want. My government doesn't tell me to believe anything. The government itself is made up of people with different opinions on all kinds of issues. As an American, I have the right to question anything I please. That's more than anyone can say about the Arab world."

"Okay, honey. Whatever you say," Imad said contemptuously. "Seriously, for as many problems as Arab countries have, Arab people are a whole lot more free there than they are in America. It's very easy for you to talk about personal freedom and all your rights. You're a Jew. Maybe it's like that for you. Jewish people control everything in the US. One of my American professors even said so in class."

While I hadn't the slightest inkling who her professor was, Imad's claim didn't shock me. My Canadian-born instructor for a course on the political economy of the Arab world spent a full week covering the likelihood that a manipulative Jewish lobby dictated all US foreign policy. Based on the readings he assigned and the discussions he led in class, it was probable students would conclude that Jews were actively undermining US democracy.

Unfortunately, other North American political science and history professors at AUS were also prone to endorsing conspiracy theories, either inadvertently or not, that often confirmed Arab students' worst nightmares about American intentions in the Middle East. My professor for a course about US relations in the Middle East stated during his first lecture of the semester, perhaps somewhat jokingly, that he chose to move to Sharjah because he "couldn't stand the thought of living in America anymore under the tyrannical dictatorship of George W. Bush."

I assumed he didn't fully understand that despite the Arab students' American-accented English and obsession with McDonald's Big Macs, they weren't American and wouldn't necessarily understand the context of his jokes or over-the-top criticism of US leaders. After all, most AUS students weren't raised in societies where criticizing authority was accepted.

As the semester progressed, his colorful pronouncements continued and I realized he uttered many of them in all seriousness. He compared the US Congress to the Reichstag of the Weimar Republic, the weak German parliament that allowed Adolf Hitler to seize absolute power in Germany. He alleged that the American-led war in Iraq was solely an effort by American neo-conservatives to "spread Evangelical Christianity throughout the Middle East." His statements convinced students that America was a terrible place with no rule of law, run by a man threatening to destroy modern Arab civilization.

"Michael, when Bush calls the war in Iraq his 'crusade' he really means it," Imad declared before lighting up her third cigarette of the conversation. "Even you have to agree that America doesn't care about freedom or democracy for the Arabs. America just wants to make the Arabs weak."

"Saddam Hussein was very bad for Iraq," Rima chimed in. "But Saddam was ours. Now, there is only trouble in Iraq because of America. We are weaker than ever. We see now that Bush is more dangerous than Saddam ever was."

"If Bush wanted to he could stop the violence in one day," Imad said smugly. "He's behind everything. We all know that as the violence goes up so does the price of oil. Violence in Iraq just makes the Americans richer."

"Who told you that?" I asked.

"My American professor," Imad answered. "He says he tells us things he can't say at universities in America. Wake up, Michael. America is a lie!"

With these professors fanning the flames of Arab paranoia, it started to seem more logical to me that some students avoided me, the AUS Jew, like the plague.

However, it still surprised and disappointed me that the day after the PCC event, all I'd heard was that the students who attended reacted to my being there with anger. Regardless of their preconceived notions of me, these were still young people in the midst of the most impressionable period of their lives. Yet none of them gave in to youthful curiosity and asked me why I'd attended the event.

Two nights after the PCC event, I was finishing up some readings for class on a sofa on the second floor of the library when I heard my cell phone ringing from inside my backpack. I pulled my phone out, glanced at the unfamiliar number buzzing me, pushed the green "talk" button, and said hello. The timid female voice on the other end said her name was Noura and that we'd never spoken before. She said she was a half-Syrian-half-Palestinian sophomore pursuing a degree in international relations. She'd gotten my phone number from Mo. She had questions for me, she said. She asked if we could meet up, so I invited her to come join me at the library. I told her I'd head to the front entrance when she arrived, so she wouldn't need to go searching for me.

"No," she said. "I know exactly where you are. I can see you right now."

A few moments later a stocky, light-skinned girl with brown hair and black glasses emerged from behind a tall bookcase, walked over, and parked herself in the chair opposite me. She looked scared to death. Her cheeks were flushed red and she smiled nervously. As soon as she opened her mouth, she began talking a mile a minute.

"Just so you know I wasn't following you, I swear," she said. "I just happened to see you sitting here awhile ago. I didn't call at first because you looked really busy and I didn't want to bother you. Then I thought, 'no that's dumb.' People are always talking to you, so you probably wouldn't mind talking to me too. But then I walked around the area trying to make sure you weren't like super busy or anything. You're not super busy, are you? We don't have to talk now. It's fine. I can leave."

"Whoa! Calm down!" I urged. "What do you want to talk about?"

Noura inhaled deeply, rubbed her hands together, and slowed her speech.

"When I first heard about you being a Jew I stayed away. I was afraid. People said you were dangerous. They said you support Israel. Right away I knew that I would never talk to you because I'm part Palestinian and I love Palestine too much. I love Palestine so much that I even want to run for a position on the PCC board next year. I didn't even like seeing other Palestinians talking to you. You are the enemy, I thought. But then you came to that event. I didn't understand why you would come. Then, I realized that maybe I didn't understand because I didn't really know what people who support Israel really think about anything. I also decided that as a student of international relations, I should get to know the perspectives of different kinds of people, in particular those who I might disagree with. So, if you don't mind, will you please explain to me why you came to the event and how people who like Israel see the conflict with the Arabs?"

"Sure," I answered full of glee for the opportunity. "I came to the event because I wanted people like you to come talk to me. So far you're the only one who has. I am a Jew who supports Israel and I want peace between Israel and the Arabs very much. I believe that peace between any two peoples can only happen if they meet, discuss, and get to know each other's story."

"But Arabs really don't want peace with Israel!" she objected.

"Perhaps not now," I said. "But maybe that would change if they knew Israel's side to the story. Do you still want to hear it?" She nodded her head. "Okay, but this could take a while. How long are you willing to sit here and listen to a history lesson?"

"As long as it takes for you to finish."

It took almost three full hours for me to exhaust my knowledge of Middle East history. I dove into the historical and religious attachment the Jewish people have to the land of Israel and the justification for modern political Zionism. I told her the story of each Arab-Israeli war from Israel's vantage point. I described Israel as I personally perceived it: as an insecure, beleaguered nation with good intentions that had been forced to surpass its Arab neighbors in military prowess, economic strength, and social stability to prevent its own demise. Israel had, like every other country, pursued its share of misconceived policies that had yielded tragic results. But, many of Israel's greatest blunders vis-à-vis the Arabs were committed when Israel was placed in difficult situations by hostile forces, where the correct courses of action were never obvious.

Noura listened attentively and asked questions throughout. The only time we got sidetracked was when I was describing the Oslo peace process and one of Noura's friends interrupted us.

"Noura, what are doing?" a girl standing behind me shrieked in Arabic in a high-pitched, squeal. "Why are you sitting with *him*?"

Noura's face turned a ghastly white, and she froze, too staggered to speak. Even in Arabic, I immediately knew who was behind me.

"Hello, Haneen," I said as she stomped her way over to Noura's side. "Would you like to join us?"

Without even acknowledging me, Haneen scowled at Noura with a look of furious disapproval.

"You must stop talking to him right now!" Haneen commanded as she switched over to English.

Noura slumped in her chair and stared down at the floor.

"Who do you think you are?" I yelled angrily. "Last I checked, Noura's allowed to talk to whoever she wants."

"I heard what you were talking about with her! I heard you spreading your lies. You're trying to brainwash her. You're giving her all these new ideas!"

"Well, isn't that what going to college is all about?" I asked jokingly. "Look, Noura asked me to share my opinions with her. There's no problem with that."

"There's a huge problem with that. You shouldn't be allowed to say anything to anyone. I know you aren't who say you are. I know you're working with some agency abroad."

"You are nuts. I'm sitting here in the library having a conversation with someone and you rudely interrupt to accuse me of being a spy? You don't know even know me. That's not fair."

"Fair? You know what's not fair? Nothing about what Israel does to the Palestinians is fair. Palestinians have nothing while America pays for Israel's entire health care system."

"You think America pays for Israel's health care? America doesn't even pay for its own healthcare."

"That's enough!" Haneen said. "Noura, stand up. You're coming with me so that we can talk in private." But Noura remained planted in her seat. "Noura, we're going."

"I'm still talking to Michael right now," Noura said. "I don't know how much longer it's going to take."

"Stop talking to him now!" Haneen yelled. "Come with me."

Noura gazed up at Haneen with a blank expression on her face and bravely uttered four words that booted Haneen out of our conversation for good.

"See you later, Haneen."

Haneen marched off frustrated and Noura asked me to continue right where I left off. About a half hour later, after I finished analyzing the Second Lebanon War, Noura and I wrapped up the history lesson for the evening.

"That was long, but interesting," she said. "I don't agree with everything you said, but I'm glad I got to hear it. I think other students need to hear what you have to say too. You know, I have other friends who were at the event who were also interested in talking to you."

"So why didn't they stalk me at the library with you?" I asked jokingly.

"They wanted me to talk to you first. Some of them were too scared. It was very hard for me to come talk to you. And standing up to Haneen was very hard too. But I'm glad I did. I still believe Israel is the enemy, but I can appreciate the Israeli perspective on some things."

"I think that when someone chooses to appreciate their enemy's perspective, that paves the way for peace."

"Maybe that's true. I'll get my friends to go talk to you. I promise."

Noura kept that promise. On her urging, three of her female friends who had also attended the PCC event tracked me down over the next few days. They each accosted me in the library and asked me to deliver the same tutorial that Noura had received. Although it was a bit grueling to repeat, I did so gladly. Their desire and willingness to hear me explain myself and my views gave me additional reason for thinking that I could have a positive effect at the university.

A week after my talk with Noura, I was finishing up dinner in the dining area in the main cafeteria when I saw Samira out of the corner of my eye. I tried to ignore her presence entirely. I was sick of her acting like a drama queen every time she made eye contact with me. If we were ever going to talk, she had to be the one to take the initiative, not me.

"I want to talk to you," she said somberly while she stood a few feet from my table's edge. "Can I sit with down you?"

"If you'd like," I said as I pushed out the empty chair across from me. "What would you like to talk about?"

She sat down slowly, took a few seconds to gain her composure, and put on a fake smile to hide her nervousness.

"My name is Samira," she said. "I know you're Michael. I'm sorry for how I've acted around you. I want to explain."

"What is there to explain? You think I'm a monster and you treat me like one every time you look at me."

"Listen, before I met you I'd seen you on campus a lot," she said. "You seemed nice. Other people said you were funny. But a lot of my friends said it was all a trick and that you shouldn't be trusted. They said it's impossible for an Arab and a Jew to be real friends and that when people least expect it you would do something bad. I didn't really believe any of it. But when we met I didn't want to take any chances. So I ran off. Then, at the event, all my friends I sat with were shocked and angry that you showed up. Since you and I had already sort of met the day before, I was afraid you were going to come up to me to say something. I didn't want to be caught with you in front of my friends."

"Your friends sound very open minded," I said sarcastically.

"Well that's just it. I realized how stupid it is that all these people who don't know you are saying such bad things about you, especially the board members of the PCC. They're supposed to be leaders."

"Yeah, I've become very aware that people like Hassan and Haneen aren't such big fans of mine."

"What they were saying about you after the event was crazy. I live on the same floor as Haneen. After you talked to Noura that night Haneen was very angry. She was screaming about you to a group of girls. She yelled, 'That Jew is such an asshole! He is pure evil. Why did Allah have to make such a terrible person like him so good looking?' Then another girl spoke up and said, 'This is Allah's test. He is not the only good-looking Jew. There are others too, especially in Hollywood. You must not be deceived by his looks or his charm. He will use it to lead the Arab women away from their religion.' All the girls agreed with this."

"I'm glad to know I'm giving the Jews a pretty face," I replied.

She cracked a smile. Then I did too.

"Hassan and those other Palestinian boys just talk, talk, talk," Samira continued. "The Jew is deceiving, the Jew is tricky, don't trust the Jew. Michael, you came to AUS. You came to the PCC event. You stand up for what you believe in. You are a person who acts. They just talk and do *dabka*."

"I see. Why are you sharing all this with me?"

"Because none of it's right. None of it's Islamic! It doesn't matter what you believe about Palestine or Arabs because it's all these other people who are acting like monsters, not you. And I decided I don't want to be like them anymore. You're interesting and I want to get to know you. If I'm going to hate you, it'll be for my own reasons, not because someone else told me to."

"There are plenty of good reasons to hate me," I joked.

Samira laughed again and at last looked totally comfortable being around me. We sat there for the next two hours together talking about anything and everything besides the AUS gossip and Arab-Israeli politics. By the end of the night, we'd formed the basis of a real friendship. Before we walked out of the cafeteria to bid each other good night, Samira asked me if there was anything she could do to make up for her behavior.

"Don't worry about it," I said. "It's over."

"Are you sure?" she asked. "Nothing?"

I took a quick glance around and, after spotting another vending machine, I said, "You could treat me to a Coke."

Chapter 9
A Man of Virtue

Sharjah, UAE
September–October 2006

M ICHAEL, DO YOU BELIEVE IN THE *JINN*?"
Mo posed the question spontaneously and initially I thought I'd misheard him. We were sitting in a cream-colored taxi sedan, Mo in the front passenger seat and Samira and I in the back, en route to the Deira City Centre shopping mall in Dubai. It was a Monday night and, like on all nights, traffic on the main highway linking Sharjah and Dubai was a mess. Our taxi wasn't moving faster than fifteen miles per hour. The surrounding cacophony of horn-honking and brake-screeching made holding a conversation difficult unless we practically screamed. I yelled out to Mo to repeat his question.

He angled his head towards me and shouted out the question again to make sure I heard him loud and clear. "DO YOU BELIEVE IN THE *JINN*? DO YOU HEAR ME?"

Apparently, I'd heard him correctly the first time. Still, the term *jinn* had never been mentioned to me before, so I couldn't say whether I believed in the *jinn* or not.

"What the hell are the *jinn*?" I asked.

"Michael!" Mo screamed. "You can't say hell and *jinn* in the same sentence. It's very dangerous. It will bring you bad luck!"

"Uh, sorry. So what the . . . I mean, what exactly are the *jinn*?"

"The *jinn* are powerful creatures made of smokeless fire," Mo said matter-of-factly. "We can only see them if they show themselves to us.

They can change their shape and copy anyone's voice. They can even travel at the speed of light and fly great distances without ever getting tired. If you become friends with a *jinn*, he'll help you get anything you want in the whole world."

"You mean like a genie? From the movie *Aladdin*?"

"Similar, but not really."

Though I loved the thought of one day stumbling upon my very own flamboyant blue genie whose only duties were to grant me wishes and burst out in Disney songs, I didn't think it was likely to happen.

"Well," Mo continued. "Do you believe in them?"

The expression on Mo's face suggested he was being dead serious, which made it harder to tell if this was all a joke. I glanced over at Samira for a sign but, strangely, she seemed equally curious to hear my answer, as if it weren't already obvious.

"No, I don't believe in the *jinn*," I said.

Mo blew a gasket. He unbuckled his seat belt, turned around to face me, and leaned forward over his seat. Our driver, an old Pakistani man well beyond normal retirement age, grabbed Mo by the back of his t-shirt and urged him to sit properly. Mo spat out a curse in Arabic and slapped the driver's hand away. He then gazed at me intensely and pointed his right index finger straight at my nose.

"You must be crazy!" he scolded. "You are crazy or very, very stupid. You must believe in the *jinn* for your own safety. Not all *jinn* are good. Most of them are very bad. The *jinn* will attack you if you say you don't believe in them. They will abduct your body and you'll lose all control of everything. My brother Hassan saw it happen once. His friend said he didn't believe in the *jinn* and two minutes later he fell to the ground. He couldn't stop shaking. My brother and his friends had to call an ambulance."

"Are you sure he didn't have a seizure?" I asked.

"No! It was the *jinn*. *Jinn* attacks are real. The *jinn* even rape girls. There are girls who have gotten pregnant by the *jinn* while they were sleeping."

"You've got to be kidding."

"This is no joke. We even know where the *jinn* live. There are many old, abandoned buildings that are full of them. Sometimes the *jinn* will attack people just to get them to move out of their homes. There are dorms at the universities next to AUS that have no students living in them? Do you know why?"

I stared at Mo skeptically and rolled my eyes before taking a guess. "*Jinn* attacks," I offered.

"Exactly!" Mo cried. "Now you understand. There are also *jinn* who live in unclean places like garbage dumps and bathrooms. There could even be a *jinn* in your toilet."

That was the last straw. I'd done my best to humor Mo as he delivered a litany of zany facts about the *jinn*. I wanted some proof.

"Forget the mall!" I yelled. "Let's go find some *jinn*. Mo, grab a flashlight and a plunger. We're going *jinn* hunting tonight!"

Mo's cheeks reddened and he clenched the headrest of his seat. He clearly feared the *jinn* a great deal. But before Mo suffered a complete panic attack, Samira intervened and dumped my idea in the waste bin.

"We're going to the mall and that's it," Samira asserted defiantly. "We will not be meeting any *jinn* tonight."

Mo relaxed and breathed a sigh of relief.

"Michael, I know all this talk of the *jinn* sounds strange to you," she continued. "But many people take this very seriously. You can't make fun of these things."

"Are you telling me you believe in this stuff too? You think the *jinn* get women pregnant?"

"People say a lot of things about the *jinn*. I don't believe everything. But I do know they exist because the Qur'an mentions them. Some *jinn* are even Muslims. The Prophet Muhammad himself was given the Qur'an to deliver to both mankind and *jinn*. Haven't you read the Qur'an?"

I shook my head and told her I hadn't. The truth was I'd been planning to pick up a copy for a long time. But actually going out to an Islamic bookstore, purchasing the Qur'an, and sitting down to read it had thus far evaded my consciousness.

We arrived at the Deira City Centre and Samira split off from Mo and me for about a half hour to take care of some "personal shopping" needs. I assumed that she'd gone off to buy feminine health care products or try on lingerie, activities she certainly preferred to engage in without men around. When Samira met up with us later on at a table at a Starbucks in the mall, she carried a large, pink shopping bag with the Victoria's Secret logo plastered on the sides.

"Michael, aren't you going to ask me what's in the bag?" she asked as she placed it on the table and sat down across from me. "I bought something for you."

"For me? From Victoria's Secret? They never have my size!" I joked.

"I didn't buy you anything *at* Victoria's Secret," she said. "I just asked them for a bag. Look inside."

Since the bag was too tall for me to peek inside of while seated, I removed it from the table and placed it on the floor.

"No!" Samira screamed. "Pick it up, pick it up! You can't do that! The Qur'an is inside. You can't put the Qur'an on the ground!"

My mother taught me when I was young that if I ever accidentally dropped the Hebrew Bible or a Jewish prayer book I should pick it up and kiss it out of respect. Not knowing what else to do to rectify my inadvertent transgression, I pulled the green hard-cover Qur'an out of the bag and planted a smooch right on the front cover. My act left Mo and Samira momentarily speechless and attracted the stares of a few curious Emirati men sipping hot drinks at the next table over. I nodded at them, holding the Qur'an up in the air.

"*Al-hamdu lil'aah!*" I said emphatically. Praise God!

The Emirati men nodded back at me, raised their cups, and responded in unison with an "*Al-hamdu lil'aah!*" of their own.

"Michael, that was beautiful," Samira said as she fiddled with her hijab. "You showed the Qur'an so much respect. You must be a Muslim at heart. If you became a Muslim for real, it would make me so happy."

I didn't doubt that for a second. Since sparking our friendship, it was obvious almost immediately that a different sort of spark was lit between Samira and me as well.

Most days we'd send each other a flirtatious text message or two during class and hang out for hours afterwards talking in quiet, secluded corners of the Student Center. Sometimes before seeing Samira, my stomach filled up with butterflies. Judging from the anxious smile she wore whenever we met up, I figured hers must have too. Other Americans who befriended Samira poked fun that she talked to them only so she could talk about me. It didn't take long for them to start playfully referring to her as my girlfriend.

Yet the notion that Samira, a Palestinian Muslim and I, an American Jew, could ever become romantically entwined was preposterous. Both Judaism and Islam frowned on inter-faith dating and, in Muslim countries in particular, the consequences for flouting such a social norm could be severe.

"A Muslim girl can't do whatever she wants," Samira explained to me once. "If her family discovers she's been dating a non-Muslim man or had sex before marriage, her father and brothers can kill her. No one would stop them. They may try to kill the man too, but that's messier because he's not always a relative."

The only way Samira and I could have ever dated without the peril of death looming over us would be for one of us to switch religions. In the UAE, the penalty for abandoning Islam for another faith was capital punishment, so even joking about Samira becoming Jewish was not funny. However, she was free to encourage me to accept Islam.

"Just read the Qur'an with an open mind," Samira pleaded while she pointed down at the holy book in front of me. "That's all."

I glanced down at the Qur'an and stared at its long title printed in gold-typed font. It read *The Noble Qur'an: Transliteration in Roman Script with Original Arabic Text and English Translation of the Meanings*.

"It was printed in Saudi Arabia. The man who sold it to me said it has the best English translation of any Qur'an," Samira continued.

I looked up at Samira, thanked her for the gift, and promised her I'd get started reading when I had time.

"You'll have time over Ramadan when it starts later this week. Muslims must read the Qur'an during Ramadan, more than once if possible, and give their friends and family presents. Consider this Qur'an an early Ramadan present from me to you," she said with a wink. "Have you ever celebrated Ramadan before?"

No, I hadn't, but I knew all the basics. Ramadan is the month during which Muslims believe the Prophet Muhammad received the first transmissions of the Qur'an from Allah. Throughout this period, devout Muslims refrain from eating, drinking, smoking, and sex from sunrise to sunset and go out of their way to perform acts of charity.

Samira wasn't alone in presenting me with a religious text in honor of the holiday. Two days before the start of Ramadan, on a day when I wore my *kandura,* I left Dr. Muntassar's classroom after a lecture to find a grinning Muhammad bin Raheem and three equally cheery, identically-dressed Emiratis waiting for me in the adjacent hallway. After dropping my backpack and politely bumping noses with each of them, Muhammad bin Raheem reached into the left pocket on the side of his *kandura,* pulled out a small black paperback book, and placed it in my hand. The book was called *Fortress of the Muslim: Invocations from the Qur'an & Sunnah.*

"This is a present from us," Muhammad bin Raheem explained as he scratched his wispy black moustache. "This book has many prayers. Ramadan is a very important time for prayer. So we think this is good for you. Inside you will find prayers for everything."

I opened up to the table of contents and saw that was no exaggeration. The book was a collection of one hundred thirty-two prayers that ran the gamut of daily life. Included were prayers I expected to see, such as those uttered before performing ritual washing and entering a mosque, and others I never thought of, like what to say when you have a nightmare or hear a dog barking at night.

"Take the book to the mosque and learn to pray like real Muslim!" Muhammad bin Raheem advised.

"I've prayed in mosques before," I said to impress them.

Muhammad bin Raheem put his arm over my shoulder.

"I think you will become Muslim very soon. I believe it," he said.

I tried setting the record straight that becoming a Muslim wasn't on my agenda, but he refused to listen. "Read the Qur'an and pray. After this, you will be Muslim. I'm sure of this."

I dropped the subject, slipped the book into my backpack, and strolled with the four Emiratis across a much more festive looking campus to the Student Center to kill time before our next classes. In honor of the start of Ramadan, ornamental white lights were hung between academic buildings and two forty-by-sixty-foot white circular tents, one for each sex, were set up near the AUS mosque to host *iftar,* the evening meal marking the end of each fast day.

When we reached the Student Center, we had to push and shove to get through the front door. Dozens of students blocked the entrance and packed the main lobby to sneak a peek at a two-person camera crew preparing for a shoot. I wanted to get a better view of what was going on, so I instructed my Emirati friends to form a human chain by linking arms, which I then dragged to the front of the crowd.

As soon as the last of my local pals emerged from the thicket of students, the pretty female reporter preparing for the segment approached the five of us looking quite confused. Tall with wavy black hair and a face caked with makeup, she gripped her corded microphone with both hands and, referring to me, asked my friends in Arabic, "Is he one of you?" Too shy to say a word to such an assertive, unfamiliar woman, the Emiratis stared at the ground and offered conflicting answers. Muhammad bin Raheem and the guy next to him nodded their heads in the affirmative while the other two shook their heads from side to side. This didn't adequately answer the reporter's question, so I spoke up.

"I am not an Emirati," I said in Arabic. "I am a student from America. But I feel like an Emirati when I am with my friends."

"You're perfect," the reporter said, suddenly switching to English.

She introduced herself as Reem, a journalist for CNN's Arabic Edition, and said she and her cameramen had come to conduct interviews with students about their thoughts on Ramadan. "I'd like to interview you first with all your friends standing with you. Please smile a lot."

Reem lined us up in front of the camera with me in the middle. When the camera started rolling she began the segment and held the microphone up to my mouth. With a big smile on my face, I said my name and where I was from, and clarified as best I could in my hodge-podge of Arabic dialects that I was very excited to experience Ramadan in a Muslim country and learn more about Islam. I thanked my Emirati friends standing with me for making me feel at home in the UAE and offered each of them a customary nose bump.

Student onlookers clapped when I finished speaking and Reem asked the Emiratis up there with me if they had anything to add. Not surprisingly, the four of them froze in place, too nervous to answer. While I understood that none of them had much public speaking experience,

I thought it would have been a shame if I hogged the limelight completely. So, I pushed Muhammad bin Raheem forward, draped my arm around him, and urged him to say something profound.

At first, all Muhammad bin Raheem could do was giggle fretfully with his teeth clenched together. But then, an early Ramadan miracle occurred right there on camera. Unexpectedly, Muhammad bin Raheem received a burst of inspiration and delivered a passionate thirty-second speech that drew raucous applause from everyone watching. When we walked away from the shoot, students from all directions patted us both on our backs, reached out to shake our hands, and told us how moving our interview was.

Since he spoke in the Gulf Arabic dialect, which I didn't understand well, I missed the gist of his message. I heard my name pop up a few times along with the words Ramadan and Qur'an, but couldn't decipher the link between them. Only after the attention faded did I pull Muhammad bin Raheem aside and ask him for a translation.

"I said that Ramadan is *the* time to be with Allah," he said. "I explained that you are foreign and not Muslim, but I believe you have a Muslim soul."

"Uh huh. Was that all?"

"I said very soon you will become a real Muslim and one day you will build a Muslim family. I said you already have a Qu'ran. This means it will happen. I know it. And I told everyone to make you feel a part of the *ummah* (family of Islam) during Ramadan."

A part of me wanted to scream at him. Muhammad bin Raheem had no right to make any kind of public declaration about my religious status without my consent, least of all on international television with millions of Muslim viewers potentially tuning in. I thought about berating him right then and there in the Student Center lobby, so that everyone in the vicinity would hear me refute his comments. But I couldn't. I just didn't have the heart. Muhammad bin Raheem had treated me like family since the day we'd met and the last thing I wanted to do was lose my temper and publicly humiliate him.

I said nothing. I knew he meant no harm and that he'd only said what he had from a sincere desire to share something beautiful with me that served as a major focal point of his life. To him, Islam was truth. No matter how much I denied any interest in becoming a Muslim, he would always insist there was hope that one day I would see that truth. Additionally, I did appreciate his efforts to make me feel included in the holiday festivities. It was a certain sense of community, after all, that was very noticeably absent from my life.

That year Ramadan and Rosh Hashanah, the Jewish New Year, started on the same night. Both Muslim and Jewish calendars run on a lunar cycle, so holidays begin based on where the moon sits in the night sky. Not knowing any other Jews in the UAE, I felt for the first time totally disconnected from the wider Jewish world. I was forced to acknowledge that I'd be spending a major Jewish holiday all by myself.

I considered asking some of the American students to celebrate with me, but I opted not to. Rosh Hashanah is foremost a religious and spiritual holiday, not a purely cultural one.

The afternoon before Rosh Hashanah and Ramadan commenced, I went to the campus grocery store to buy some important Rosh Hashanah items such as candlesticks, grape juice, apples, and honey. Barely bigger than my dorm room and carrying mostly snack foods and ice cream, the store sold neither candles nor grape juice. The closest things I found to apples and honey were two small boxes of Apple Jacks and Honey Nut Cheerios cereals. I bought them both, since I didn't have time to get to a real supermarket off campus.

Right after sunset, I welcomed in Rosh Hashanah in my room by reciting the blessing over wine over a bottle of orange juice and the blessing over bread with two slices of whole wheat. I sat at my desk and feasted on my Apple Jacks and Honey Nut Cheerios to symbolize my wish for a sweet new year.

Following my festive meal, I lay on my bed on top of my covers, and tried praying. I wanted to focus on the spiritual significance of Rosh Hashanah, whatever that meant. But, after only a few minutes, I couldn't concentrate and felt that lying in bed was just making me sleepy. Determined to connect with the Divine, I returned to my desk and took out a Jewish prayer book I kept in the top drawer. I didn't have a special prayer book Jews use during the High Holy Days, so I browsed through this regular prayer book, searching for something inspiring that would pull me out of my spiritual funk.

Unfortunately, that didn't do the trick either. I read through a few lofty-worded essays about prayer, but still felt numb. It just didn't feel like Rosh Hashanah locked away by myself in my dorm room with only a few uneaten bits of cereal to keep me company. Judaism specifically encourages its adherents to celebrate holidays with others precisely because public worship strengthens the spirit and shows people that they share a common life and purpose.

Through my open window I heard the chanting of the *adhan*, the Muslim call to prayer, and saw a few students speedily walking in the direction of the AUS mosque. If it hadn't been Rosh Hashanah, I probably would have been on my way to a mosque as well. I was on exchange in a Muslim country, and I believed that meant I should experience Muslim holidays firsthand.

Muhammad bin Raheem had invited me to join him and his family for prayers at their Dubai mosque and for *Iftar* afterwards. Additionally, Ahmad Jew had invited me to Abu Dhabi where he would honor the first day of Ramadan with his extended family that lived there. I declined both their offers because I thought it would have been wrong to mark their holiday at the expense of my own. But, as I stared at the walls of my dorm room, I grew tired of my Jewish solitude and began considering how I could celebrate Rosh Hashanah alongside my Muslim peers celebrating Ramadan.

I thought about how much Rosh Hashanah and Ramadan had in common. Both holidays emphasized the importance of repentance, of improving one's character through introspection, and of increasing one's commitment to doing good deeds. Since Judaism didn't explicitly prohibit Jews from entering mosques, I wondered how kosher it would be to conduct my Rosh Hashanah prayers at one.

Like Jews, Muslims were monotheists and surely, I told myself, it was preferable to pray to God in a communal setting with other monotheists than to completely isolate myself. With no synagogues to be found, I concluded that a mosque must be the next best place for a lonely Jew to worship.

But, if I tried to enter the AUS mosque would I even be let inside? I wasn't some anonymous foreigner like I was in Cairo. In Sharjah, I was infamous, known to all as the outspoken Jew. What if some of the more extreme students objected to me being there? What if someone accused me of desecrating the mosque with my heretical non-Muslim presence or worse, of insulting Islam?

Then again, what if my concerns were entirely unwarranted? What if praying at the mosque was actually seen by other AUS students for what it was: a showing of my desire to learn about Islamic culture and rejoice over Islam's similarities with Judaism? What if, by not going, I was forfeiting the chance at having a tremendous cultural and religious experience by wasting time wondering 'what-if?' I decided that a healthy compromise was to go take a walk by the mosque and wait to see if someone invited me inside.

With my plan finalized, I snatched my *Fortress of the Muslim* book and headed toward the mosque. Just in case I made it in time and was invited inside, I intended to participate properly by reading the prayers in my little black book. I was convinced that would show any naysayers I was there to learn and show respect, and not as part of some practical joke.

Looking up at the darkening sky, I could see time was not on my side. The *Maghrib* prayer service, the fourth Muslim prayer service of the day, finished up at dusk. I presumed that, it being the first night of Ramadan, there was a good chance prayers would run longer than usual. Maybe the imam of the mosque would even deliver an extensive sermon.

I started to sprint, and when I arrived at the mosque, I was covered in sweat and out of breath. I rested for a minute on the second of three steps that led up to the mosque entrance. I admired the intricate, carved patterns decorating the mosque's exterior walls and tried to hush my panting so I could listen for any signs of activity. But there was nothing going on, not even a faint whisper as far as I could tell. I turned around with my back facing the mosque and bent my head towards the marble pavement feeling dejected.

Without me noticing, the mosque's main door suddenly opened and a man with a deep voice spoke to me in Arabic from behind.

"You are too late for the *Maghrib* prayer," he said. "But return for the *Isha* prayer (the fifth daily prayer said late at night). *Ramadan Kareem.*" Happy Ramadan.

Before I could put together a coherent Arabic response, the man walked down the steps and looked down at me to see who I was. The instant we saw each other, we both gasped.

"It's you!" he said visibly startled. "I can't believe it's you."

I thought about saying the same thing to him. For a few seconds, I couldn't tell if my eyes were playing tricks on me or not. I wondered if I was hallucinating or if I needed to spend less time in the sun. Standing before me was none other than a young man who looked exactly like a younger version of the mastermind of the 9/11 terror attacks, Osama bin Laden.

He had it all: the tall, lanky figure, the thick, scruffy black beard, the pointy, downward-sloping nose. He wore a long white *kandura* and *ghutrah* that, though different from the Emirati style, did nothing to downplay the resemblance.

"You look surprised to see me too. Do I look like my father?" he asked with a mischievous smirk.

Was he serious? Was he the son of Osama bin Laden? If he was and held information that could have led to the capture of the world's most-wanted man, alerting the American authorities to his presence would have made me a hero. I needed to get the Pentagon on the phone pronto!

"The answer is yes," he said. "I do look like my father. But my father's name is not Osama bin Laden. A lot of western people who see me think we look similar. I promise we're not related. But my name is Osama and I am from Saudi Arabia."

"You definitely have a famous face. Sorry for being startled," I apologized. "But it's nice to meet you. My name's Michael by the way."

"I know who you are. You're a famous person here. And now you're a television star too. That must be very exciting."

"You saw that clip on CNN?"

"No, I try not to watch TV. It is *haram* in Islam. But some of my less strict friends from home told me they saw it and asked me if I knew you. They said you and your local friend spoke beautifully."

"Thanks. Tell me, why were you so surprised to see me?"

"Because I didn't think it was true."

"If what was true?"

"That you are becoming a Muslim."

"I'm not becoming a Muslim. Don't listen to what my friend said on TV."

"You're not?' Osama posed skeptically. "Then why are you sitting here on the steps of the mosque holding a book filled with Muslim prayers? Am I imagining all this?"

I glanced down at my *Fortress of the Muslim* book in my hand and realized how I may have given him that impression.

"I want to learn about Islam and Ramadan," I said. "But I'm a Jew and tonight is the beginning of a holiday for my people too. I thought it would be good to come to the mosque to pray."

"Join me for dinner in the *iftar* tent and then we'll come back afterwards for the *Isha* prayer. Does that sound good?"

It sure did. Apparently, the dinners in the *iftar* tents were free and distributed to anyone who showed up. We went inside the tent reserved for men and picked up two pre-packaged greasy chicken and rice meals from a long serving table. There were no chairs or tables, so we sat down by ourselves on one of the thick, colorful carpets that covered the marble-tile pavement.

A few dozen other male students also took advantage of the free food, nearly all of them sporting beards of various lengths and wearing some version of the *kandura*. Five guys who looked strikingly similar to Osama were eating their meal fifteen feet away from us. They all had thin frames, dark brown skin, and thick black beards. The six of them could have passed for sextuplets. When they waved at Osama, he waved back. I asked him if he preferred we go sit with them, but he said no.

"They are great guys," he said. "But I prefer we eat alone. I want to talk to you first before you go off talking to everyone else. I have heard that you like talking to people and I don't want to lose you so fast."

Before we opened our pre-packaged meals, Osama offered me a reddish-brown date from a plastic bag he had in his pocket and urged me to eat it.

I submitted to his command and started to peal the date fruit off its pit.

"The Prophet Muhammad ate dates," he explained.

"So?" I asked.

"So we eat a date before we break our fast, even if the fasting has not yet begun. The Prophet Muhammad was the most perfect human being to ever walk the Earth. Every one of his acts must be emulated by mankind. Even the things that seem insignificant, like eating dates."

When Osama and I finally got down to devouring our meal, he told me that his main goal in life was to live exactly how he thought the Prophet Muhammad would if he were still alive.

In practical terms, that meant Osama committed himself to praying in a mosque five times a day, avoided what he called hedonistic temptations like television and music, and taught Islam to anyone who would listen. His family was very religious, he insisted. His father taught Islamic studies at a university in Riyadh. Still, he strove to be more devout. Though he studied engineering at AUS, his real dream was to bring Islam into the world like few others ever had.

"I want to build heaven on Earth," he said. "Islam is the means to achieving this. Would you ever consider becoming a Muslim?"

"I really admire a lot about Islam," I answered. "But I'm not shopping for a new faith."

"My friends told me you said on TV that you're reading the Qur'an."

"My Emirati friend said that I *have* a Qur'an," I corrected. "I haven't started reading it yet."

Osama leaned in towards me and made sure I paid close attention to what he had to tell me next.

"The Qur'an is flawless," he declared. "It doesn't have one single mistake. If you are a man of virtue, you will see this when you start reading. You will believe in Islam. Let me ask you. Are you a man of virtue?"

I didn't like how Osama set up that question. Answering "no" would have sounded idiotic. Who denies being a man of virtue? But answering yes would have been de facto agreeing with him that all men of virtue eventually become Muslim.

"I try to be a man of virtue as much as anyone else," I answered as a compromise.

"You are modest," he retorted. "That is a Muslim quality. I look forward to the day when I can count you as a brother. In Islam, faith is the basis of brotherhood."

When the foreign workers began cleaning up the tent, I returned to the mosque with Osama for the *Isha* evening prayer. Aside from us, only ten other students joined in. We removed our shoes and Osama reminded me how to ritually wash before prayer, something I hadn't done since Egypt.

Throughout the ten-minute service, Osama kept a watchful eye on me as I struggled to follow along in my *Fortress of the Muslim* book. Whether we were standing, bowing, kneeling, or sitting, he constantly verified that I was reading the right prayer on the right page. Osama probably thought my problem was that the prayers were written in hard-to-read tiny Arabic calligraphy. I didn't tell him I was actually concentrating on my own improvised Rosh Hashanah prayers. I wasn't hiding anything from him per se. I just didn't see the need to rub his nose in the fact that I was praying to the god of Isaac, not the god of Ishmael.

After the service concluded and people started wandering back to their dorm buildings, Osama took my hand and held it firm.

"I know you wanted to come to the mosque for different reasons than the rest of us," he said. "I know that the prayers you normally say are different from ours too. It is no problem. Come as you are and you will be accepted. We are all children of Allah. I also hope being here tonight has helped make your holiday meaningful."

"It definitely has," I said.

"But start reading the Qur'an immediately," he prodded as he let my hand go. "Do not delay. Ramadan is a busy time. You'll see."

Chapter 10
I Caught Osama

Sharjah, UAE
October 2006

B UT I DIDN'T SEE AND IT WASN'T BECAUSE I WAS BLIND. IN fact, as the month of Ramadan carried on, the opposite seemed to be the case. The AUS campus became all but a ghost town.

Ramadan is often called the month of heat. The word itself is drawn from the Arabic verbal root *"ramada,"* which means to bake or to be heated up by the sun. Some Muslims contended that the word "Ramadan" should have been understood only metaphorically for the reason that, throughout the month, one is supposed to "burn off" bad deeds with prayer and by abstaining from addressing worldly needs. I speculated that most AUS students would have strongly disagreed with that opinion.

One of the supreme challenges for Muslims celebrating Ramadan anywhere in the world is upholding the holiday's restrictions while maintaining a normal routine. Just because they're fasting doesn't mean they stop going to work or school for a month. That is, unless they live in a place like Sharjah, where the suffocating humidity saps the energy of anyone but the most properly hydrated individual. When drinking water during the day isn't an option, getting out of bed to face the heat becomes the ultimate test of will power.

So many AUS students didn't get out of bed. The number of empty chairs during classes increased exponentially as Ramadan progressed. The dedicated students who did attend classes seemed constantly on edge from hunger, thirst, and sleeplessness. No doubt it was doubly hard for the smokers. As soon as a lecture wrapped up, the students with time on their hands would race back to their air-conditioned dorm rooms to rest. Those pressed for time would snatch chairs and couches wherever they could be found and doze until their alarms woke them up for their next classes.

Carrying out daily responsibilities was certainly easier for non-Muslims like me, but being a non-Muslim in Sharjah during Ramadan presented its own set of hardships. All campus restaurants were closed throughout the day, so the option of grabbing a quick bite to eat in between classes didn't exist. The tiny grocery store where I'd done my Rosh Hashanah shopping was open for only a few hours in the mornings. Each time I made it there, the selection of food was disappointing. For a month I had to be content eating sugary cereals and tuna and mustard sandwiches.

However, just because non-Muslim students were technically permitted to eat during the day didn't mean they could eat anywhere they pleased. Although drinking water was tolerated, eating in public during Ramadan anywhere in the UAE was explicitly forbidden to accommodate the sensitivities of those fasting. Getting caught out in the open with a Snickers bar in hand could have resulted in a fine or jail time.

Given that campus was dead and my dorm room was the only place I could safely eat during the day, I ended up just staying there during the day when I didn't have class. With nothing to distract me, I finally opened *The Noble Qur'an* and started reading. And once I started reading, I could hardly put it down. While attending classes and keeping up with my assignments, it took me only five days to finish all one hundred and fourteen *suras* (chapters) and 6,346 verses. No, this was not because I discovered the Qur'an to be the most captivating work ever to be unleashed on man (and *jinn*), whose author could only have been Allah.

I'm no expert and these are merely my opinions, but from a literary perspective, the Qur'an was unimpressive. It wasn't written in chronological order, so I didn't find the storyline clear or easy to follow. It jumped around between various biblical narratives seemingly at random and didn't properly introduce or give context to the lives of the prophets of the Abrahamic faiths. To me, the Qur'an read like a series of long rambles.

"No tongue besides Arabic could ever capture the beauty and brilliance of the Qur'an. Not even the most meticulous translation could do it justice."

That's what more than a few of my Muslim friends from the US had said over the years about reading the Qur'an in a language other than the original. The translation of any document is problematic because the original meaning is changed. However, after reading the Qur'an, I found this argument shallow. Nothing, literally nothing I came across in the Islamic scriptures even remotely measured up to the hypnotizing language of the Bible, both Old and New Testaments. Putting personal theology aside, I thought the stories and poems of the Bible to be extremely powerful in their examination of morality and human nature in any language, in ways the Qur'an could not compare.

That's not to imply that the Qur'an was an amoral document. Arabian society before Islam was a scary, lawless place. With the arrival of Muhammad and the Qur'an came the foundation for building a more just society that accorded substantially more rights to women, the poor, and other previously disenfranchised people. But for all these advancements, I didn't run into one law or moral concept in the Qur'an that hadn't already been addressed the same way or better by the earlier monotheistic faiths. Simply put, Islam didn't offer the world anything new.

Then, what was it about *The Noble Qur'an* that entranced and compelled me to blaze through it so, dare I say, religiously? The answer is cut and dried. I was shocked to find out that the book in my hands served as a vilifying polemic against non-Muslims and, in particular, my people, the Jews.

I'd been taught that Islam was a religion of peace and that it was only fanatics who distorted the faith who made international headlines. Up until then, whenever I engaged in a terrifying conversation with a Muslim consumed with anti-Semitism, I very much wanted to believe their politics was the problem, not their religion.

But then I read that "the Jews are men who listen much and eagerly to lies" (5:41) and "you will find the strongest among men in enmity to the believers (Muslims) the Jews" (5:82). This Qur'an advised Muslims to "take not as friends the people who incurred the wrath of Allah (i.e. the Jews)" (60:13) and promised that they "will find them (the Jews) the greediest of mankind for life" (2:96). I even recognized a passage that could easily be twisted to give Islamic credibility to a modern anti-Israel political stance: "And we decreed for the Children of Israel in the Scripture: indeed you would do mischief in the land twice and you will become tyrants and extremely arrogant" (17:4). For any Muslim holding a personal grievance against Israel and hell bent on its destruction, this verse added scriptural justification.

Non-Muslims as a whole didn't fare well either, as far as I could tell. Although the Qur'an stated that "there is no compulsion in religion" (2:256), it also warned those who refused to accept Islam that "when the angels take away the souls of those who disbelieve (at death), they smite their faces and their backs (saying): Taste the punishment of the blazing fire" (8:50), "whose fuel is men and stones, prepared for the disbelievers" (1:24). In this world too, non-Muslims were not always safe from Allah's wrath since the Qur'an urged Muslims to "fight those of the disbelievers who are close to you and let them find harshness in you" (9:123).

Needless to say, reading these passages bothered me. I was aware that plenty of other world religions offered blessings for faith and damnation for heresy. I'd just never read anything that summed up hellfire in as colorful language as the Qur'an. However, what disturbed me about the Qur'an was also what spurred me to read more of it and to jot down notes about what I read. The sooner I finished reading the whole thing, I reasoned, the sooner I would be able to ask educated questions about it. I wasn't so naïve as to think I was capable of fully understanding an unfamiliar religious text without the slightest bit of assistance. I wanted help. I wanted to talk to someone about it. But, was there anyone I could really ask?

Since my arrival at AUS, many Muslim students had invited me to ask them questions about Islam I might have had. But when I took them up on their offers, the conversations always headed south.

"Do Muslims consider the prophets who lived before the time of Muhammad to be Jewish or Christian *and* Muslim at the same time?" I posed to Deilal, a petite Kuwaiti girl with braces.

It was the first week of the semester and we were in the Student Center enjoying a KFC dinner she treated me to as a way of welcoming me to Sharjah.

"No, Michael. All the prophets were Muslims, only Muslims," she corrected as she pulled a piece of chicken out of one of her bottom braces.

"How were they all Muslim if there was no Islam yet?"

"There was Islam already. There just wasn't the Qur'an yet. So they were Muslim, you see?"

"But don't Muslims believe that Judaism and Christianity were Islam before the time of Muhammad?" Deilal nodded in agreement. "Then doesn't that mean you could say that Abraham, for example, was Jewish and Muslim?"

My question caught Deilal off guard and she became upset. She blinked her eyes rapidly and smiled uncomfortably.

"We shouldn't speak about this anymore," she decided. "What you are saying is *haram*. I don't like these ideas of yours."

Not only did Deilal and I never again speak about Islam, we barely spoke at all after that.

Another time I asked an overweight, goateed Lebanese Shia named Ali to explain to me the differences between the dozens of sects of Islam. Since Ali was a Shia living in the UAE, a predominantly Sunni country, I imagined he had a unique perspective on divisions within Islam.

"Know this," he said when we were hanging out in my dorm room. "The Sunnis take the Qur'an and they shit on it."

"Huh?" I said in disbelief.

"That's all they do, Michael. That is Sunni Islam. Shitting on the Qur'an. They shit and they shit and they shit some more. They take the pages of it and they wipe their asses. That is all."

"So you mean to say there's nothing legitimate about Sunni Islam?"

"Exactly."

"What about the other Shia sects, like the Ismailis, Alawis, and Twelvers."

"There are no variations!" he claimed. "Shia Islam is the only true way. It is unified and one."

"But all these groups have different customs and beliefs!" I protested. "Everyone knows they don't all practice the exact same thing."

"Yes, they do!" he yelled. "What is this? Are you criticizing Islam? Are you saying that not all Shia Muslims believe in the Qur'an?"

"I'm not saying that at all. Islam isn't black and white. I was just asking you to help me understand it better."

"Stop criticizing Islam! You must never criticize Islam. Just stop."

So I stopped. I changed the subject to beautiful Lebanese pop singers to get him to calm down lest he accuse me of shitting on the Qur'an too.

While the intensity of my exchange with Ali was unusual, I found that his and other Muslim students' refusal to speak critically about Islam was not.

My peers at AUS weren't raised to subject the Qur'an or any Islamic topic to scholarship or skeptical analysis. They viewed Islam as perfect in every respect and the Qur'an as a physical manifestation of that perfection. If anyone had a bad word to say about either, they were deemed a threat.

I knew that discussing my concerns about the Qur'an with the wrong person would have been like pouring gasoline on a raging inferno. But I had to speak to someone. The thought of accepting what I'd read at face value only raised disconcerting questions. If Muslims were forbidden from taking Jews as friends, then were all my meaningful relationships with practicing Muslims total shams? Were they even capable of truly trusting a Jew? Could I trust any of them?

I tried my best to maintain my composure, but it was tough. What I thought about the Qur'an became the main topic people wanted to discuss with me.

"Do you like what you've read so far?" one person asked.

"Don't you think it's wonderful?" another inquired.

Their questions made me uncomfortable because they weren't really asking me for an honest assessment. They merely hoped I'd say something that matched up with their own opinions. So, I described the Qur'an as "amazing" and "very inspirational." I hated concealing my actual thoughts, but I had no choice.

I opted to bring my concerns about the Qur'an to none other than my friend who was using Islam to build heaven on Earth, Osama. I considered approaching someone I was more familiar with who was also extremely devout, such as Muhammad bin Raheem, Samira, or Kareem. But I ruled out each one. I wasn't interested in alienating any close friend over religion. I still didn't know Osama all that well, and that was part of the appeal. Plus, he was an aspiring Islamic scholar.

Since Osama hadn't given me his cell phone number, I went to the *iftar* tent late one evening towards the end of Ramadan to find him.

It was long after the conclusion of the *Maghrib* prayer service and I was carrying my backpack with *The Noble Qur'an* and *Fortress of the Muslim* books inside. When I walked through the entrance, a Sri Lankan foreign worker with disfigured teeth waved his hands at me, signaling that they were out of food. That was fine, I tried to tell him. I'd planned for that to be the case.

It was obvious to me that soon after I tracked down Osama, he would ask me how my reading of the Qur'an was going. I was aching to tell him, but would only do so if there weren't many other people around us. Therefore, I purposely skipped out on the free meal and came to the *iftar* tent when I was sure it would be relatively empty.

Just as I'd hoped, I caught Osama sitting on the far side of the tent with a few other bearded guys. As soon as Osama and I made eye contact, he jumped up and dragged me over to the rest of the guys. Immediately, I knew I'd made the right decision.

"You should not be so late," he chastised light-heartedly. "You missed *Maghrib* and dinner. But anyways, I am glad you have come. Have you started reading the Qur'an yet?" I told him I had. I even mentioned that I had my Qur'an in my backpack. "Excellent. We will look through it and discuss. I will answer any questions. But only after the *Isha* prayer. You remember how to do that one, yes?"

I did more or less and I think that showed while we prayed. Osama still checked up on me every now and then while I followed along in my *Fortress of the Muslim* book, but he seemed a lot more confident that I had a grasp of things. After the conclusion of the service, Osama sat me down outside the mosque on the front steps, the place we'd first met, removed my copy of *The Noble Qur'an* from my bag, and carefully examined it.

"This is a Saudi Qur'an, Michael," he said while he flipped through the pages. "That means it is the best. Not every copy of the Qur'an has the right translation. This one does."

"Osama, is everything in the Qur'an meant to be taken literally?" I asked.

"Of course. Allah was not careless with his words. He chose every word for a reason."

"But is it possible that it was written for a different time? That some parts of the Qur'an are not meant to be taken as literally today?"

"Michael, the Qur'an is timeless. It is perfect and can never be changed."

"I see," I murmured as I momentarily looked away.

"Something bothers you. You have read the whole Qur'an? All of it?"

"To the very last *surah*."

"Ah, but you have found parts that trouble you. Some say those are the good parts," he laughed. He sounded like he was joking. I started to feel relieved. "But then, as you Americans say, 'the truth hurts, don't it?'"

"What do you mean?"

"There are many parts of the Qur'an that don't speak very well of non-Muslims, in particular Jews. I am not surprised that this hurts you. Let this be your wakeup call. It's better that you learn the truth now."

"What truth?"

"The truth that people who do not accept Islam are cursed. When a person rejects Islam he declares war on all Muslims."

"The Qur'an says there is no compulsion in religion," I argued.

"True, but it also says terrible consequences befall the disbelievers."

"It's written in the Qur'an that Muslims can't be friends with Jews," I said aggressively. "If you try to obey every law of the Qur'an, then how can you be friends with me?"

Osama sat there on the step still holding my Qur'an. He looked totally calm, like nothing we were talking about fazed him in the least.

"I am friends with you, Michael, because I believe that one day you will become a Muslim."

"No!" I yelled before consciously trying to compose myself. "I will never become a Muslim," I declared unruffled. "Ever."

Osama smirked.

"Michael, my brother. You have all the traits that the Qur'an describes the Jews as having. You are clever and quick on your feet. You are a real cunning Jew. But I see something in you. You are very curious about Islam. You learn our customs and traditions. You even pray in the mosque. One day I know you will become a Muslim, and when you do, your skills will be of great service to us."

"So you're saying the only reason I have any friends at AUS is because people are counting on me to convert to Islam?"

"I'm not saying that. I'm saying that's why I'm friends with you."

"And what if I never convert? What if I stay a Jew my whole life?"

"Then you are my enemy."

"And what is a Muslim supposed to do to his enemy?"

"Kill him."

"Osama, I'm telling you right now. I'm a Jew and I will stay a Jew. What's stopping you from killing me right now?"

"My belief that you will change your mind. But, even if I didn't think you would become a Muslim, I wouldn't kill you anyway. It would ruin my plans. I want to be a leader. I want to do great things. I want to give the world the wakeup call it needs to turn to Islam. Throwing away my future for you or any one person doesn't interest me."

"What happened to all of us being children of Allah?"

"Every father knows it's their responsibility to punish their children when they do wrong. I merely act on Allah's wishes."

"You know when you talk like that you sound a lot like the other Osama, the one you look like."

"That's great. If I could one day be a leader like Sheikh Osama bin Laden, then I'd be very happy."

"You want to be like a man who mass murders as many people as possible? How do you think that's going to make anyone see the beauty of Islam? People see what Osama bin Laden did and think Islam is bloodthirsty and obsessed with death."

"Some do."

"Then why would you say you want to be like him?"

"Some of what you say is true. Many people do believe Sheikh bin Laden only wanted to kill. But that is not the case. The purpose of his actions was to give the world a wakeup call to Islam, the same wakeup call I am trying to give you now. After the Twin Towers fell, many western people became interested in Islam. People began to learn about the Middle East and to speak Arabic in great numbers. What was sad about 9/11 was that it took so many people dying for Sheikh bin Laden's message to come through. Do you think you'd be learning Arabic and living in Sharjah if 9/11 never happened?"

"I don't know."

"In Riyadh, I have met many western people who found Islam after 9/11. Many started like you. They came to the Middle East to study Arabic and to discover why Muslims would do such monstrous things. But then they saw the truth and changed. Now, they are my brothers and sisters. I pray you will be like them. I pray you too will be my brother, my real brother."

"I don't think Allah's going to answer your prayers."

Osama rose from the step and handed *The Noble Qur'an* back to me.

"Maybe not, but I will still pray for you," he said. "If the Qur'an calls out to you, answer it. I have nothing else left to say. That's it."

Maybe that was it for him, but it definitely was not it for me. Osama's perspective on Islam, and apparently the world, was clearly warped. I'd heard plenty of Muslims over the years condemn Osama bin Laden and other Islamic terrorists.

If those people disagreed with my Osama about that, then maybe they disagreed with him about his interpretation of the Qur'an too. Lacking any other bright ideas, I rang up Kareem right after Osama left and asked to meet.

"Why? Can it wait till tomorrow?" he asked. "I'm about to go to bed."

"Kareem, it's about the Qur'an," I said. "I need to talk someone about it. I'm at the mosque."

Immediately, his attitude changed.

"Stay where you are. I'm on my way!" he shouted before hanging up the phone.

I knew I could count on him. I noticed Kareem walking speedily towards my position in front of the mosque less than five minutes after our call. He was wearing a tight, black, long-sleeved shirt that outlined his massive, bulging arm muscles. I started to worry that if Kareem held the same beliefs as Osama, then angering him with criticism of the Qur'an might put me in serious physical danger. However, I set aside my paranoia and resolved not to pull any punches with what I had to say.

Kareem took a seat on the same spot where Osama had been sitting only minutes before. He propped up his chin with his right fist, which indicated he was ready for me to begin. With my Qur'an in my hands, I explained in detail which parts bothered me and why. Afterwards, I rehashed my conversation with Osama, which only confirmed my worst fears.

To my relief, Kareem didn't jump up in rage or pummel me to death. All he did was demand to see my copy, so I handed it off to him without question. He glanced at the cover and looked up a few of the phrases that troubled me. In less than thirty seconds, he diagnosed the problem.

"This is a Saudi Qur'an," he said, holding it up in the air. "That means the translation is totally biased. You shouldn't read any garbage that comes from Saudi Arabia. There are other versions of the Qur'an that take into account the actual context."

"But Saudi Arabia is the world center of Islam. That's where Mecca and Medina are. It's the land of Muhammad. Why shouldn't I read anything that comes from there?"

"Saudi Arabia is all those things, but it's controlled by Wahhabis. Wahhabis are extremists that teach Muslims to remove themselves from all 'contamination' with non-Muslims. They are intolerant, narrow-minded, and completely against any form of modernizing. Your Qur'an was translated by men who want Muslims to fear non-Muslims very much, especially the Jews."

"Are you telling me that all the negative things I read about Jews and other non-Muslims aren't really in there? It was all made up by the Wahhabis?"

"No, that's not what I'm saying. The Prophet Muhammad fought wars against Jewish tribes and pagans. That is true. But anything negative you read about Jews or anyone else in the Qur'an only refers to *those* Jews or *those* Christians or *those* pagans from that time. Relax and don't take it so personally."

Kareem's last comment made me laugh. He was so nonchalant about discussing this issue that I felt silly for getting so worked up. Unfortunately, my euphoria lasted only a few moments before another alarm rang off in my mind.

"Do you think most Muslims see things like you or like the Wahhabis?" I asked.

Kareem winced at my question and I prepared myself for the worst.

"I used to be just like your friend Osama," he confessed. "For about a year or so, I identified as a Wahhabi. Osama and I were also good friends then. We used to spend time in the mosque together. This mosque!" he emphasized while pointing at the building behind him. "For a while I stopped talking to a lot of my other friends because I disapproved of how they lived. I thought I knew what was best for everyone. I became passionate about jihad and even considered dropping out of school to go fight the Americans somewhere."

"What changed you?"

"One day I was in the mosque listening to some imam speak. The imam talked about what a disgrace it was that there were so many girls walking around AUS wearing tight jeans and showing their hair and skin. He said that any Muslim girl who wears shorts or mini-skirts should be executed."

"What happened then?"

"The administration heard about the incident and banned him from ever coming back. But something changed in me after that. I thought about my female friends and cousins who are not so religious. I wanted them to be more religious, but I didn't want them to die if they chose not to be. I started to realize I supported an Islam that focused on the positive in people, an Islam that is tolerant."

"So what happened to your relationship with Osama?"

"We don't speak anymore. I don't come to this mosque either. Most of the students who pray here think like him, like how I used to be. Now, I pray in my room, read the Qur'an, and try talking to students who come to the Islamic Club meetings."

"That goes back to my original question. Do you think most people stand with you or with Osama?" It was clear Kareem didn't want to actually answer the question. From his tense facial expression, I read that coming up with a positive response only invited agony.

"The Saudis are very wealthy," he continued. "They send money to build mosques and schools that teach their ideology all over the world. Moderate Muslims are also afraid of speaking out against the Wahhabis. They are afraid that if they come out too hard against them, the less open-minded Muslims will accuse them of being traitors and treat them as enemies. I think that today most Muslims are caught in the middle of these two forces. Take you, for example."

"Me?"

"Yes. Islam teaches Muslims to honor Jews because they are *Ahl al-Kitab* (People of the Book). When you came to AUS, many students welcomed you in and treated you as Islam commands. But others only gossiped about you and started saying stupid things. They said that you were treacherous and not to be trusted because of some verses in the Qur'an that have been twisted around. Many Muslims today are stuck between what Islam really intends and what the extremists say."

"Kareem, every religion in the world is defined by its followers. If every Muslim was like you, then Islam would be as you describe it. But if every Muslim was a Wahhabi, then Islam would be synonymous with Wahhabism. How do you think moderate Muslims are going to convince people that they have the real Islam if they're too afraid to stand up to the extremists? Isn't being afraid a sign of lack of faith?"

Kareem rose to his feet looking glum.

"It is," he said softly. "I'm very afraid what will happen to Islam if the moderates lose."

As was I.

After my talk with Kareem, I was much more comfortable telling AUS students the simple truth: I'd read the whole Qur'an, or at least one version of it, and had chosen to stick with being the other kind of son of Abraham, the Jewish kind.

Most of my friends, like Samira and Ahmad Jew, accepted my decision without objection. Other friends, those particularly those who saw me as more of a brother than a friend, had a more difficult time with it.

Muhammad bin Raheem found out about of my rejection of Islam at an *iftar* dinner held at one of his stepmothers' houses in front of most of his family, including his eighty-three-year-old father. I preferred telling him one-on-one, but I was basically forced into coming out with it right then and there.

When the first tray of appetizers was brought out, his elderly father asked me in Arabic, "You are a Muslim?" I didn't want to lie so I said no, which led to his next question of, "You will be a Muslim later?" When I responded in the negative to that question too, he ended our conversation saying, "*Inshallah*, tomorrow you will be."

His father probably had some form of dementia because after every one of the following five courses was served, he repeatedly asked me those same two questions with no apparent recollection of my previous answers. Muhammad bin Raheem sat next to me throughout the evening. He smiled the whole time, but I knew he was faking it. I could only imagine how tough it must have been for him to hear me turn down his belief system six times.

Close to midnight, he drove me back to the AUS campus. He was mum during the ride, preferring to listen to a CD of Arabic folk music rather than talk. Therefore, it surprised me when he parked his Range Rover in front of my dorm building and escorted me to my room. The short walk there he barely said a word. Only when I opened my door and was about to tell him goodnight did Muhammad bin Raheem pour out his heart.

"I am very sad," he bemoaned with his eyes glued to the floor. "I am in pain that you are not Muslim. I want us to live in paradise together one day. You read all the Qur'an? All the words?"

"I did," I answered.

"I don't understand. I don't understand this."

I understood why he didn't understand. Besides interacting with their servants and teachers, Emiratis like Muhammad bin Raheem weren't accustomed to developing close relations with non-Muslims. I didn't think most of them, except for the true elites of their society, ever fathomed it was possible for a non-Muslim to experience Emirati hospitality, read the Qur'an, and then to decide not to embrace Islam. I was sorry to crush Muhammad bin Raheem's hopes, but he had to learn that most people would never see a lot of issues through his eyes.

"What will change your mind?" he asked. "There must be something."

"Muhammad, stop it!"

Suddenly, he perked up and a genuine grin returned to his face.

"Stop what? Stop this?" he asked as he jabbed my side with his index finger. "And this also?" He poked at both my sides at once. "This too?" That time he went for my armpit.

That was it, I ruled. Three jabs and you're out. It was time to take this Muhammad down. Within seconds, we'd wrestled each other to the floor in our sleek, white *kanduras* and were tickling each other without mercy. I don't know what flipped the switch in Muhammad bin Raheem's brain. All I knew was that I preferred to make him writhe in agony from tickling rather than continue talking about Islam.

Our hyena-like shrieks attracted the notice of ten other local guys hanging out in the common area.

When they came over and watched us rolling around torturing each other with tickles, the ten of them joined the frenzy. Before long, there were a dozen men in white robes tickling each other in that narrow hallway.

We put an end to the madness less than a minute later when someone got injured. The chubbiest guy in the group sliced his hand open on someone's watch. The second we saw blood we halted the mayhem.

"Michael, tell me! Tell everyone!" Muhammad bin Raheem shouted. "How we can change your mind about Islam?"

Geez, this guy didn't give up. I wanted to bury the hatchet on the subject once and for all. I decided the only way to do that was to attach some impossible stipulation to my acceptance of Islam, something along the lines of "when hell freezes over" or "when pigs fly."

"I'll become Muslim when you show me a *jinn*," I proclaimed. "No *jinn*, no deal."

"Ohhh!" the Emiratis moaned in unison.

A fully-bearded local named Faisal stepped forward to confront me. He was much paler than most UAE nationals, which suggested he was of Persian stock or maybe a half-breed, like the kind of local I sometimes passed for.

"The *jinn* are very dangerous," Faisal warned. "They are everywhere all the time and they don't like to be bothered."

"Are you saying you won't show me a *jinn* because you're afraid?" I challenged. "Does that mean you could show me a *jinn* if you wanted to?"

"I am a little afraid. I have never done this. But I know how." An apprehensive little smirk surfaced on his lips and he nodded his head slowly. "If this means you will become a Muslim, then I will do it."

"Ohhh!" the Emiratis moaned again. "*Illa al-hamam!*" one of them yelled in Arabic. To the bathroom!

Everyone except Faisal hurried into my dorm room and stood around looking jumpy.

"If a *jinn* comes out really you will believe in Islam?" Muhammad bin Raheem asked me hopefully.

"If this works I'll believe anything," I said.

Faisal appeared in my room several minutes later with a large pot, a bottle of cooking oil, a box of salt, and oven mitts. He set all the equipment down next to my small stove and went to work while the rest of us observed.

To start, Faisal filled the pot with water and heated it on the burner. I tapped Muhammad bin Raheem on the shoulder and asked if he'd ever done this before. Suddenly tongue-tied, he shrugged his shoulders and let out an exasperated cackle. I assumed that meant no. When the water began to boil, Faisal dumped about half the box of salt in the pot and turned off the stove.

"Come," he ordered pointing at me. "Take this pot to the toilet."

I walked over to my little kitchenette, slid my hands inside the oven mitts, and brought the big pot of salty water into the bathroom while all the locals waited in the bedroom.

"Look into the toilet and pour the water in. Then say '*jinn kharooj*' (which literally means 'Out *jinn*') three times," Faisal instructed. "Doing this will wake up the *jinn*."

"You're sure there's a *jinn* in *my* toilet?" I asked.

"If you use your toilet often and it is a dirty place then there must be."

"I use my toilet like it's my job."

"Then know that when you are there you are not alone."

I moved towards my toilet and stared down into the bowl. Pouring in the hot, salty water from the pot I cried out, "*Jinn kharooj, jinn kharooj, jinn kharooj.*"

After a few suspenseful seconds the experiment looked like a dud.

"Wait!" Faisal roared. "This is only the beginning. The *jinn* is awake. I know it! Now we must heat the oil. Only when you pour hot oil into the toilet will the *jinn* come out."

I felt myself rapidly losing patience with this silly *jinn* game. It seemed Faisal was making this stuff up as he went along in a last ditch effort to convert me to Islam. Still, the Emiratis in my room were eating this nonsense up like it was candy.

Sure enough, after heating up the cooking oil, adding salt, pouring it all into the toilet, and crying out "*jinn kharooj*" three times, the only thing that emerged was an overflowing concoction of murky water and bubbling, yellowish oil.

"This isn't working, guys," I said as I stepped out of my bathroom. "There is no *jinn* in my toilet. Good night."

"Wait Michael!" Faisal yet again objected. "You should not say such things. If there is a *jinn* in the toilet he will not like it if you say you do not believe he is there. He will attack you when you are alone. You must bring him out now while you have friends here to help you."

"So what do we do?" I sighed skeptically.

"Go back to the toilet and yell three times, '*jinn tha'ayif*' (which literally means 'weak *jinn*'). This is a big insult to a *jinn*. He will come out of the toilet to hurt you and will see how many of us he must fight. We will defeat him because we have the power of Islam. We will not fail you, Michael!"

"Faisal, if you've never done this before, how do you know so much?"

"This is what my grandfather says he did to meet the *jinn* when he was young."

"Faisal, there were no toilets in the UAE when your grandfather was young. What the hell are you talking about?"

"Let us try it anyway."

All the Emiratis in my room clapped their hands and promised to save me in the event that I was attacked by a supernatural demon capable of traveling at the speed of light and possessing my body but, for some strange reason, preferred living in my toilet. If that isn't unconditional friendship, then I don't know what is. Nevertheless, the cynical side of me yearned to put their promise to the test and the practical joker in me craved to have some fun.

So, as the Emiratis beckoned each other to remain silent, I returned to the toilet, bent over, and placed my hands firmly on the seat. Closing my eyes, I breathed in deeply and tried one last time to invoke the *jinn* of my toilet.

"*Jinn tha'ayif,*" I said softly. I let a few seconds pass before emitting a soft growl. "*Jinn tha'ayif,*" I said again with slightly more gusto. I growled once more just a bit louder and twitched my head erratically. I heard some of the locals standing behind me start to move backwards. "*Jinn tha'ayif!*" I suddenly screamed at the top of my lungs.

Heaving for breath, I staggered to my feet and gave the noisiest, most animalistic growl that I could. I turned around slowly with my head a bit crooked and my hands shaking at my sides. I stared upwards so that all who fixed their eyes on me could see the whites of my eyes.

"*Ana jinn!*" I screamed in Arabic at the onlookers. I am a *jinn*! I grabbed Faisal by his *ghutrah* and howled whatever improvised, unintelligible gibberish I could muster.

Instantly, he ran away in a state of panic, leaving his *ghutrah* behind in my hand. His panic only induced greater panic among the rest. Every one of the nine other Emiratis followed his lead and shrieked and cried as they ran out into the hallway, pushing each other up against the walls and tripping over each other's feet. So much for saving your friend from an evil *jinn* with the power of Islam, I thought.

I chased the stragglers at the end of the pack, thrashing at their *kanduras* with my nails. The last Emirati out attempted to slam the door shut, leaving me behind in the room. But alas, he was too slow and too weak for a powerful *jinn* like me.

I pushed the door open and he rushed off to join his friends huddled ten feet away. Once out in the hallway, I halted my act.

"It was a joke, guys," I called out to them.

Hesitant for a moment, the ten locals walked up to me with exasperated expressions still plastered on their faces. Faisal smacked me on the neck and took back his *ghutrah.*

"If you choose not to be a Muslim, that is fine," he conceded. "We can live with this. We are very happy you are not a *jinn.* That would be a bigger problem."

I thought my complicated saga with Islam was nearing an end. But as the news that I'd read the Qur'an spread outside of my immediate circle of friends, students who hated me used that information against me. Random students, not just Mo, approached me to confirm or deny increasingly preposterous rumors swirling around campus. Not surprisingly, most of these rumors were started by Hassan and his friends.

"Hassan said that after you read the Qur'an, you used it as a plate and a foot rest. Is this true?" a gullible Egyptian girl asked me in a hallway one morning.

I carefully responded that her accusation didn't even make sense. Why would someone eat on something they rested their feet on? She accepted my response, and informed me it was also being said that I was feverishly plotting with Christian students against Muslim ones.

"Plotting what?" I asked.

"Just plotting," she shrugged. "I don't really know what it means. But it sounds bad. Please don't do it!"

Exhausted with facing down these indictments and feeling the need for some camaraderie, I spent the last week of Ramadan afternoons with Jake, the other American student constantly accused of being a Jew. Jake wisely refrained from delving too deeply into topics of religion with other AUS students, but was often pulled into discussing religious topics anyways by his roommate, Salim.

Salim was a short, but strong Indian Muslim who grew up in Saudi Arabia. Since both sides of his family had lived there for three generations, he was granted a Saudi passport at birth. Salim had a difficult time finding his place among the AUS student body. He wasn't culturally Indian enough to fit in with the other Indians and many of the Arab students viewed him as an unabashed status seeker due to his hard-to-come-by Saudi citizenship.

Salim found solace for his social woes in two things: weight lifting and Islam. Salim had won numerous amateur body-building competitions and planned to go pro. That is, he did until the night a drunken Emirati girl crashed her convertible into him while he crossed a street on campus.

As the daughter of a prominent Emirati, she went unpunished for her intoxicated assault. He ended up in the hospital with two shattered legs. With his body-building career on indefinite hold, Salim's be-all and end-all became Islam.

"The day I moved in with Salim, I knew he wasn't just a Muslim by association. He was a real believer," Jake recounted one night when Salim wasn't around. "He walked in the room when I was putting my things down and started looking underneath the beds and desks. Then he stopped and said, 'My grandfather was an exorcist and I have a really bad feeling about this room.'"

Normally, when I went to their room to chill out, Salim was asleep. I'd check email on Jake or Salim's computer, and then Jake and I would binge watch television. But, as one might expect, when Salim was awake he'd try to engage me in religious discussions too. At first, he'd preface our talks with a warning.

"Just so you know, I'm not supposed to trust people like *you*," he'd say.

Most of our first conversations focused on his conviction that Jews were inherently a manipulative and deceiving people. To my satisfaction, through his day-to-day interaction with me, he began to see things differently. He'd tell me that I was his friend, that maybe not all Jews were the same (though most were still very, very bad), and he'd even speak to me about non-religious subjects that interested him too, like the sexual habits of American women and legal steroid use.

Still, the miserable reality was that being friends with me made his reputation even worse than it already was. One afternoon while Jake and I feasted on tuna and mustard sandwiches in their dorm room, Salim walked in, angrily slammed the door shut, and tossed his backpack on the floor.

"People are saying I'm a Jew!" he stammered as he leaped onto his bed. "They're saying you made me one."

"Why would anyone say you've become a Jew or that I made you one?" I asked in disbelief.

"It's because of that stupid shirt I was wearing."

Salim went through his closet and picked out a black t-shirt with a five-pointed silver star emblazoned in the middle.

"People are saying this is the star of the Jews!" he cried. "But even I know this isn't how it looks. It's just a shirt with a star on it. How can people say that I've become a Jew? How can people say such a crazy thing about me?"

Now you know what's it's like for me, I wanted to say to him. It wasn't that I had no sympathy for Salim. I empathized with him. But, the reality was that I was burnt out from all the rumors and conspiracy theories. I'd had it. Deep down, I felt like I was reaching my breaking point. I knew it wouldn't be long before I went on a critical rant about something.

In the middle of one of Dr. Muntassar's lectures during that last week of Ramadan, Aisha, an Emirati girl who wore designer clothes underneath her black garb, asked the professor for his view about the university policy of expelling any student for any sort of public protest. The question made Dr. Muntassar noticeably uncomfortable, since he understandably preferred not to comment about such matters in front of students. So, instead of taking a stance, he asked her what she thought about the matter.

"I think it's wrong!" Aisha asserted in her ultra high-pitched voice. "Last year I tried to organize a student protest against the Danish and the university blocked it. I don't understand the problem with protesting our enemies who make fun of the Prophet Muhammad and insult our religion."

Aisha was referring to the infamous Danish cartoon scandal that broke in September 2005. The Danish newspaper *Jyllands-Posten* published twelve inflammatory editorial cartoons about the Prophet Muhammad in what was claimed to be an effort to contribute to the debate over criticism of Islam. The cartoons were re-printed all over the world, leading to violent protests and attacks on Danish embassies in Muslim countries.

"Aisha, if your government let you protest that issue, they'd have to let you protest anything else you wanted," I interjected.

"No, this is different!" she insisted. "What these cartoons did was show that Denmark hates Islam. If that wasn't true then the Danish government would have stopped it from being printed."

"Hold on, Aisha!" Dr. Muntassar chimed in. "In the West, there is a difference between a newspaper and a government. In Denmark, the government has no power to stop these things."

"Unacceptable!" Aisha yelled. "This is about respect and pride. They cannot be allowed to print these kinds of cartoons. If they act as enemies of Islam then they should be treated as enemies of Islam."

"Hey, Aisha. Here's a news flash!" I said somewhat condescendingly. "There are people in the West who believe that Islam is a violent religion, that Muslims support terrorism, and that all Arabs a bunch of nutcases. The purpose of printing these cartoons was to expose Muslims for what they believe they are. When Muslims riot and burn down Danish embassies and call for a jihad against Denmark, it proves your opponents right. If Muslims are portrayed as violent and unreasonable and then act violently and unreasonably, wouldn't that mean that Muslims are violent and unreasonable people?"

Rami, a thin, scruffy-faced Palestinian who I'd seen hanging around with the likes of Hassan and his crew, gave me a mean glare before opposing my point.

"This is an assault on Muslim sensibilities," he argued. "If cartoons like these were printed about Christians, western countries would bomb us to death."

"What you're saying has no basis," I replied. "Go inside almost any book store in the Muslim world and you'll find books and newspapers with terrible cartoons vilifying Christians and Jews. How can people in Muslim countries criticize Denmark or any other nation when they're guilty of doing the exact same thing to other religions?"

"The cartoons of Jews and Christians are cartoons of men," Rami alleged. "It's different when it's a picture of the Prophet Muhammad."

"How? Western newspapers have drawn caricatures of lots of biblical figures. But even if they hadn't, the cartoons of Muhammad were also of a man. That's the point. Muhammad was a man. Muhammad wasn't God. Drawing Muhammad shouldn't be considered worse than drawing a picture of anyone else."

On that note, despite the pleas of various objecting students, Dr. Muntassar ended the discussion and returned to the topic of his lecture. I was glad I'd been given the last word and that my points would be the ones that would stick out in my classmates' minds. I felt relief knowing I hadn't minced my words. Of course, that didn't stop my detractors from distorting what I'd said to unleash the most dangerous allegation against me yet.

The next night, when Jake and I were finishing off the third season of *Lost* on his computer, a startling knock interrupted us. Jake got up and opened the door.

"Michael is here? He must speak to us," a male voice demanded urgently.

Jake turned towards me apprehensively and motioned for me to come to the door.

Roughly a dozen male AUS students were standing there arms-crossed with very disgruntled looks. The speaker for the group was Alaa, an incredibly tall Palestinian with glasses and the longest nose this side of Arabia. I was on cordial terms with Alaa, but I couldn't exactly say we were the closest of friends.

"Michael," he said. "We have heard that you have defamed the Prophet Muhammad."

"Huh? What?" I asked flabbergasted. "What does that mean?"

"You have spoken out against the Prophet Muhammad. You have accused the Prophet of being a wicked man and a thief."

"And a sorcerer!" a voice from behind Alaa yelled out.

"First of all, I have nothing bad to say about the Prophet Muhammad, peace be upon him, nor have I ever had anything bad to say about him," I contended. "He lived over fourteen hundred years ago. I didn't know him personally. How could I speak badly about someone I never knew?"

Alaa relaxed the muscles in his face and took a quick look at his posse behind him before returning his gaze to me.

"I guess that's true," he admitted. "But it is being said that you publicly accused the Prophet Muhammad of these things in class. Do you deny this?"

"Of course I deny it. Let me ask you some questions, Alaa. Who told you that I defamed the Prophet Muhammad? Who's the liar that's spreading this shit? Was it a guy named Rami by any chance? Or Hassan? Tell me!"

"We will not say. It would not be right to tell you. Defaming the Prophet Muhammad is very serious. There is no greater offense to Muslims. If these charges were true, then something very bad could have happened to you."

"Alaa, that's exactly why I want you to tell me who it was. It's not fair for the accused to not meet his accuser. You tell whoever's been saying all this shit behind my back that he's a coward for not showing his face."

"We will tell him what you say. I believe you did not say these things. But if you did or you ever do, you could die because of it."

I told Alaa and his friends good night, and I went back to watching television with Jake feeling stressed-out and aggravated. I couldn't continue with all this madness indefinitely. I needed a break from Sharjah. No, I needed a break from the entire Arab world. It didn't have to be a long break. Just long enough to clear my head. So, I went where tens of thousands of other nice Jewish boys went when they wanted to get away for a while.

Chapter 11
A Strange Jewish Wonderland

India
October–November 2006

INDIA." MO SAID THE WORD IRRITATINGLY SLOWLY. HE LET EACH syllable linger like this: In. Dee. Ah. Then he said it again. "In. Dee. Ah." And again. "In. Dee. Ah." I tried to ignore him but I felt that, if he didn't stop soon, I'd have to duct-tape his mouth shut to save my sanity.

It was ten at night and I was on the floor of my dorm room packing up my large travel backpack. Mo had phoned me to ask if he could stop by to see me before I left. I consented, not knowing what a pain he would be.

Ramadan was almost over, and in honor of *Eid al-Fitr* (commonly just called "*Eid*"), the three-day festival marking the cessation of fasting, AUS gave students and a faculty a full week of vacation. I, therefore, seized the opportunity to go travel.

"And you chose India?" Mo spouted disdainfully as he looked down on me sitting in the chair at my desk.

That I had. In just a little while, a taxi was scheduled to pick me up and whisk me away to the Sharjah airport, where I'd catch a midnight flight to Jaipur, a sprawling metropolis in northern India.

"I don't understand," he said. "You live in the UAE. There are tons of Indians here. And you feel like you need to see more of them? Everyone knows you only go to India if you want aggravation."

"Sharjah's pretty aggravating at the moment too," I shot back.

"Still, you're going for two weeks?"

Traveling for only the one week we were allotted didn't seem long enough. I needed more time than that to detox, so I decided to ditch classes for an extra week and indulge my wanderlust. I bought a cheap flight to Jaipur, known as the "Pink City" for its abundance of pink-painted architecture, and was planning on going with the flow.

"So you're just going with no plan?" Mo asked alarmed. "Are many other Jewish people as crazy as you?"

They certainly were. India was appealing to me because of the 50,000 Israelis who traveled there each year. I wanted to experience Indian culture to the fullest, but I couldn't deny feeling extra giddy about the prospect of mixing with other Jews. I didn't let Mo in on that piece of information though. He would have jumped to other conclusions.

"Some people say they don't think you'll come back after the break," he said. "They say this is your best chance to get out of the UAE. Otherwise you'll have big trouble when you come back."

"Mo, I'm definitely coming back," I replied. "My mission isn't complete. If another spy was sent to Sharjah in my place, he wouldn't know where to start."

Mo suddenly went quiet and looked away. A part of him still suspected I wasn't who I claimed to be.

"Mo, you're crazier than your brother!" I yelled. "At least he's smart enough to stay away from me. You know I was joking. My name is Michael and I am not a spy."

Instead of responding to my proclamation, Mo changed the subject.

"Will you celebrate *Eid* in India?" Mo asked.

I nodded yes, but I didn't mean it. I really didn't care at that moment about Eid or anything else remotely connected to Islam.

Shortly thereafter, the taxi driver I was waiting for called to say he was parked out front. I said goodbye to Mo, locked up my room, and rushed outside.

About an hour and a half later, I boarded my flight and found myself seated next to a large, older Indian man with a red mark on his forehead, signifying that he was a Hindu.

Right before takeoff, I received a text message from Salim. He wrote, "Be safe in India. Never trust a Hindu. He'll steal the shoes off your feet."

The absurdity of his message and seeing the smiley face at the end made me laugh out loud. The Hindu man next asked me what was so funny. I thought it was better not to tell him, so I said it was nothing and tried to fall asleep. Thinking of Salim, I glanced down at my sneakers before closing my eyes.

I woke up a few hours later, well before dawn, in what seemed like a strange Jewish wonderland. I stepped off the jet and all through the airport I saw bright lights in the shape of Jewish stars dangling from the ceiling and stuck to the walls. Feeling dazed, I continued walking to Immigration and was waved over to a booth where a baby-faced male passport agent spoke to me in Hebrew.

"*Boker tov,*" he said. Good morning. "I am learning Hebrew. *Hakol b'seder?*" Is everything okay?

Surprised, I responded in Hebrew that yes, everything was. I handed him my ticket stub and my American passport. He raised one eyebrow confused.

"You are an American. You are coming from the UAE. And, you speak Hebrew?" he asked.

"It's a long story," I said.

"Your family is Jewish or Arab?"

"Jewish. Do I look Arab?"

"Yes. To Indians you all look the same. Next in line please."

"Wait! What are all these stars hanging from the ceiling about?"

"The star is a religious symbol. I thought all Jewish people know this kind of star. They always point to it and laugh. Good day."

I took my passport back, exited security, and had a three-wheel auto rickshaw taxi drop me off in Jaipur's pink city center. It was four o'clock in the morning and still dark outside. The streets were mostly empty, except for stray cows and piles of garbage everywhere. Dozens more Jewish stars of all different colors hung on lamp posts and buildings, along with thousands of other tiny yellow lights. It was like Hanukkah in Jerusalem, with the addition of cows and trash.

I saw a young girl, no older than fourteen, preparing spiced tea from a cart on a street corner. I approached her, put my backpack down, and bought a cup. After she served me, I pointed to all the lights and asked her what was going on.

"It is the 'Festival of Lights,'" she said.

What universe had I been transported to? More perplexed than ever, I slung my backpack over my shoulders and walked off sipping my tea. I strolled a few more blocks down until I spotted a group of buildings with black swastikas painted on them. Of course, they were Hindu swastikas, not the Nazi ones tilted at a forty-five degree slant. Nevertheless, I didn't see any Jewish stars next to them, so I turned around and marched back in the opposite direction. In my exhausted stupor, I concluded that I hadn't yet adequately learned the rules of this bizarre place and thought it was best to stay out of questionable areas until I had.

I felt sleepy even after drinking the spicy tea. So I lied down on a clean street bench and snoozed.

Just after sun-up I was awoken by the trumpeting of six grand elephants draped in jewelry with intricate artwork painted on their skin. Sitting on top of them were bearded men sporting long white robes and red turbans. Dozens of women in colorful dresses with jingling bells attached danced all around them. Trailing behind was a group of a few hundred Indians, singing hymns and banging on drums and tambourines.

Near the end of the pack were two young male travelers, one of them short and the other tall, moving forward with the crowd, and clapping their hands. A person with an untrained eye might have believed they could have come from any western country. But I knew better. The long hair wrapped up in buns, the unusually unkempt facial hair, the t-shirts with the collars ripped off. To me, it couldn't have been more obvious. They were Israelis.

Excited to finally meet Jews and seeking answers to my questions about the baffling scene around me, I rose from the bench, snatched my backpack, and greeted them as if they were my long-lost brothers.

"Tell me my brothers, what's going on here?" I asked in rapid-fire Hebrew. "All I see everywhere are swastikas, Jewish stars, and elephants. Am I on drugs?"

Both of them bowled over laughing.

"My brother, relax," the short one urged.

It was good advice. I stopped talking, took a deep breath, and they explained that that day was the start of a five-day Hindu festival called *Diwali*, which, like Hanukkah, is called the "Festival of Lights."

They'd woken up at dawn specifically to be a part of the elephant parade, which formally inaugurated the celebration. The six-pointed star, they said, is a prominent symbol in the Hindu faith, not just the Jewish one.

My new friends were twenty-two year old ex-infantry men. Assaf was the name of the shorter of the two and his taller friend was named Omri. Childhood best friends from Ramat HaSharon, a suburb of Tel Aviv, they'd been touring India for six months already, experimenting with psychedelic drugs and going wherever the Hindu gods took them.

While we followed the elephant parade around town, I told them about my life in Sharjah, my friends, my enemies, the accusations that I was a spy, and my efforts to learn about Islam. As people banned from stepping foot in the UAE because of their Israeli citizenship, they were floored hearing about my experiences.

"You're doing something no Israeli has ever dreamed of," Omri said. "My whole life I've wondered what people in the Arab countries are like. I've just had to believe that people there wonder what Israelis are like. Do they?"

I didn't know what to say in response. Most questions I fielded from AUS students about Israel had to do with conspiracy theories and political leaders, not average Israeli citizens. I didn't want to make everyone at AUS sound like a bunch of closed-minded bigots, but they weren't open-minded enough for me to give them any undue credit.

I gave them some brief answer and tried to steer clear of talking about Arabs and Islam. I hung out with Omri and Assaf for the next few days.

We got to the Taj Mahal twenty minutes before sunset. After we bought admission tickets, two cheeky elementary school-age kids peddling informational booklets about the complex darted towards us to pitch their merchandise. They dressed identically in brown slacks and white button-down shirts and spoke charming, but grammatically incorrect English. One wore thick eyeglasses while the other had carefully slicked-back hair.

I asked them both to read the cover of one of the books they were marketing. Neither could. Clearly, they'd picked up English from working the tourist circuit, not from being in school. Whoever they worked for was exploiting their look of innocence for profit and was keeping them from having a future. That was something I was unwilling to support and I was up front about that from the start.

"Please misters, please buy for the mothers!" the one with glasses pressed. Omri and Assaf refused to make eye contact with them, much less issue responses. I volunteered to give them a verbal rejection only to help them practice their English.

"We're not buying anything from you. Give up," I said.

"But your friends at home? They love Taj Mahal. It is a beautiful and interesting, the Taj Mahal!" he countered.

I shook my head. I admired his persistence, but I wasn't going to budge. I had, so I thought, already heard every clever sales pitch out there.

"Your enemy, sir," the one with slicked back hair shrieked as he hurried alongside me. "Buy for your enemy. It is perfect gift for man you are hating."

Now that was something new. They both grinned after he said it, which meant they understood the irony. Impressed with their tongue-in-cheek salesmanship, I offered to let them tag along with Omri, Assaf, and me as we walked around the area. The two boys agreed in a heartbeat.

"We're not giving you any money," I reiterated. "If you want to make money you should go find other tourists."

"It is no problem," the one with glasses reassured me. "We are making same money every day. It is only important talking with white people. Fine?"

It was fine by us. The two boys gave us a private tour of the grounds. Evidently, they also operated as tour guides when they ran out of booklets to sell. At sunset they brought us to the famous garden reflecting pool and started discussing religion. I felt a knot tightening in my stomach.

"I am Muslim," the one with glasses announced.

"I am Hindu," the youngster with slicked back hair said. "You are what?"

"We are Jews," Assaf answered.

"What is Jews?" they both asked in unison.

I considered taking a rock and drawing a Jewish star on some gravel, but immediately remembered why that would prove useless. Instead, I asked them if they knew what Christians were. They did.

"First there were Jews and then there were Christians," I said.

They narrowed their eyes looking confused. Maybe they really hadn't heard of Jews before. Indeed, India had no gory history of anti-Semitism. Maybe India was a country where people didn't think one way or another about Jews.

"In India all the people are okay," the Muslim boy said. "Hindu, Muslim, Jews. It is no problem. Today is holy day you know?"

"Yes, it's *Diwali.* We're also celebrating *Diwali.*"

"Not only *Diwali,*" the Hindu boy corrected.

"Also *Eid!*" the Muslim boy stated. "You also celebrate *Eid* is very good. You will do *Eid*?"

I said I would, and to my own surprise, I actually meant it. Religion is so often used as a means of dividing people. Hearing those boys talk with such open enthusiasm about each other's religious holidays uplifted me. I realized it had been silly of me to purposefully disregard the holiday altogether. The month of Ramadan in Sharjah may have brought me a fair share of negative experiences, but that didn't justify disregarding all the positive ones I'd had. Plus, I reasoned that if I met other Indian Muslims as tolerant as my little street salesman friend with glasses, then finding a way to authentically mark *Eid* might be worthwhile.

I split off from Assaf and Omri in the Main Bazaar in Delhi, an area teeming with shoestring hostels, street hawkers, and leprosy-infected beggars. Craving to get out of the city, I wandered around various tour company offices in the area to see if I could negotiate a decent price to travel somewhere far off and interesting.

As I strolled the jam-packed streets, it was difficult keeping my eyes peeled for opportunities because I was forced to scan the dilapidated sidewalks for cracks, potholes, broken glass, and any other recklessly strewn object capable of causing me injury.

Despite my precautions, I still succeeded in smashing my right foot into a sharp rock. When that happened, I keeled over in pain. An Indian man standing nearby pointed and laughed at my misfortune. He looked to be in his mid-thirties, had wavy black hair, and a cocky smile.

"I hope you had a nice trip," he teased.

"Very funny," I said as I sat on the pavement clutching my bruised foot. "What's your next joke?"

"How about, 'How can I take your money today?'"

I laughed, though I learned afterwards he wasn't kidding. He helped me to my feet, lifted up my bag, and brought me to his shop next door to sit and have some tea. His shop turned out to be a tour agency he owned, specializing in package trips to Kashmir, a Muslim-majority region in the northern-most part of India famous for suicide bombings and insurgency.

"It is a land of snow-capped peaks, quiet lakes, glittering rivers, and majestic gardens," the man said dramatically as he stood in front of a wall covered in brochures and pictures. "It is paradise, my friend. It is the 'Switzerland of the East.'"

Yeah, maybe if Switzerland had been locked in conflict for sixty years.

After India and Pakistan gained independence from the British in 1947, both countries claimed sovereignty over Kashmir. Their dispute led to three bloody, intractable wars, numerous Islamist insurgencies, and an ugly division of the territory.

"Kashmir sounds dangerous," I said while seated in a creaky, wooden chair across from him.

"No, no, no!" he said defensively. "Kashmir is a very safe place, I promise. I am the sultan of safety. I am telling you there are many soldiers in Kashmir. Over 600,000 Indian soldiers are there right now."

"That doesn't mean it's safe. That means there are big problems there."

"Sir, Kashmir is my homeland. I promise if you go you will not regret it."

He offered me a five-day package tour of the Kashmir valley, which included two days of exploring the capital Srinagar, three days of hiking in the Pir Panjal range, a one hundred dollar one-way flight from Delhi, and all food, lodging, and other transportation logistics.

"All for only five hundred US dollars," he asserted confidently.

No deal. Even after taking out the cost of the flight, that would still have been an eighty-dollar a day excursion, too expensive for a budget traveler like myself. I got up to leave and told him I couldn't pay that kind of money.

"Wait, let's negotiate!" he urged. "Don't you understand how wonderful Kashmir is right now? It is a holiday. They are celebrating *Eid*."

Of course, those were the magic words. Instantly, my ears perked up and I returned to my seat.

"*Eid Mubarak*," I said back to him.

"Ah, you know *Eid*, do you? Kashmir is a great place to be for *Eid*. But you must leave tomorrow. I will give you everything for four hundred dollars." Again, I rose to leave. "Three hundred and fifty!" he shouted in desperation.

"I'll do it for three hundred," I offered.

He scowled at me for a few seconds before grudgingly nodding his head.

"You will leave from here at six in the morning. Please don't be late."

I ran off to an ATM close by to withdraw cash to pay the bill. When I returned, I asked if I could lock up my backpack at the agency until the morning since I hadn't booked a hotel room for the night. It was already late in the afternoon, and, frankly, I preferred to spend the remaining hour of daylight touring Delhi, not hostel hunting.

"It is no problem. This agency is as safe as Kashmir!" he joked.

I didn't laugh. I dropped off my backpack in a corner of the agency beneath a five-foot tall poster of the most breathtakingly ornate mosque I'd ever seen before. The roof supported eight white and purple marble domes and was surrounded by tall minarets made of white marble and red sandstone. In the picture, thousands of worshippers crowded a massive courtyard in front of the mosque itself.

"That is the Jama Masjid," he said. "It is the largest mosque in India. Twenty-five thousand people can fit in that courtyard. It is a very big tourist attraction in Delhi. You should go see it."

Two and a half hours later, after slugging through Delhi traffic in the back of a bicycle rickshaw, I was let off at the eastern entrance to the Jama Masjid. I was met immediately by two stout security guards sitting on stools opposite the two massive iron doors leading into the mosque.

"You cannot enter," the guard on the left said as I approached. "No tourists now, no tourists."

"Why not?" I asked.

"Today is a holiday. You cannot enter. It is for Muslims only."

"I know it is a holiday. *Eid Mubarak*. I am a Muslim!"

Truth be told, I don't recall what I was thinking when I told that little lie. It was like the words flew out of my mouth on their own without receiving any instructions from my brain. But once I'd said it, I couldn't take it back. I had to back it up. I knew it would be difficult because of my non-orthodox outward appearance. I stood there wearing a yellow t-shirt and khaki shorts, and had very visible piercings in both my eyebrow and ear.

I clearly wasn't religious and wouldn't have been able to pass as a recent convert. I knew that whatever explanation I'd give would have to remove all doubts about my Muslim status. The passport official at the airport told me Indians couldn't tell the difference between Jews and Arabs. Thus, I determined that for one night I would borrow the identity of my good Palestinian-American friend from high school.

"My name is Joe Barkawi," I said. "Youssef in Arabic. I am an American, but my family comes from Palestine. It would make me very happy to celebrate *Eid* with other Muslims at this great mosque."

To give my claim a bump of credibility, I recited the *shahada* and initiated an Arabic conversation with them in the best accent I could imitate. Just as I suspected, they could pray in Arabic, but they couldn't speak a lick of it. The two guards then discussed the matter in Urdu. Half a minute later they waved me into the complex without bothering to ask me for ID.

Relieved that the guards bought my story, I thought the most difficult task of the evening was behind me. I walked into the massive courtyard I recognized from the poster and tried to keep a low profile, which proved to be impossible. Although the courtyard was packed with thousands of men and women, I was by far the lightest-skinned person around. Everywhere I went people pointed and reached out to touch me. Some even aggressively pulled me by the shirt and poked my butt as I passed. This was not the kind of welcome I was expecting.

To protect myself, I stayed close to the main wall surrounding the complex. Eventually I wound up in front of a long elevated platform with a podium and attached microphone sitting on top. Near the platform stood an assembly of five prominent-looking bearded men wearing stainless white *jalabiyyas*.

When they saw me saunter past them, one of them, an extremely tall and fat middle-aged man with yellow teeth, stormed up to me and grabbed me by the wrist. Terrified, I tried to pull my hand away. But it was too late. I'd been caught.

"Who are you? What is your name? What are you doing here? Are you a Muslim?" he shouted.

"Yes, I'm Muslim. My name is Joe Barkawi. I came to celebrate *Eid*," I answered as my whole body trembled.

"What is your country?"

"I'm an American."

Right away, the big man loosened his grip and patted me on the shoulder.

"You are American? And you are Muslim?" he asked surprised. I nodded my head. "You must speak about this to the people. Wait here."

He ran off to huddle up with his colleagues to tell them about me. He returned a moment later with a simple request.

"Go to the microphone and speak to the people about the life for Muslims in America," he pushed. "Those four men over there are trustees of the Jama Masjid. I am Aakef, their assistant. This is a very rare opportunity. We do not see many Muslims from America. The trustees agree that Allah has brought to you to this podium and they feel it is important for the people to hear your words."

"Oh, but I don't have much to say," I said. "I'm not very religious."

"It is okay. Come up with me. You will speak and I will translate into Urdu. I am a very good translator. I studied translation in the university. I will not confuse your words. Now come, brother."

Before I could process what was about to happen, Aakef had already pulled me up onto the platform, escorted me to the podium, introduced me as Joe, and gestured for me to start talking. I can't say that the thousands of people in the crowd quieted down for me, but the microphone was connected to a speaker system so powerful that they didn't have to.

Without having any experiences of my own to draw from, I spoke in general terms about the position of Muslims in the United States as I saw it. I talked about what a great nation America was because of the freedoms and equal rights it accorded to all its citizens, including Muslims. I said that Muslim life in America was thriving. New mosques, Muslim schools, and community organizations were being established every year, largely thanks to the financial success many Muslims in America had achieved. Perhaps most crucially, I said I understood that while America's image in the greater Muslim world was not very positive because of its occupations of Iraq and Afghanistan, America had gone to war to overthrow those countries' dictators who used Islam to justify egregious rule and terrorize their people.

They didn't buy my pro-America propaganda. When I jumped down off the platform, a swarm of dozens of people encircled us and a few feisty listeners asked me heated questions in English.

"You are wrong about everything!" a pudgy man with a scratchy voice roared. "America is the enemy of all Muslims. They are killing Muslims everywhere. If you are a good Muslim, you will bomb yourself in America. Put on a bomb and bomb yourself in Washington. Why do you not do this?"

"We must bomb America until it becomes a Muslim country," a woman wearing a black hijab argued. "We must take control away from the Jews. The Jews control America and hate Muslims. Death to the Jews! Death to the Jews! Why do you not kill Jews?"

Their comments infuriated me, not least because I knew that, if they were serious, then the thousands of Jews traveling around India were in real danger. These people were obviously in need of a strong dose of Kareem's moderate Muslim medicine. I decided to try and administer it to them.

"My brothers and sisters," I said to the crowd. "What these people are suggesting I do will only bring upon Muslims pain and destruction. Bombing America and killing Jews will do none of us any good.

Is anyone here really surprised that when a Muslim puts on a bomb belt and blows himself up, the non-Muslims attack us with even bigger bombs? There are many people in this world who hear the word Islam and equate it with bombs. I am telling you that if we are serious about making Islam thrive in the West, then we must put our bombs aside and prove to people through our good deeds that Islam is the true path to a life of decency and satisfaction."

"Joe, how can Muslims do this?" Aakef asked.

"I propose we launch a jihad, my friends. A jihad with our words. For us to have the influence we need in this world to spread our faith, we must become better organized and involved in politics, journalism, and lobbying wherever we live. We must raise money for our cause. This is the only way to spread Islam's message!"

"But how we can watch America and Israel kill so many Muslims? How you can tell us not to fight them?" a pimply-faced teenager posed.

"Muslims love to mention how America and Israel kill Muslims, but they never want to talk about when Muslims kill other Muslims," I rebutted. "Muslims are killing each other right now in Iraq, Pakistan, and Palestine. We must stop blaming America, Israel, and everyone else for the problems of the Muslim people. We must take responsibility for ourselves. Don't tell your sons to strap bombs to their chests. Tell them to study, get jobs, read the Qur'an, and be examples to the world. This is the only way Islam will triumph."

Aakef translated my words into Urdu as fast as he could for the non-English speaking listeners. When he finished, numerous people clapped, including the four trustees of the Jama Masjid. Men flanked me on all sides to shake my hands and kiss my cheeks and, as corny as it sounds, even a few small children were thrust into my arms.

"All the people loved your words very much," Aakef said. "When I was translating into Urdu, I felt like the angel Jibril was talking through you."

Feeling a sense of accomplishment, I continued shaking hands with my adoring admirers until a few minutes later when the thousands of people in the courtyard began making a mad rush to leave.

"Everyone is going home now for dinner," Aakef told me. "You will come with me to eat with my family?"

"Oh, I would, but I need to find a hotel for the night and get some sleep. Tomorrow, I leave very early for Kashmir."

"You will eat with me. You will sleep with me. You will get to Kashmir. If you don't come, I will be very offended. So you see, you have no choice."

Yet again, Aakef seized my wrist. To make sure I didn't run off, he refused to let go of me until we'd safely exited the compound, walked about ten blocks to his modest four-room ground-level apartment. When he pushed open the front door, his wife, four sons, and two daughters were lined up in a row in their sparsely decorated living room waiting to greet him. Aakef gave his family a lengthy introduction about me in Urdu in which he said God knows what.

"I told them you are Joe the hero," he said as he reached for my wrist once more. "When you speak, you make the ground shake."

Aakef seated me next to him at their round white plastic dinner table in the living room where a meal of spicy lamb biryani and naan bread was already set. While we ate, Aakef's wife and children remained silent, only making noise to swallow their food.

"They understand that a man needs quiet to get know his guest," he explained.

And get to know me did, or rather the person he thought I was, a Palestinian-American Muslim named Joe. He asked me all kinds of questions about my childhood in America, my family, and my connection with my supposed homeland of Palestine.

"It surprises me you don't hate the Jews," Aakef stated as he gnawed on a lamb leg. "I thought all people with Arab blood hate the Jews."

"I don't hate anybody," I said. "When a person hates he is bound to make mistakes. He is incapable of thinking clearly. Hatred is the weakness of the Arabs."

"You are very wise, Joe. I hope your approach to life will lead to many Muslim victories. At the mosque, you described new ideas for defeating our enemies. The Jews are an especially tricky people to defeat. They bring so many problems to Muslims in this country. Perhaps with your tactics we may overcome them."

"Aakef, I'm confused. What kinds of problems do the Jews bring here?"

"Powerful Jews ruin everything. The Jews created all the problems between Pakistan and India. Without them, India, Pakistan, and Bangladesh would still be one country. Look at Kashmir. You know that without Jews, there would be no war in Kashmir. In Kashmir, the people are hungry for revenge against the Jews. You will see when you go there tomorrow. In Kashmir, there is a thirst for Jewish blood."

Just like that, I lost my appetite. I started feeling light-headed and sick to my stomach. Aakef sensed that I wasn't feeling well. His wife brought me a bottle of Coca Cola and I downed it in less than a minute. The ensuing sugar rush helped me perk up and feign interest in my conversation with Aakef. When it was time for bed, one of his sons hauled a thin mattress and some blankets into the living room and set them up near the door.

"You will sleep here, not in the boys' room," Aakef settled. "You will have privacy. I promise to wake you tomorrow very early."

That was nice of him to say, but I was out of his apartment long before he got out of bed. I had trouble sleeping, so in the middle of the night I just left. I wandered the streets for a while contemplating Aakef's chilling words: "In Kashmir, there is a thirst for Jewish blood." I couldn't make any sense out of why Kashmiris might believe Jews were responsible for their political problems.

I had decided to spend this break from school in India to get away from the Jewish conspiracy theories of the Arab world. But now I was about to go somewhere that was possibly just as bad, if not worse.

Most of the Arab world maintained some semblance of order, but rebel-filled Kashmir sounded like a lawless place, the kind where people took matters of vengeance into their own hands. It was a place where I didn't want trouble, so I'd have to exercise caution at all times. Once there I wouldn't tell a soul about my Jewish identity for any reason. When I arrived in the Kashmir capital, Srinagar, later that morning my anxiety was only heightened.

After the plane landed, a group of six armed Indian soldiers boarded to check every passenger's travel documents before allowing anyone to disembark. When one of the soldiers got to my row, he looked at me surprised, took my passport, and called his superior officer over. The officer marched up and ordered me to stand up from my seat, take my backpack, and follow him off the plane to a tiny cigarette smoke-filled office adjacent to the runway.

"You must register with the military," the officer said. "We haven't seen someone like you for a few weeks."

"Like me? An American?" I asked.

"No. A white man."

He then photocopied my passport, finger-printed me, took some additional headshots, and warned me about taking unnecessary risks in the area.

"Sir, now is a very volatile time in Kashmir," he said. "Just a few weeks ago there was a big attack on a tourist hotel in Srinagar. Ten people died. It is very important that you stay safe. In Kashmir, it is against the law for any tourist to be unaccompanied at any time. Here you don't trust anyone."

I was given permission to leave the office when a gruff representative from the tour agency, named Abdul, came and signed me out.

Abdul was short, but tough and sturdy, and had a thick black mustache and a permanently grumpy facial expression. I found out later he was only thirty, but his rough skin made him look a couple decades older than that. When he entered the room, he gave me no sign of acknowledgement. Instead, he pointed at me, mumbled something to the Indian officer, and reached for a pen. I felt like I was stuck in a neglected daycare for hapless tourists or something. I would soon learn that feeling would only get worse.

Abdul had been assigned to be my personal guide for my five-day tour. He was clearly not thrilled about that. He griped to me later that he had been promised tourists for weeks, but none had come. Then, the day before I booked my tour, Abdul bought an expensive bus ticket to go back to his native village far off in the mountains where his wife and children lived. When Abdul was told he had to be my guide, he couldn't get a refund for his bus ticket.

It didn't help matters that I was coming by myself. With big groups, Abdul could expect to get a big tip. With just me though, his profit potential was small. All this frustrated Abdul a great deal and he took it out on me.

For the two days I stayed in Srinagar I was put up in a room on a houseboat in the middle of Dal Lake, a beautiful eighteen square kilometer body of water famous for its floating gardens. Getting from the shore to the houseboat and back required hiring a *shikara*, a small wooden paddled taxi boat.

Any miscellaneous transportation I needed during the trip was supposed to be included in the fee I'd paid in Delhi. Abdul even assured me of that the first time we took a *shikara* to the houseboat. However, every time thereafter that I wanted to leave the houseboat to go off into the city, Abdul changed his tune and yelled at me to pay up.

"If you are wanting to see your bag and your things again, you will give the money!" he threatened before one *shikara* trip back to the houseboat.

Needless to say, seeing the sights of Srinagar with Abdul was less than pleasant. At a large street festival in honor of *Eid*, he rebuked me whenever I haggled with craftsmen over souvenirs. At every one of the famous gardens and palaces I requested to see, he demanded that I put up the cash not only for my own entrance fee, but for his as well.

"I am with you always. Without me, you no go in!" he stated.

Unfortunately, Abdul took his responsibility to accompany me everywhere very, very seriously. Sometimes I tried wandering off when he stopped to talk to someone he knew. But every time I did, it only led to more confrontation.

"You no respect me? You no respect me we have big problem!" he warned.

I tried my hardest to remain upbeat. I reminded myself that I still had three days of scenic hiking to look forward to. I told myself that, perhaps once Abdul and I were out of town and surrounded by glorious nature, we might get along better. It wasn't like he had a personal vendetta against me of any kind. Or did he?

The night before we left for the wilderness, Abdul and I were sitting in silence on the floor of the houseboat eating a meal of mutton and rice by candlelight when he initiated a very peculiar conversation.

"I am thinking about you today," he said. "I think you are Jew!"

"I'm not a Jew, Abdul," I denied.

"You are sure? If you are Jew, I must know."

"Abdul, I'm a Christian," I lied.

"Tell me again if you are Jew!" he insisted without answering my question. "Tell me if you are Jew."

"I'm not a Jew!" I snapped back. "Nothing about me is Jewish, Abdul. Nothing. I am not a Jewish person. What the hell is your problem?"

Abdul refused to answer. He just glanced at me with cold, heartless eyes and laughed while he stuffed rice into his mouth. He didn't say another word to me for the rest of the night. Suddenly, I was even less excited about wandering through the Kashmiri wilderness with him as my guide. Nevertheless, I went.

The next morning Abdul drove us in a dilapidated, 1980s-era Fiat about sixty kilometers on a muddy, barely passable road to a small wooden cabin in a tiny village that served as our base for trekking. The village was inhabited by only a few dozen people from the Gujjar tribe, a people of traditionally nomadic shepherds that included Abdul as a member. While Abdul spoke with the spry four-and-a-half-foot-tall elderly woman who would be cooking our meals during our stay, a group of three small boys with yellowish snot dripping from their noses ran up to me to give me high-fives.

"Islam, Islam! Muslim?" one asked me as he wiped his nose and slapped my hand. When I shook my head to say that I was not a Muslim, he screamed *"Baksheesh!"* The other boys screamed *"Baksheesh!"* after him and they all stuck out their hands demanding a cash reward. I pretended like I didn't understand and just patted them on the heads.

During the trek that day, I did my best to keep some distance between me and Abdul. I stuffed iPod headphones into my ears even when my iPod was turned off. I made sure that wherever we walked, whether over a steep forested slope or through a flower-filled meadow, Abdul was always at least ten feet ahead of me. Still, I think that being in the mountains actually had a soothing effect on him. During some of our water breaks, he started some friendly conversation with me. Specifically, he let me know I was welcome to collect hashish if I saw it growing in a field somewhere and that if I wanted to pass the night with one of the village prostitutes I just had to tell him and he'd set it up.

"If you no sleep with village lady you are crazy, crazy man!" he emphasized.

It was only on our way back to the village that evening that Abdul returned to the disturbing topic of the night before.

"If you are Jew I must tell the village people," he told me. "They must know there is Jew here."

Feeling a little nervous that Abdul might confess his thirst for Jewish blood right there on the spot, I diverted the conversation back to hashish and prostitutes, a subject I knew interested him a great deal.

We reached the village soon after dark. It being right on the cusp of winter, the temperature dropped to well below freezing, and the sky opened up with light snow flurries. Our cabin wasn't well insulated so I put on every piece of clothing I had. After eating dinner, Abdul said that most of the other residents were going to spend that evening drinking chai and enjoying the warmth of the only cabin in the village with a functioning indoor fireplace.

"It is the home of the village leader," he clarified. "He is very wise man. Very important for Gujjar people. We go there now."

"Sounds good. What's this leader's name?" I asked.

"He is called Bob."

"Bob?"

"Yes, Bob. You are guest in the village. You must meet him. You must give Bob respect."

Not wanting to show any disrespect, I braved the bitter cold and marched with Abdul a few hundred feet to a cabin with smoke billowing out of its chimney. When we got within a few feet of the front door, I saw a strange sticker pasted on it that I never expected to see in Kashmir. Though it was very small and the colors were faded, it surprised me more than all the six-pointed stars, swastikas, and Hebrew-speaking Indian passport officials put together.

"Abdul, why is there an Israeli flag on the door?" I asked, truly befuddled.

"Israeli flag is the flag for Gujjar people," Abdul said. "Israeli people and all Jew people are brothers to Gujjar people. I like them very much."

"Abdul, I'm Jewish!" I shouted ecstatically. Once again, I couldn't keep my mouth shut.

"You are Jew? Before you say you are not Jew. If you are Jew, then I like you very much. You are my brother."

Abdul opened the door and brought me inside the cabin, where a group of about fifteen villagers were huddled inside. An old, bald man with black glasses with frames in the shape of ovals sat on a creaking rocking chair bundled up in wool blankets. Abdul whispered to me that this was the incredible Bob and that I should go introduce myself to him at once.

"Hello Mr. Bob," I said standing over him. "My name is Michael. Thank you for having me. I wish you could speak English so we could communicate because I have no idea what's going on here."

Bob looked up at me and waved for me to come close to him.

"I speak English fine," he declared in a surprisingly authentic-sounding British accent. "I learned English from working with British officers who lived here before Indian independence. They gave me the name Bob because they didn't like my Kashmiri name. That is why I am called Bob."

"I see," I said as I sat on the ground next to him. Abdul, who was suddenly smiling at me, came over to hand me a cup of chai. "Why do you have an Israeli flag on your door? My guide Abdul said Gujjars and the Jews are brothers?"

"Yes, of course we are. All Gujjar people are part of *Bani Israel* (the local pronunciation of "*B'nai Israel*," Hebrew for the "Children of Israel"). We are part of the nation of Israel. The Jews and the state of Israel are blessed. We love all Jews who come. We put the flag up to show Israeli people that Kashmir is like their home."

"Bob, you and all the other Gujjar people are Muslim?"

"Yes."

"Interesting. I haven't heard too many Muslims speak about the Jews and Israel like you do. I am a student at a university in the UAE. The people there don't think the same way as you."

"In the Qur'an, it says that the Jews are Allah's people. It says that the land of Israel belongs to them. Many Muslims today have problems with Jews because of all the problems the Arabs make. The Arabs mix up their political problems with religion. Sometimes men from Saudi Arabia come here to teach us their ways. We chase them out of here. They are men who believe they have the real Islam. But they do not. They use their religion to hate and destroy. That is not Islam. In

Kashmir, we have a saying about the Arabs. 'The Arabs were the first to receive the Qur'an and the first to toss it away.'"

"I was told by someone in Delhi that people in Kashmir don't like Jews very much."

"There are those people. In Kashmir we have our problems. Those are the ones the Saudis talk to when we kick them out. But don't fear. In Gujjar territory, the Jews are safe. When a Jewish person comes here the people become extremely happy. You will see. You will be like a celebrity here when they find out."

So I was. For the rest of my time based there, I spent my days hiking with Abdul through more places of breathtaking beauty and my nights meeting villagers intent on welcoming me. No one besides Bob and Abdul spoke much English, so conversation was fairly limited. Thankfully, Abdul truly turned over a new leaf with me. He stopped being bitter about not being able to make much money off me and looked on the bright side.

"I bring Jew to the village. For this the people like me. So everything is okay," he said.

The morning I was set to leave the village with Abdul to return to Srinagar and catch a bus out of Kashmir, Bob stopped by my cabin to see me off.

"After India, will you be going back to the UAE?" he asked. "You're going back to all those Arabs?"

"Yup," I answered."

"Good. You must show the Arabs that the Jews are their brothers, not their enemies. Enjoy your remaining time in India. I hope when you go back to the UAE, the people there greet you with open hearts."

I did too.

Chapter 12
The Chocolate of the Jews

Sharjah, UAE
November 2006

MY FIRST DAY BACK IN SHARJAH IN EARLY NOVEMBER I MET UP with Ahmad Jew right outside the classroom where my course on US-Middle Eastern relations was about to start. He and Ahmad Greasy had spent the *Eid* break visiting their families in Jerusalem, and they kindly smuggled in a few Israeli chocolate bars to give me as presents. The UAE, like most members of the Arab League, boycotted all Israeli products and decreed possession of them illegal.

"You should eat them all now," Ahmad Jew advised as he handed them over to me. "The longer you wait to eat them, the more likely it is you'll get in trouble for having them."

As I put the chocolate bars in my backpack, an Emirati from my class named Saad walked up to us with a surprised expression on his face.

"Now that looks like something I've never tried before," he said.

For Saad that was saying something. Born into one of Abu Dhabi's wealthiest and most influential families, he was assertive, savvy, and spoke English with a perfect American accent. He was used to the finer things in life and was the type of person that had to have whatever caught his attention, even if it came from Israel.

"Can I take one?" he asked. I offered him an Elite milk chocolate bar with popping candy inside. "You have a lot of candy there. Would you mind sharing some with the rest of the class too?"

I told him I didn't mind. I thanked Ahmad Jew and followed Saad into the classroom, where he immediately made an announcement to the seven students already seated.

"Listen everyone!" he yelled. "Michael has brought us the chocolate of the Jews. It comes from Jerusalem! Take some now. You might not get another chance to try it ever again!"

Immediately, everyone came up to get an up-close view of my forbidden fruit. After removing a chocolate bar from my backpack, I tried passing it to a secular Saudi girl, but she moved her hands away frantically, as if the candy was radioactive. When I offered it to the Kuwaiti guy next to her, he refused to touch it as well.

"You're all babies," Saad declared as he bit into the popping candy chocolate bar. "Oh my God," he then yelled sarcastically. "The candy is exploding in my mouth! I'm going to die. The Zionists have done it again!" The other students froze. "I'm just joking. It's not poison. Just eat the Jewish chocolate already."

With that, the other students grabbed all my chocolate bars and passed around samples of the different types to each other.

"I'm not dead," the Saudi girl confirmed. "And these are pretty good."

Seeing that the only ones not partaking in the chocolate feast were Rania and Yasmine, the two Lebanese girls who told me Starbucks is evil because it supposedly supports Israel, I brought a candy bar over to them and offered them a taste. Rania glanced down at the chocolate and cautiously put a piece in her mouth. Yasmine immediately scolded her.

"You shouldn't eat that!" she chided. "It's from Israel. What about the boycott?"

"We didn't buy it ourselves. Besides, the wrapper was already open," Rania said defensively. "But it's good. Try some."

Yasmine broke off a tiny piece, examined it carefully, and placed it between her lips.

"*Walla*, this Jewish chocolate is amazing!" she announced a moment later. "I shouldn't be eating this, but it's like really good. Israel may be bad, but it makes great chocolate."

As surprising as this mellowing of anti-Israel sentiment was, it was nothing compared to what an Emirati named Maher expressed a few nights later when we drove around in his Ford Bronco. A brawny local enrolled in the AUS intensive English program, he dreamed of getting a degree in international relations and serving as a diplomat. Since his English language skills weren't adequate to represent anything other than himself, he'd invite me to join him on long drives, where he would practice his English.

That night we were driving on a rural desert road when he flipped on his car stereo to a pre-selected song. Blasting from the speakers a few seconds later was a Hebrew prayer.

"*Baruch ata adonai. Baruch ata yerushalayim.*" Blessed are you, God. Blessed are you Jerusalem.

Then, reggae beats boomed and I realized it was the song "Jerusalem" by the reggae singer Alpha Blondy.

"I was reading about Israel," Maher said. "You tell me all about Israel before, so I go to websites to learn about this country."

"Really? What did you find out?" I asked.

"I read about Israel's government. They have parliament there with prime minister and elections. I like it. I want to take Israeli government style and put it in UAE. But shhh. It is important you don't say I say this!"

"Your secret is safe."

"Michael, I also look up what Zionist is, but it is confusing. What is Zionist?"

I understood why Maher was confused. Zionism has never been a monolithic ideology with one simple set of ideas and principles. There are secular Zionists, religious Zionists, socialist Zionists, revisionist Zionists, neo-Zionists, and post-Zionists all with their own nuances and differing outlooks. I answered Maher's question by emphasizing the one value I believed all Zionists had in common.

"A Zionist is someone who believes the Jewish people have the right to live in their homeland like all other peoples," I said. "The Jewish homeland is Israel. Zionists believe that, just like Emiratis have the right to live in the UAE and Egyptians have the right to live in Egypt, Jews should have the right to live in Israel."

"Michael," Maher whispered.

"Maher," I whispered back.

"I am Zionist!" he yelled before erupting in laughter. "Shhh!" he said holding his finger to his mouth. "It is important you don't say I say this to no one. But I think Israel is good. Maybe one day I can be UAE ambassador to Israel."

"That would be great."

"I am Emirati Zionist. I will make UAE and Israel very good friends."

"Go talk to the sheikhs and make it happen."

"I will. You will see."

That was a day I very much looked forward to. Although the UAE and Israel had no official diplomatic ties, they'd also never been actively at war with each other. The notion that, in the future, Israel and the UAE could establish full diplomatic and commercial relations excited me and I was glad I knew one Emirati who was supportive of the idea.

True to Bob's words, the tide even seemed to change with some of those people who had expressed deep hatred of me.

At the free dinners held in the *iftar* tent during Ramadan, I had occasionally conversed with a short, pudgy Iraqi guy named Nawar. Originally from Iraq, Nawar's father had held some high-up position in Saddam Hussein's government (though Nawar refused to divulge what it was). He and his family defected to the UAE when coalition forces invaded Iraq in 2003. The sudden upheaval from his homeland had left Nawar bitter and angry. He remained an ardent supporter of Saddam Hussein and frequently declared Sunni Islam to be the one legitimate religion of Iraq. He also mistrusted anyone he perceived as being responsible for the removal of Saddam Hussein from power, namely the US government, Shiites, and Jews.

When I first met Nawar during Ramadan and acknowledged being the Jew of Sharjah, he told me exactly what he thought of my tribe.

"The Jews are the enemies of all true Iraqis," he alleged. "I have no choice but to hate them and you. A true Iraqi must hate his enemy."

"You hate all Jews?" I asked. "Even me? You don't even know me."

"I hate all Jews. I have no choice."

That lack of choice, though, didn't stop Nawar from sitting and talking with me in the *iftar* tent. Most of the time, our conversations would involve him spouting some kind of insensitive anti-Jewish vitriol, and me refuting it.

"Jewish people always talk about the Holocaust," he said once. "Everyone knows it didn't happen like they say it did. Jews exaggerated it to control America and conquer Palestine."

"I'm going to tell you this once," I replied. "The Holocaust was the most well-documented genocide in human history. Most people in the West don't question that it happened because there's so much proof."

"Fine, let's say it did happen the way the Jews say. So what? Everyone always asks what the Germans did to the Jews. No one has the guts to ask what the Jews did to the Germans. That's the problem. I want to know more about what the Jews did to deserve what the Germans did to them."

Most of my conversations with Nawar gave me headaches. But when I bumped into him in the Student Center cafeteria shortly after I returned from India, he had some pleasing things to tell me.

"I've been thinking about you a lot," he said. "I decided I don't hate you anymore."

"That's great, Nawar. What made you decide this?" I asked.

"We don't agree about many things. But every time we talk you are still very nice to me. I could not understand how a person can be a Jew and be a nice person at the same time. I realized I must accept it is possible to be both."

"I'm glad you finally see that."

"That's not all. I told my family about you too. I told them I know this Jew who is actually a nice person. They were very interested. They said they would like to meet this Jew. I asked if I could invite you for dinner sometime next week and they said yes. Will you come?"

"Of course."

"Excellent. I am very eager to have a Jew in my house."

To my astonishment, this new openness towards me didn't end with Nawar. The day after Nawar extended the invitation to his home, a devout Lebanese Shiite girl from Abu Dhabi named Hala called me up to ask me to meet her in the library.

"I need your help with something. I can't talk about it on the phone," she said.

A short, pale-skinned girl who tucked the earpieces of her eyeglasses safely inside her hijab, Hala was one of the sweetest people I'd met during my time at AUS. She always made sure to say hello to me whenever she saw me, even if I hadn't noticed her, and she regularly offered me cookies from the most recent batch she'd baked.

Despite Hala's kindness, I was apprehensive about spending time with her one-on-one. Our only substantial private conversation hadn't ended well. Shortly after the ceasefire between Israel and Hezbollah took effect right at the start of the term in late August, Hala and I were sitting on a couch in the Student Center when she revealed her identification with Hezbollah and her admiration for its leader, Hassan Nasrallah. She asserted that Hezbollah militants were the "eternal heroes of Lebanon" and that "Hassan Nasrallah is the most righteous man" she could think of.

"Do you think so too?" she asked me naively.

Not wanting to crush her spirit with details, I replied with a simple no.

"Why not?" she asked. "Do you believe Hezbollah is a terrorist group?"

"I do," I affirmed.

"But why?"

"Hezbollah is a terrorist group because it conducts terror attacks and targets innocent civilians. In Argentina, it blew up a Jewish community center and the Israeli embassy. In Israel, their fighters routinely murder women and children in cold blood. Hassan Nasrallah tells his followers to destroy Israel and kill as many Jews as possible. As a result, I don't like Hassan Nasrallah or Hezbollah."

Hala began to bawl in response. She wasn't angry, just very, very hurt. Hezbollah clearly meant a great deal to her. I reassured Hala that my opinion of Hezbollah had nothing to do with her personally and that I very much wanted us to be friends. She removed her glasses to wipe the tears from her eyes.

"I hope we can be," she whimpered. "But you are also my enemy. I don't hate you even though I know I should hate my enemy. Is this what people mean when they call someone a 'frenemy?'"

"I don't think so."

When I met her in the library for our second chat, we sat down across from each other at a table near some bookshelves. I felt slightly anxious wondering what she wanted to talk about, since I didn't need another conversation to end with her in tears.

"I have to do a presentation for my English literature class on a foreign language of my choice," she started off. "I chose Hebrew. Will you teach me about Hebrew?"

"Hala, why Hebrew?" I asked. "Why not French or Swahili or Thai or something?"

"Because I think Hebrew is important. I don't know anything about it. Since Israel is a country in the Middle East, it would be good for people at AUS to learn about it too. The professor said it was okay, so that's what I'm going to do." And, if that was what she was going to do, then I was of course going to assist her.

Her presentation was set for a week later and, every day until then, I got together with Hala to teach her the Hebrew alphabet, basic sentence structure, and the history of how the modern Hebrew language came into being. I avoided discussing topics of a political nature with her during our meetings, but sometimes it was inevitable. The more she learned about Hebrew the more she wanted to know about Israel. She asked me about the different kinds of people who lived there, how the political system worked, and what Israelis thought about Lebanon. She even confided that she had family members who spoke Hebrew from the days of the Israeli occupation of southern Lebanon.

"They did not like the Israelis, but they respected them," she claimed. "When the Israeli army was in southern Lebanon, there was order. If someone stole something from you the Israelis would find out who did it and return your property to you. I am jealous that my cousins know Hebrew and I don't. Maybe if my Hebrew gets good enough I can speak it to them. Maybe I will have the chance to speak Hebrew to an Israeli one day." Little did Hala know she might get that opportunity sooner than she realized.

I sent Guy an email from Salim's computer briefing him on all the remarkable developments in Sharjah. Guy answered that he wished he could book a flight to see Sharjah for himself. To this I encouraged him to come visit in early December on his American passport. Since Guy used his Israeli passport to travel in and out of Israel, his American passport was clean of any Israeli stamps. After some more back and forth, Guy purchased a round-trip plane ticket from Amman to Sharjah.

Our plan was spontaneous, but we thought we could pull it off. Obviously, once Guy stepped foot in the UAE, his Israeli identity would be our little secret. He was only going to be in Sharjah with me for four days. I was sure nothing would go wrong. Unfortunately, almost immediately after Guy booked his trip, the newfound openness I'd started to witness around me at AUS came to a grinding halt.

Nawar never picked a day for me to join him and his family for dinner. I didn't know why, but I had a bad feeling something was not quite right. When I bumped into him in the cafeteria the next week and asked him about it, he became visibly anxious and was incapable of looking me in the eye.

"Listen Michael," he mumbled. "I'm very, very sorry, but dinner isn't going to work out. My parents changed their minds. They wouldn't agree to having a Jew eat with us at our table. My father said the Jews are the enemy and that this would not change for as long as he lived. I was going to call you to tell you, but I was too embarrassed."

"Don't worry about it," I said.

"No really, I'm *very* embarrassed. Let me take you to dinner tonight. Please. I must make this up to you. I insist."

Since he insisted, I consented to going out with him that evening to a traditional Arabic restaurant. However, while I shoveled down lamb meat and rice, Nawar barely ate. He just sat across watching me anxiously. I tried reassuring him he had no reason to feel embarrassed and that he had already more than made it up to me. But his mood remained unchanged. He simply watched me eat and stared repeatedly at his watch.

"Are you okay? Do you have to go somewhere?" I asked.

"No, no!" he denied.

"Alright. You're acting weird. Are you sure everything's fine?"

 He paused and looked away.

"I think you are a spy!"

"You and who else?" I asked as I leaned back in my chair.

"My father too. We were talking about it. That's the other reason you can't come over."

"How sure are you that I'm a spy, Nawar?"

"Um. About seventy percent."

Ugh. This was crazy. I was fed up, so I decided to have some fun.

"Only seventy percent, Nawar? Well, if I'm a spy then tell me who you're working for."

"I am not a spy!"

"Come on, Nawar!" I yelled. "Tell me the truth. Tell me who you're working for and we'll settle the score once and for all. Who knows? Maybe we're working for the same people."

"I am not a spy. It's the truth."

"Neither am I, Nawar."

"Yes, you are. Listen very carefully. My father wanted me to give you a message to deliver to your Jewish bosses."

"My Jewish bosses? You can't be serious."

"Listen!" he said intensely. "My father and I hate Israel very, very much. We hope that one day the Arab people destroy Israel once and for all. But, we hate the Shiites more. If Israel bombs those Shiite sons of bitches in Iran, we will tell all true Iraqis to raise and salute the Israeli flag for three days. After that we will continue fighting our war with the Jews."

A few days later, after Hala gave her presentation on the Hebrew language to her English literature class, I learned how far Nawar was willing to go to display his hatred of Shiites and Jews.

I called up Hala after her presentation to find out how it went. No answer. I called again. She picked up the phone for a split second and hung up without saying anything. I thought I heard sobbing in the background, but I wasn't sure. She sent me a text message fifteen minutes later asking me to meet her outside the library. When I got there, I found her crying her eyes out with her hands covering her face. A few people standing around hurried inside the building to avoid the awkwardness of being near a weeping girl they didn't know.

"The students . . . yelled at me . . . the whole . . . time," she cried. "They . . . wouldn't . . . let me . . . present."

"What did they say?" I asked.

"'You are . . . a traitor. Why did . . . you pick . . . this horrible language? It's an . . . evil language.'"

"Didn't your professor step in? Didn't he try to quiet them down?"

Slowly, Hala started regained some composure.

"He tried, but then they started yelling at me in Arabic," she said. "He's an American, so he didn't know what to do. He told me I could do my presentation for him later in his office."

"I'm sorry it didn't go well."

"The worst one in the class was this one Iraqi boy, Nawar."

"Nawar? I know Nawar. What did Nawar do?"

"He screamed at me in Arabic. He said, 'You are a Jew lover! You are working with the Jewish spy to destroy all of us. The Shiites will work with the most treacherous enemy to harm the Sunni nation.'"

"Nawar is nuts. Surely people know that. Don't worry about it."

"People listened to him. They hate Shiites and Jews and they hate me. I hate Nawar more than anything."

"It's over, Hala. Don't worry about what Nawar or anyone else says about you. Words can't hurt you."

Unless they were backed up by very real threats that is. Partially due to Hala's presentation, more nasty rumors spread about me on campus. According to Mo, Hassan and company were saying I was brainwashing students with hidden messages in Hebrew and handing out Israeli chocolate bars laced with hormones specifically engineered to make Arabs infertile. I intended to let these rumors pass unanswered and carry on with my normal routine. I didn't care anymore who listened to Hassan and his drones.

"You should care," Mo told me over the phone one night. "They're planning something crazy. We need to talk. I'm at the picnic tables outside the Student Center. When you get here I'll tell you what's going on."

In spite of the urgent tone of Mo's voice, I didn't dash over as quickly as I could have to get the latest scoop on the silly conspiracies of Hassan and his friends. I took my time and strolled over to meet Mo feeling completely calm and relaxed. By then, I was totally desensitized to Hassan's antics. Whatever it was that Mo had to say would have to be truly shocking to elicit more than a yawn from me.

"Hassan and his friends are talking about taking you to the desert and doing something bad to you!" Mo said emphatically, leaning against one of the tall orange sidewalk lamps that lit up the area. "If they invite you to the desert, don't go with them. Promise me! If they try to grab you run as fast as you can."

"Whoa, whoa, whoa, Mo!" I retorted. "What exactly do they want to do to me?"

Right away, images of the scene from the 1962 film *Lawrence of Arabia*—in which Turkish soldiers brutally whip and rape T. E. Lawrence—flashed through my mind. Was something like that going to happen to me?

"All I know is that nothing good happens in the desert. If you go with them it will be bad for you. Hassan says what you're doing at AUS is out of control. He says your Jewish presence here pollutes everything, and that he'd rather have your blood fill the sands of the desert then let your voice utter another word of evil."

"If he has this much of a problem with me then why has he never come to talk to me? Why have none of them ever come to talk to me?"

"They're scared of talking to you. They're scared of arguing with you. Look, they probably won't do anything. I just felt like I had to tell you. It's probably all talk like it always is."

Probably wasn't good enough for me. I could deal with Hassan and company slandering me behind my back. I could not, however, live knowing they were possibly coordinating a plot to physically hurt me, or worse. I considered immediately reporting the threat to the AUS administration or the police. I opted not to only because I thought Mo's testimony was too vague to be taken seriously, and I didn't want to create an incident that would make Hassan and his friends look like martyrs to the rest of the student body. Instead I decided that before I took this issue to the powers that be, I had to confront my foes and try to make peace. That was, after all, what I'd gone to the Arab world to do in the first place.

I located Hassan and most of his crew the next evening. They were sitting around a bunch of pushed-together tables in the mostly empty cafeteria. For a while, I watched them from a place where I could see them, but they couldn't see me, and tried to prepare myself for a tense encounter. The more I watched them, the more I despised them.

They were laughing and smiling and enjoying each other's company, as if not a thing in the world bothered them. Hanging around these enemies of mine were a few not-so-religious-looking girls wearing tight jeans and loose blouses. Small speakers perched on one of the tables played a mix of rap music. They were hypocrites, I thought. For people that constantly preached about upholding Islamic values and protecting Islam from heathens like me, they appeared awfully secular.

When I finally felt ready to face them, I walked over with a strut in my step and a cheerful smile on my face. When they saw me, all conversation ceased and at least one person gasped. I said hello and asked everyone how they were doing. A few uttered incoherent responses and the rest remained speechless. They looked anxious. I could tell they were scared. So was I.

After a few seconds of awkward silence, Hassan, skinny, sly Hassan, stood up from his chair and offered me his hand. I shook it. It was wet with sweat, and not just because he'd been outside in the heat for too long.

"Michael, it's good to see you," he said. "How can we help you?"

"I'd like to speak with you and your friends about some things that have been bothering me lately," I said. "Would that be possible?"

Hassan glanced around at his buddies apprehensively.

"We're actually all working on homework right now. Could we do this some other time?"

"Really, this will only take a few minutes. But, if this is an inconvenient time for your friends, could I just speak to you?"

"Sure, let's go outside, so we won't disturb everyone."

I followed Hassan out the door situated just a few feet away and we stopped in front of a glass window in view of all his friends. Instead of returning to their "homework," they stared at us with a mix of curiosity and concern.

"Thanks for agreeing to speak with me, Hassan," I began. "Ever since I met you the night before classes began, a lot of very nasty rumors have gone around about me. Everyone tells me these rumors were started by you. What I want to know is why you and your friends choose to say things about me behind my back instead of saying them to my face."

"I don't know what you're talking about," he responded dryly. "I only say good things about you. You are my friend, Michael."

"No, we're not friends, Hassan. Cut the crap. You have huge problems with me and I'm asking you to talk to me like a man. All I want is to work our issues out before anything bad happens. Now, stop being a little bitch and tell me what I can do to get you and your homeboys to stop talking shit."

"Why did you come to Sharjah?" he shouted all of a sudden. "Tell me why you came here."

"Seriously? What the hell is wrong with you? I came here because I wanted to meet and become friends with people like you, so that I could help make things better between Jews and Arabs. That's why I came here. How do you not get that?"

"There will never be good relations between Arabs and Jews. Or Muslims and Jews. It says so in the Qur'an. The Jews work with Satan. There will never be peace."

"Don't you realize how nutty everything you believe is? If you decide right now that all the problems that exist between Muslims and Jews are unsolvable because of your religion, then you've doomed everyone to an eternity of war."

"All Jews are liars."

"You call me and my people liars? You're the liar. You're the imposter. You smile, shake my hand, and pretend to be my friend while you talk with your friends about having some fun with me in the desert."

Hassan's eyes got big and he started to stutter.

"I . . . I don't know what you are talking about," he claimed. "That is not true."

"Coward!" I shouted with a finger pointed at him. "Listen to me carefully. I don't want to waste any more time thinking about you and your stupid friends. If I hear any more rumors about you and your friends launching a jihad or laying a finger on me, I will unleash a reign of terror unlike anything your pampered Palestinian ass has ever felt. Stop talking shit or I'll make you regret it, Mr. Al Qaeda."

Hassan's hands shook and he looked scared to death. I liked seeing him like that. I felt a perverse satisfaction making him tremble with fear. Seriously out of control, I'd lost my ability to filter my words.

"Believe me when I say this, Hassan," I concluded. "You don't know me. You don't know who I am or where I come from or what I believe in. You also have no idea who I know or what I'm capable of doing to you and to all your friends. Leave me alone or I will make you suffer."

On that note, I went back inside the Student Center with a smile on my face, waved to Hassan's friends watching me with their mouths gaping open, and said "see you around" before walking off.

I never had another problem with Hassan or his friends again. Still, the confrontation jaded me and depleted me of any desire to remain in Sharjah for any longer than I had to. All I could think about after that was making another escape.

Chapter 13
Real Men of Hezbollah

Lebanon and Syria
November–December 2006

THEY WERE THE TWO ARAB COUNTRIES MY PARENTS SPECIFI-
cally forbade me from visiting before agreeing to let me traipse
around the Arab Middle East.

"If you go to Lebanon and Syria and you survive the trip, I'm going
to kill you," my father told me before I left for Sharjah, while a massive
blue vein bulged from his forehead. "I'm serious. If you come back
with Lebanese and Syrian stamps on your passport, I'm going to put
your head on a stick."

Lebanon and Syria weren't like Egypt and Jordan, which had peace
agreements with Israel or even the UAE, which, despite not having relations with Israel had never participated in a violent struggle
against it. Lebanon and Syria were self-declared enemies of the Jewish
state, committed to its destruction and, technically, still in an active
state of war with it.

Syria had a policy of granting Americans tourist visas only from
official consulates in the US. Since I wasn't about to mail my passport
across the world for a visa, travel there didn't seem likely. Lebanon
didn't require Americans to get a visa, but even I thought it was too
risky to dare a trip there. In the aftermath of Hezbollah's 2006 summer
war with Israel, Lebanon's economy had tanked, its infrastructure was
wrecked, and its government and population were heavily divided. It
didn't seem to me like the kind of place one went for a good time.

"What are you talking about?" Rania fired back at me in class days after sampling the Israeli chocolate. "Lebanon's got everything: weather, beach, skiing, night life. The parties never stop in Beirut. Ever."

Despite her enthusiasm, I didn't buy it. Yes, Beirut, the Lebanese capital, had once been called the "the Paris of the Middle East," and was known for its culture, secularism, wealth, and social scene. But that was back when Lebanon had a secular Christian majority and before it plunged into decades of civil war. While it had been reported that Lebanon had done an admirable job rebuilding itself as a tourist destination before the Israel-Hezbollah war, I was certain it was once again starting from scratch.

"You must believe me when I say Lebanon is the best Arab country," Yasmine added. "You have to go there to understand. There's a saying about Lebanon: 'Some days bring war. Some days bring peace. But every day brings a party!' In Lebanon, no one cares what your religion is. Everybody just wants to have a good time."

What Rania and Yasmine were saying contradicted every version of Lebanon's modern history I'd ever learned. Maybe there was truth in these contradictions, particularly because Rania and Yasmine seemed to symbolize that truth. Although Rania was a Sunni and Yasmine was a Shiite, they were best friends as far as I could tell. Neither one being especially religious, they left their hair uncovered and wore skin-tight outfits to show off their figures. They smoked cigarettes, drank alcohol, and worked as bartenders in Beirut during their summer vacations. To sum up, they did just about everything nice Muslim girls were supposed to avoid.

They told me they were planning a visit to Beirut for the few days we had off from classes in honor of the UAE National Day.

"You should come too," Rania said. "We'll take you to the best parties in Gemmayzeh and on Rue Monot. You'll meet so many people. You'll love Lebanon."

"If you don't go now, when will you?" Yasmine asked.

That was a fair question. If I didn't at least investigate the possibility of going to Lebanon, my wanderlust would nag me to my core.

Quite a few AUS students were arranging trips to Lebanon for the break. Everyone I talked to promised me that if I came, I'd always have a place to sleep as well as access to a refrigerator. That made me feel more secure, but I still felt the need to have a constant travel companion.

So, I invited Jake and Ahmad Jew to come along. Ahmad Jew said yes immediately. To be clear, he held serious grievances against the Lebanese for their treatment of Palestinians. Of the 400,000 Palestinian refugees living in Lebanon, most were deprived of basic rights, such as working in numerous professions, not having the right to vote, owning property, access to high-quality health care, or traveling without special permits. Nevertheless, Ahmad Jew had friends of friends in Beirut and was eager to experience the city's nightlife.

Jake was more hesitant about my proposition. For him, planning a trip to Lebanon meant having to go through the hassle of ordering a new passport. He'd traveled to Israel and Egypt during our *Eid* break and an Israeli border official had stamped his passport, rendering him unable to visit countries unfriendly to Israel, such as Lebanon and the UAE. Only thanks to Allah's good graces did the UAE immigration officials fail to notice the mark of the Zionist entity on his passport and let him back into the country.

"I'm just glad they didn't search my stuff and find my Israeli coins," he'd said.

Lebanon, we thought, would be far more thorough in its screening process.

When I found round-trip airfare to Beirut for one hundred and twenty dollars per ticket, Jake agreed it was a steal. We bought the tickets, and Jake applied for and received a new US passport shortly thereafter. Ahmad Jew, on the other hand, told us he'd buy his ticket later after he figured out how much time he could take off from classes.

Jake emailed his parents right after making the purchase to let them know of his plans. Jake's parents, unlike mine, had no personal ties to any place or anyone in the Middle East. Lebanon, Israel, the UAE—all those countries were one and the same to them. They had no apprehension about their son roaming around countries hostile to Israel and Jews. Therefore, they could handle the truth.

Mine could not. If my parents knew I could so blatantly go against their one demand of me, they would have fought with me every day until the trip. They might have cancelled my credit and debit cards, leaving me stripped of cash. And if I managed to find a way to access money and went to Lebanon anyway, they would have worried non-stop.

I hated the thought of causing my parents unnecessary stress. So, like a good son, I lied.

"I'm going on a camping trip for a week in the Omani desert with some friends from school. We'll be somewhere near Muscat," I explained over the phone the week before the trip. "There won't be any reception, so I won't be able to call or email you. Don't worry. I promise I'll be alive the next time you see me."

As my departure date approached, I began to fear that was one promise I might not be able to keep. Lebanon's government came out of the 2006 war more fractured than at any point since the end of the civil war in 1990. Hezbollah, though badly weakened by Israel, emerged from the war more politically emboldened than ever. Hezbollah's leadership demanded the creation of a national unity government that would have granted them a third of the cabinet seats, veto power, and the ability to bring down a governmental coalition. When Lebanese Prime Minister Fouad Siniora rejected these demands outright, Hassan Nasrallah called on Hezbollah's loyal followers to get ready to take to the streets.

On November 21, 2006, Hezbollah-allied pro-Syrian gunmen assassinated Pierre Gemayel, a young Cabinet minister from one of Lebanon's most prominent Christian families, in his car. Eight hundred thousand people staged an anti-Syrian political rally at Gemayel's funeral, and the remaining members of the Lebanese Cabinet voted to create a UN-sponsored tribunal to investigate the assassination of former Lebanese Prime Minister Rafik Hariri, long suspected to have been carried out by Hezbollah and Syria. That slap in the face led Hezbollah officials to announce that protests would be launched any day and without warning to bring down the government.

This left the entire Arab world, not only Lebanon, gripped by a sense of impending doom. King Abdullah II of Jordan publicly stated that Lebanon might be on the brink of another civil war. Egyptian President Hosni Mubarak expressed concern that protests would lead to

Lebanon's complete destruction. Friends of mine at AUS urged me to change my plans.

"Don't go to Lebanon," Samira wrote in a text message after hearing the news about the Gemayel assassination. "Stay here! If anything happens to you, I will never forgive you."

"Don't worry," I wrote back. "I bet it's not as bad as it sounds. I promise I'll be careful. I'll have Jake and Ahmad (Jew) around to keep me out of trouble."

That ended up being only half true. Ahmad Jew ended up not buying the plane ticket to Beirut.

"I'm not going," he said, dejected, when he told me over the phone. "It's too dangerous for me. What if people try to hurt me because of my citizenship?"

"No one has to know you're Palestinian," I argued. "You have a Jordanian passport."

"No, I'm scared of them finding out I'm Israeli. They'll kill me."

"But you're an Arab. You're not an Israeli Jew."

"They don't see a difference. If things were calmer in Lebanon, I would go. But, with the way things are now, I can't risk it."

No big deal. It would have been nice to bring him along, but it wasn't like Jake and I wouldn't have anyone else in Lebanon to look out for us. At least that was what we thought. Then, a few days before we were set to leave, we found out that every person we knew who planned to travel there at the same time as us had already cancelled their trips, including Rania and Yasmine.

"It wasn't our fault," Rania swore when she broke the news to me in class days before our flight. "Our parents are overprotective."

"You should still go," Yasmine insisted. "There will still be parties going on for sure. Our parents are traumatized from the civil war. They worry that every time something bad happens in Lebanon the whole country will be thrown into chaos."

On November 30, 2006, Rania and Yasmine's parents' worries seemed legitimate. While we were already at the airport to catch our flight, Hezbollah leader Hassan Nasrallah gave a speech on television urging all opposition supporters to occupy downtown Beirut and launch street demonstrations the next day to force the Lebanese government out. Jake and I didn't find out until we were at the gate waiting to board our flight. We agreed it was too late to turn back.

Our plane itself was almost entirely empty of passengers, which gave us an eerie feeling. Around midnight we touched down. While Jake and I stood in the aisle waiting to get off the plane, we started talking to a tall, muscular man in his mid-thirties with American-accented English. He was a Lebanese Christian named George who had graduated from the University of Michigan with an engineering degree. He was now plying his trade in Ras al-Khaimah, one of the lesser-known emirates in the UAE, while his wife and son stayed in Beirut.

"My situation isn't so bad," George said. "I get to come back to Lebanon every month or so. This time I came back a few days earlier than my wife expects so I can party and meet some ladies."

George looked like someone ready to party and meet some ladies. He reeked of cologne, his hair was all gelled up, and he wore a light blue, button-down shirt half-way open, which exposed his clean-shaved chest. We went through passport control, where the border agent gave our passports half a glance, grabbed our backpacks at baggage claim, and walked out the airport exit with George. One solitary taxi driver waited outside to pick up customers.

"This is weird," George said. "The airport's usually packed with taxi drivers. I'm going to a club over on Rue Monnot. Come along and I'll help you find a hotel afterwards."

Jake and I said yes and George rushed off to get a rental car. He pulled up in front of us ten minutes later in a sleek black BMW X5 SUV. George drove us through the nicely-paved streets of Beirut like a mad man, accelerating down narrow one-way streets and pressing on the gas during sharp turns. Fortunately, there wasn't much risk of us crashing into anyone because we were practically the only ones on the road.

"What is going on here?" George asked furiously. "It's Thursday night. Why is this city so dead?"

George parked the SUV across from a club near Rue Monnot with thumping techno music blasting from inside. I looked up and down the street and didn't see anything else open. Every one of the dozens of other clubs, bars, and restaurants in the vicinity had shut their doors. George led us to the entrance and began chitchatting in Arabic with a surly bouncer with his bulky arms crossed.

"Sorry guys," George said after wrapping up their conversation. "I can't get you in because you didn't come with girls."

"You didn't come with girls either," I objected. "You came with us."

"Yeah, but I know people here. Let me go inside for a couple minutes to see what's going on. If it's good, I'll talk to my people. If it's not good, we'll go somewhere else."

Just like that George disappeared inside the club. Feeling lousy about being ditched, we walked back to the BMW and watched vehicles pass by. Taxi, taxi, tank, military jeep, tank, armored personnel carrier, tank, tank. The preponderance of military vehicles made Jake and me anxious. We paced around until George returned fifteen minutes later.

"There's hardly anyone in there!" he lamented obnoxiously as he unlocked the car's driver-side door. "Everyone's saying that tomorrow Hezbollah is going to blow this city up. I'm getting out of here. Take your bags. Good luck finding a hotel."

"But you said you'd help us find a hotel," I protested.

"Yeah, sorry. I can't do that anymore. I'm going home."

"Can you point us in the right direction at least?" Jake asked.

"Just go anywhere," George said. "I'm sure you won't have any trouble."

As ordered, we grabbed our backpacks from the trunk. George, the one person we knew in Beirut, drove off, leaving us alone in Beirut on a night when every local resident seemed to have the common sense to be at home. Well, except for those celebrating the last hours of stability before all hell broke loose.

As Jake and I scoured the thin Lebanon section of our *Lonely Planet Middle East* book outside the club, a light-skinned Christian named Pierre stepped out with his girlfriend, gave her a kiss goodbye, and came over to offer assistance. We explained we were looking for a hotel. He just frowned and raised an eyebrow.

"That's going to be tough at this hour," he said. "Right now, I'm actually supposed to go meet some friends at a restaurant. Tomorrow no one knows if there will still be a Lebanon, so we thought we'd celebrate this life with a last meal. If you come with me I will help you find some place to sleep afterwards."

Lacking any alternative, we followed Pierre to his family's luxurious penthouse apartment. He snatched the keys to his Audi and drove us to a twenty-four-hour fast food joint called "Zaatar With Zeit." We walked inside to a packed restaurant filled with young people in western garb talking, laughing, and eating what could only be described as fast food with a Lebanese twist. The three of us ordered French fries and sodas and sat down in a leather booth with two more of Pierre's Christian guy friends: Michel, a dark-skinned fellow with wavy black hair, and Bashir, who was shorter, had a beard, and brown hair parted down the middle.

They'd already begun wolfing down their zaatar-covered pita bread, chicken sandwiches, and cheese sauce-drenched pork hot dogs. Until that moment I hadn't encountered any type of food product with pig in it since leaving the US.

"You two are very brave and very stupid for coming to Lebanon now," Michel proclaimed. "What were you thinking?"

"We didn't know what was going on here until we couldn't turn back," I said.

"That's funny and sort of sad. We're going to the mountains tomorrow until everything calms down. My only hope is that Hezbollah doesn't throw a fit and ruin this country. The people who support Hezbollah think they can threaten anyone and get them to give in to their demands. I wish Israel had just finished them off this summer. Even if the Israelis had destroyed more of Lebanon, it would have still been better than waiting for Hezbollah to destroy everything now."

"Whoa!" I replied flabbergasted. "Are you saying you wanted Israel to destroy Hezbollah?"

"None of us wanted Israel to attack Lebanon," Bashir piped in before taking a quick bite of his chicken sandwich. "But we also didn't want Hezbollah to attack Israel. Hezbollah attacked and took those soldiers, Israel responded, Hezbollah survived, and Lebanon's going down the toilet. Muslims everywhere believe Hezbollah is this great hero even though all their territory in southern Lebanon was flattened."

"Was the war really terrifying?" Jake posed.

"No, not really," Pierre said while he glanced over at his friends for approval. "The media exaggerated everything. We all went up to the mountains and smoked *shisha*."

"But how did you know Israel wasn't going to bomb you there?" I interjected.

"Because the Israelis told everyone where they were going to bomb. They dropped leaflets with messages and instructions. The war wasn't a big deal if you knew where not to be. If you were Lebanese, you knew exactly where not to be."

"How did you feel when no Arab country intervened to help Lebanon?"

"It's always better when the other Arabs stay at home!" Michel asserted. "Most Christians don't care what happens between the Israelis and Palestinians. Let them fight their own fight. We also don't want to see one patch of Lebanon's grass get blown up ever again. But, if Israel could have defeated Hezbollah and really given it a knockout punch, it would have been okay. But Israel didn't do that. Israel hurt Lebanon without finishing off Hezbollah. Now, Hezbollah is stronger and Lebanon is weaker. And tomorrow Lebanon will pay the price once again."

"What will happen if we go to the protests tomorrow and tell people we're Americans?" Jake asked.

"Hezbollah will probably kill you."

True to his word, Pierre stuck with us until we found a room in a tiny hotel at four in the morning and collapsed into bed.

"Just so you know, this hotel is really close to the Lebanese Parliament building," Pierre told us before he left. "That's where the protests will be. I think both of you are out of your minds for being here, but I understand you're looking for some action. If you really want to see things get out of hand, go to Dahieh. It's a Shiite neighborhood in the south of the city. That's where the protests tomorrow will start. If you go there, try not to die. Tomorrow Dahieh will be a war zone."

Our elderly taxi driver said the same thing when we asked him to take us to Dahieh the next morning.

"There is nothing good in Dahieh," he claimed in Arabic while he started up the engine of his 1980s Mercedes-Benz taxi. "Why do you want to go to that place?"

"For tourism," I replied.

That was the truth. Dahieh was Hezbollah's capital and the main target of heavy Israeli Air Force bombing during the war. Jake and I were interested in viewing the physical results of the war. Our driver reluctantly consented and drove us south.

Once we left Beirut's city limits and entered Dahieh, the scenery changed dramatically. Gone were Beirut's wide boulevards and elegant buildings. In their place were sewage-filled roads with deep potholes and tall, gray apartment complexes. The neighborhood's only uplifting features were the pictures of smiling, handsome teenage boys plastered on billboards, signposts, buildings, and even on t-shirts small children wore. In all the photographs, the boys looked happy and full of life, as if they knew they were about to go someplace far better than the tragic wasteland of a neighborhood where they'd grown up.

"*Shahid, shahid,*" the taxi driver said as he pointed out the photos. Martyr, martyr. "Every boy you see is a *shahid*. They died in the war with Israel. They came from Dahieh."

Hearing those words made my heart sink. Few of the boys in the photographs seemed like they'd had much experience handling a shaving razor, much less a Kalashnikov. They looked like kids on a high school JV soccer team, not bloodthirsty terrorists. And now their lives were over, long before any of them had the chance to discover why life was worth living in the first place.

Our taxi driver dropped us off before a small cluster of one-story buildings with green and yellow Hezbollah flags pasted on them.

"Wait, wait. We said we wanted to see where the war happened," I said frantically in Arabic. "Where are we? How do we know if this is right?"

"I *know* what you want to see," the driver promised. "It is here. Look up at the buildings in front of us. Do you see any tall buildings behind them?" We didn't. "You see. You are in the right place."

We paid the driver, walked into a narrow alley, and emerged a few dozen feet later in a huge neighborhood of nothingness. Aside from a few bombed-out tall buildings, the entire place had been reduced to rubble. There were no roads, almost no buildings, and not a single living soul still inhabiting the area. Not even heaps of garbage could be seen. Former residents must have collected what they could salvage and let the rest burn.

Jake and I barely spoke while we explored. There just wasn't much to say. Gradually, we got tired of wandering around the flattened ghost town and yearned to return to the world of the living. Not knowing which direction to go, we followed the sounds of beating drums in the distance to the main road where hundreds of thousands of Shiites were marching towards Beirut to launch that day's protest.

The streets were noisy and jam-packed, but the scene was much calmer than we'd expected. Shiites of all ages marched together carrying signs, waving flags, and chanting. The marchers seemed peaceful, but Jake and I still worried about angering people and getting lynched in the street. We'd seen the destruction and mayhem these people had endured. I understood why they hated Israel and realized there was a good chance they hated America too.

"We should probably say we're from somewhere else to be safe," Jake reasoned. "How about Iceland? I bet no one speaks Icelandic."

"Yeah, that'll work. Let's be Icelandic."

As two Icelandic tourists, we moseyed through the crowd of people bent on overthrowing their government. Jake and I were practicing a fake Icelandic gibberish-language to be more authentic when a group of five teenage boys rushed over to us as we reached downtown Beirut and asked in English where we were from. When we told them Iceland, they gave us a look of bewilderment, signaling they had no idea where Iceland was. Their complete unfamiliarity with our adopted glacial homeland enticed them to ask us what we and other Icelandic people thought about Hezbollah.

"Do you like Hassan Nasrallah?" one wondered.

"Of course we like Hassan Nasrallah," I answered. Jake stood by expressionless.

"*Shoof, shoof!*" the boys hollered in Arabic. Look, look. "These men like Hassan Nasrallah."

A few people glanced over at Jake and me and then immediately went back to navigating the crowd. The boys shifted their attention back to us and bombarded us with more questions.

"Does everyone in Iceland like Hassan Nasrallah?" we were asked.

"Why did your country not fight for Lebanon during the war?"

"You will make Hezbollah in Iceland?"

To free ourselves, Jake and I mumbled fake Icelandic gibberish to each other, explained that our English wasn't so good, and awkwardly ran off. From then on, we decided we'd take the risk and confess to bleeding red, white, and blue for simplicity's sake. Lying was too much trouble. Hezbollah would have to deal with it.

"I believe Hezbollah loves you *because* you are Americans!" a tanned teenage boy with large red pimples and potent body odor said in Arabic, as he draped yellow Hezbollah banners around our necks.

He was a seventeen-year-old named Mohammad (no surprises there) and hailed from the southern town of Bint Jbail, close to the Israeli border, which experienced some of the most brutal fighting of the war. I translated for Jake, whose colloquial Arabic was not as strong as mine at the time.

"Who did you come here with today?" I asked.

Mohammed moved his hand in a circle as he pointed to all the people in the immediate vicinity. "My family," he said. "My family is big. We are a big Hezbollah family. Bush does not like Hezbollah. But you are not like Bush. You are here with Hezbollah. That is very good!" Switching to English, he said, "Now you are like me. You are real men of Hezbollah."

Like most other "real men of Hezbollah" among the roughly one million people in and around Martyrs' Square, where the demonstrations were held, we were standing too far from the gold-colored Lebanese Parliament building to see what was happening at the center of the protest. Powerful but low-quality speakers blasted muffled speeches that even the fluent Arabic speakers couldn't understand. Jake and I considered pushing our way forward, but we were nervous about getting caught in potentially violent clashes.

At a minimum, Jake and I expected what the rest of the world feared: a complete breakdown of order. Angry mobs stampeding the streets, cars being lit on fire, tear gas canisters thrown in all directions, soldiers firing on protesters in desperation—these were the things I psychologically prepared myself for. Not even Hassan Nasrallah, the adored leader of Hezbollah, dared attend the protest in person.

No such chaos ensued. In fact, the protest felt more like a giant music festival than anything else. All around us people sang songs, played instruments, ate packed lunches, and generally seemed to be enjoying themselves. Even the thousands of Lebanese soldiers guarding the perimeter of the protest were smiling and having fun. At one point, a few men climbed some street lamps and pumped their fists in the air, but that was as crazy as things got.

"I don't understand," I said to Mohammed while I fiddled with the Hezbollah banner he gave me. "I thought people here were angry, but everyone looks happy."

"People are angry," he answered. "We just know Hezbollah will fix all the problems. Allah is with Hezbollah. Hezbollah gives the people everything. We are here to show we love Hezbollah. We know things will be okay."

"Are things okay now?"

"Now life is not okay. Things are very bad. In the war, we lost it all," he said as he scratched his forehead. "Our house is gone. My school is gone. We live with my uncle now. Hezbollah will give us a new house, but it will take time. But the war was not all bad. I know many people who became *shahid*."

"Were they all Hezbollah fighters?" Jake asked.

"My cousins yes, but I have one younger brother who died also. He was no fighter."

My stomach twisted when I realized that Mohammed's brother had probably been an innocent casualty of the fighting with Israel. It's easy to tell yourself when you watch the news that, in the fog of war, tragedies happen and mistakes are made. But all that changes when you stare at someone in front of you and consider that one of those casualties was someone that person loved. It's extremely strange. What's even stranger is learning his family believed his death was a good thing.

"Everyone left Bint Jibail when the war started," Mohammed recounted. "But Hezbollah picked certain people to stay and become *shahid*. They said it was important to have people stand in front of our fighters when they fight the Israelis."

Israel claimed the reason so many Lebanese civilians had been killed was that Hezbollah prevented some residents from leaving the south. It basically accused Hezbollah of using its own people as human shields to give it a strategic military advantage. Many had dismissed these claims as Israeli propaganda. I didn't know if I was happy or sad that there was truth to Israel's claim. I must have had a disgusted expression on my face because Mohammed assured me that all was right in his world.

"It is very, very good," he stated. "My brother helped Hezbollah and is a *shahid*. There is nothing better than this."

It disgusted me that Muhammed could view Hezbollah's action—essentially taking his younger brother hostage and sentencing him to death—as anything positive. I had to talk about something else.

"When will Hezbollah give your family a new house?" I wondered.

"Soon, *inshallah*."

Yeah, right. In my time in the Arab world I'd learned that *inshallah* almost always meant "never going to happen." I wanted to tell him that, but I had to be tactful.

"I am an American and I don't know a lot about Hezbollah. Help me understand. Your brother is dead, you don't have a house, and you cannot go to school. Why do you believe Hezbollah will make everything better?"

"Because Hezbollah is better than everyone else."

Sadly, that statement was almost certainly true for Shiites at least. One reason Hezbollah had been able to develop such a strong loyalty among Lebanese Shiites was because of its social service programs.

Historically, Shiites represented the poorest and most disenfranchised Lebanese citizens. Long ignored by the Sunni and Christian-led central government, Hezbollah provided Shiites with schools, hospitals, community development projects, garbage collection and, unfortunately for Israel, military protection. Lebanon's Shiites regarded Hezbollah as the only functioning government they'd ever known.

For the next two days, Jake and I used Beirut as a base to explore other parts of Lebanon. But while we were in Beirut, we could almost always be found hanging around the Hezbollah-led protest downtown since that was the only place we could find a decent bite to eat.

Unlike the rest of Beirut, where nearly all stores and restaurants remained closed and boarded up, the area around the protest reopened up for business after the first day of demonstrations ended peacefully.

Open-air cafes spilled out onto the sidewalks, people huddled around the rotating spits at greasy shawarma shops, and clothing stores featuring knock-off designer labels offered huge sales to entice Hezbollah's more image-conscious followers to make major purchases. Though some fighting did break out between a pro-government Sunni militia and Hezbollah activists, Jake and I were always far from the scene and heard about it from the news.

It was extraordinary how comfortable I felt surrounded by a million supporters of Hezbollah. Everyone I met and talked to appeared so normal, so much like myself. They seemed to have the same desires as everyone else in the civilized world: a home, an education, and a sense of community. I began to feel that even as an American Jew, I blended in with everyone at the rally. Somehow, I thought, I was almost safe in Hezbollah's company.

Almost indeed. During our third afternoon in Beirut, Jake and I walked into a tiny sandwich shop on a quiet side street recommended by a Lebanese soldier standing at a nearby guard post. A bearded, middle-aged man a good half foot taller than me, with arms as thick as a gorilla's, took our order and prepared us some fresh turkey sandwiches from behind a narrow counter.

When he was finished, I offered the man a fistful of Lebanese pounds. He seized the money from my hand and grabbed my wrist.

"You!" he said in Arabic with a freakish grin on his face. "Where are you from?" Scared and confused, I told him we were Americans and unsuccessfully tried to pull my arm away. "No. Your friend is from America. You are from Israel."

And that was the end of me, I feared. I knew that even a baseless accusation of being Israeli might be enough to get me killed right then and there. Trying to stay calm, I vehemently denied the charge.

"I am not from Israel. I am an American," I swore.

"You have the eyes of a Jew. I have seen eyes like yours. Don't lie."

"I am not a Jew," I lied. "I am an American. That's all."

Suddenly, the sandwich maker let go of my wrist, shook my hand gently, and let out a hearty laugh.

"I know you are from America," he said. "It was a joke. If I really thought you were a Jew or an Israeli, I would have already killed you."

I pretended to chuckle. "Good joke."

"I was a Hezbollah fighter long ago. In my life, I have killed three Jews. All were in the Israeli army. Two, I killed with a gun. Puh pow, puh pow," he excitedly recounted as he aimed an imaginary gun at the doorway. "But one I found alive. He was alone and lost his gun. I beat him until he was dead," he laughed as he swung his fists at the air.

"If a Jew came into your store, you'd kill him?"

"If a Jew came to Lebanon, I would find him and finish him. Everyone in Hezbollah would do the same. Before I die, I pray Allah will bring me one more Jew to kill. That is all I want."

Though Jake didn't catch every word of the exchange, he got the gist of it. We both agreed it was time for a change of scenery. We had only a couple days left until we had to fly back to Sharjah, so wherever we went had to be close by.

"Let's go to Damascus," Jake suggested later that night. "It's only two hours from Beirut."

"We don't have visas. We can't even get into the country!" I griped. "We'll just get stopped at the border and turned back."

"Maybe. But why not try?"

It wasn't hard finding transportation to Damascus the next morning. An elderly man wearing a blue flat cap guided us to his decades-old Buick station wagon taxi at the Charles Helou bus station, a large, gray building nearly deserted from a lack of tourism. The man was taking two suspicious-looking Iraqis all the way to Baghdad.

During the drive, Jake and I sat up front with the driver, while the two Iraqi men stayed in the back. At the time, Iraq was in the midst of full-on sectarian chaos. I couldn't imagine who the men were, what they'd experienced, or why they were returning to Baghdad at all. I tried making small talk with them while we passed through Beirut's eastern suburbs, but was rebuffed by silence and stares each time.

"They don't talk with you," the driver made clear in English. "They talk to nobody until they are home. No more questions."

Israel bombed all the major roads between Lebanon and Syria during the war to prevent Hezbollah from receiving weapons, so we traveled on dirt-tracked back roads the closer we got to the border.

"You see, you see," the driver said as he pointed to a section of highway piled with rubble. "Every ten years, Israel break economy. Israel afraid of Lebanon economy. Lebanon has big potential. Israel know Lebanon can be strong and rich. So every ten years, Israel break Lebanon economy. Fucking Israel!"

I certainly appreciated why that conspiracy theory made sense to many Lebanese. But no, I did not believe Israel, whose economy is largely technology driven, acted out of fear of Lebanese competition.

We passed through Lebanon's border and entered Syria's fenced-in, barbed-wire-surrounded no-man's land without incident. Signs advertised a derelict, unkempt amusement park called "Happy Land" just a few kilometers up the road. Surprised we'd even been allowed into Syrian territory at all, we felt like we were on our way to Syria's version of Disneyland. Of course, that was when the real fun started.

We followed the two Iraqis into a colorless building without central heating. There, passports were verified and stamped by a young Syrian military officer in green fatigues. He sat behind a counter next to a few extremely old army radios, which he spoke into every time he stamped a traveler's passport. His expressionless face indicated boredom. He didn't appear to be in the mood to conduct a particularly thorough screening.

The two silent Iraqis presented their passports to the officer, who stamped and returned them without a word. Jake and I stepped forward, considered the young officer's indifferent eyes, and handed him our Uncle Sam-sponsored documents hoping for an equally uneventful procedure.

"You have been to Israel," the officer stated in English.

The way he said it hadn't sounded like a question. It was a declaration. Syria, it was known, was especially strict about not allowing in foreigners with any signs of an Israeli visit on their passports.

"No, this is not true," I said in our defense. The officer, ignoring my response, looked through every single page of our passports as well as the back cover to check for remnants of glue from Israeli security stickers.

"Okay," the officer said. "You do not have visas to enter Syria. Why not?"

"We thought we could buy visas here at the border," I fibbed. "We can pay for our visas here?"

"I do not know. I must check this. You must wait."

"Do you have any idea how long we'll have to wait?"

"It depends. One hour, two hours, four hours, twelve hours. Maybe even a full day. Sit and I will call you when I know something."

Jake and I thought about just turning back to Lebanon right then, but we figured we might as well stick it out. We hurried outside to let our driver know the situation, but when we walked up to his station wagon, he seemed to know exactly what was going on.

"No visa, no Syria," he affirmed as he tossed our backpacks to the dusty ground. "You no go Syria today." Then he got back into the car and drove off with the Iraqis still in the backseat.

How encouraging, I thought. He ditched us and kept our ten dollars. For the first hour, we waited near the disinterested passport control official hoping for an update. While we sat there, a few backpackers from various European countries showed up who also needed to buy visas. They received theirs immediately. I asked a blonde-haired Swiss with thick black glasses how he'd managed to get in so easily.

"Because I am not an American," he said. "Syria likes nothing American these days."

But it wasn't true. When Jake and I craved a change of location, we wandered around the no-man's land and discovered the only place to eat in the area was, of all things, a fully functioning Dunkin' Donuts. We passed another couple hours eating pastries and playing cards while groups of hungry Syrian soldiers poured in. Syrians might have hated US foreign policy, but they sure loved our egg and cheese muffin sandwiches.

When Jake and I made our way back to the immigration hall, we checked in again to see what the status was. The Syrian officer glanced at us with lifeless eyes and informed us that there was still no change.

"Every time I try to cross into Syria they give me problems too. The bureaucracy kills me," a tall man in his mid-forties with thick graying hair said in English as we sat down in the waiting area. Wearing a pin-stripe suit and a sparkling Rolex watch, the man introduced himself as Hussein and explained that he owned a major cell phone carrier that stretched across Lebanon, Syria, and Jordan. He lamented that, despite being a wealthy businessman who invested significantly in Syria, he was always held up at the Syrian border because passport officials could never decide what his nationality was.

"I was born and raised in Lebanon," he clarified. "But I'm not Lebanese. I can never be truly Lebanese. My wife is Lebanese, my mother is Lebanese, and all my grandparents are Lebanese except for my grandfather on my father's side. He was born in Jordan. In Lebanon, you can only get citizenship if your father is Lebanese. Since my father's father was a Jordanian, my father is a Jordanian and I am a Jordanian. Since I'm Jordanian, the Syrians can't figure out why I always seem to be coming from Lebanon. The Arabs are so obsessed with tribe, religion, and nationality. Arabs are supposed to be an inclusive people, but the reality is that every Arab stands alone. Have either of you ever heard of Moshe Dayan?"

My ears perked up.

"The Israeli Defense Minister?" I asked.

"The best defense minister! He was the Israeli defense minister during the Six Day War."

Were Jake and I really about to receive an Israeli history lesson from an ethnically Lebanese Jordanian businessman in Syrian no-man's land?

"Moshe Dayan said Israel will only ever have a problem when the Arabs learn how to stand together," he continued. "But since the Arabs can't ever stand together, Israel will never have a problem. It's true. Arabs can't stand together for crap. That's why I'm stuck here waiting like a tourist."

Soon after, the apathetic officer called him up to inform him he'd been approved for entry.

"You boys really want to get into Syria?" Hussein asked us after taking his passport back. "Wait."

Hussein walked up to the officer, they conversed briefly in Arabic and a few minutes later, Jake and I were miraculously called up to take back our passports.

"Your requests for visas have been approved," the officer said without emotion. "Welcome to the Syrian Arab Republic."

Completely dumbfounded, Jake and I paid for our visas. Hussein offered us a ride all the way to Damascus in his chauffeur-driven Lincoln Town Car. Happy Land, here we come.

Once we were in the clear, Hussein explained how he got us across while he relaxed in the front passenger's seat next to his driver.

"I slipped the border guard five dollar bills for each of you and told him you were my associates. I said that the five dollar bills were your visas," he said. Was ten dollars really all it took to completely circumvent the foreign policy of Bashar al-Assad, one of the most reviled dictators in the world? "Ten dollars is a lot of money for a young officer like him. It'll pay for his family's electricity bill for a month. He would have been crazy not to take it."

"Couldn't he get into trouble for that?" Jake asked.

"Don't worry. He's protecting himself. You could be CIA spies for all he knows. I'm sure he's notified the right people that a couple of American tourists have entered the country. Believe me. In Syria, someone will be watching you."

That someone would be a member of the *mukhabarat,* Syria's secret police. The term "secret police" is deceptive because its members did not enforce actual laws or remain invisible. In fact, they could be found all over Damascus dressed in black leather jackets and black dress pants, talking to people, sitting in coffee shops, and standing on sidewalks watching and waiting.

The objective of the *mukhabarat* was to maintain the stability of the Assad regime. This was done by any means necessary: entering homes to "investigate" potential "crimes," imprisoning citizens without due process, and torturing and murdering at random to increase fear. The *mukhabarat* were there to enforce the will of the state. And what made them so effective was their visibility.

Jake and I weren't particularly concerned with the *mukhabarat.* We were tourists who'd be leaving Syria almost as soon as we arrived. We didn't have the time to get into any serious trouble. The *mukhabarat* didn't agree.

We first had an inkling we were being followed towards the end of our first afternoon. We noticed the same young agent with a short crew cut, dressed in a black leather jacket and black dress pants, over and over again. I first spotted him in the various markets walking about fifteen feet behind us. I saw him again loitering around the hummus shop where we ate lunch. While Jake and I admired the minarets of the Umayyad mosque, one of the largest and oldest mosques in the world, he chatted with a man selling fresh cashew nuts nearby.

Poor soul. His droopy eyes showed he was either extremely tired or entirely uninterested in his task at hand. Who could blame him? All Jake and I did most of the time was walk and walk and walk some more. If he'd been on our trail at all hours of the day and night, he must have been exhausted.

Jake's twenty-first birthday was the next day. As funny as it would have been to celebrate by visiting a seedy strip club in Damascus (and such places did exist), we decided that having a calmer night of festivities was a better idea.

After spending the day engaged in our endless walking while our not-so-inconspicuous friend from the *mukhabarat* crept behind us, we went searching for a nice bite to eat. In the old city, deep in the cellars of some of the most decrepit buildings, lie some extremely fancy restaurants. The problem was they were nearly impossible to find if you didn't know where to look.

Jake and I zigzagged through quiet, empty alleyways for a while until we got too fed up and hungry to search anymore. Literally, there wasn't anyone in the immediate vicinity who could have given us directions. Left with no other option, we waited a minute for our casual observer to catch up to us. Until that point, we hadn't spoken to him at all. We didn't know what his true intentions were or if engaging him would have gotten us into trouble. Maybe he really was doing his best to remain inconspicuous. Or maybe he wanted us to know he was following us, so we wouldn't try anything funny. At that point, we were too hungry to care, and didn't see the harm in asking the guy if he knew of any nice places to dine.

"Excuse me," I called out to him in Arabic when he walked up. "Where is there a nice restaurant close to here?"

The youthful field agent shifted his eyes rapidly between Jake and me and kept his arms locked at his sides. Were we up to no good? Did we have him right where we wanted him? Was he about to meet his end? He didn't know. Still, he answered my question trying to keep his cool.

"There is Al-Khawali, a very good restaurant fifty meters from here," he said.

"Thank you. After the restaurant, we will see you?"

"I don't understand," he said with a phony grin.

"We see you a lot. I want to know if we will see you again after we leave the restaurant."

"I don't understand." A bit awkwardly, he walked back in the direction from which we'd come and darted off.

He'd been right on about Al-Khawali. It was below ground in a huge building whose entrance was a nondescript rusty iron door. Jake and I enjoyed the feast of our lives there. While violinists played classical Arabic tunes, waiters in tuxedos served us massive portions of meat skewers, rice, and vegetables. When we finished our meal, our friend from the *mukhabarat* was nowhere to be found.

Less than twelve hours later, we boarded a Beirut-bound mini-bus with unhinged seats that skidded sideways from window to window. Though our trip to Syria was too short, I was anxious for us to return to Beirut, so we could catch our flight to Sharjah. The morning after getting back, my friend Guy was supposed to arrive from Israel. I still had to develop a game plan for how we'd pull off the visit successfully and remain invisible to the Emirati authorities. If anyone discovered Guy was an Israeli, who knows what kind of problems we'd face?

Before heading to the airport, we stopped by an Internet café to check email. I hoped I'd see a message from Guy in my inbox.

I did. However, the message didn't read the way I'd wished. Rather than express his excitement for our upcoming adventure in the UAE, Guy informed me that he wouldn't be coming at all. He wrote that he had a terrible feeling about the trip and felt it was simply too dangerous a mission for him to undertake. I wrote back right away that he had nothing to worry about and that I would take care of everything. Take a chance, I urged him.

My efforts to persuade him failed. Minutes later, Guy sent me an email saying there was nothing I could do to change his mind. He preferred to forfeit the money he'd spent on airfare rather than do something his gut told him was a terrible idea.

I flew back to Sharjah angry with Guy for giving in to his own unsubstantiated doubts. What was he so worried about? It wasn't like anyone knew he was coming. Right?

Chapter 14
The Good Jew

Sharjah, UAE
December 2006

WRONG. BESIDES JAKE, I HADN'T TOLD A SOUL ABOUT GUY'S plans to visit. It turned out I didn't have to for the information to get into the wrong hands. Half an hour or so after arriving back at my campus dorm room, my phone rang. It was Jake.

"Michael, you need come over to my room and talk to Salim," he said urgently. "Something bad happened while we were gone."

Confused but curious, I hurried over and knocked on the door. Jake let me in and I saw Salim sitting quietly upright on his bed, pressing his hands together. His face gaunt, his facial muscles stiff, and his eyes baggy and bloodshot, he looked like he hadn't slept for days. Jake slowly closed the door and we both sat down on his bed facing Salim.

"Who's coming here from Israel?" Salim asked me aggressively.

"What?" I responded. "No one's coming here from Israel."

That was the truth as of a few hours before.

"I know you have someone coming here from Israel!" Salim screamed. "I know because they thought I was in on it when they took me away."

"What are you talking about?"

Salim breathed deeply, exhaled, and, with a crack in his voice, told us what we'd missed while we were gone.

"Two nights ago, I was here in the room playing on my computer when someone knocked on the door," he began. "I opened up and a bunch of huge guys wearing uniforms grabbed me, told me they were the CID, put me in handcuffs, and blindfolded me. They put me in a van and took me somewhere off campus. I don't know where. When they took the blindfold off me, I was tied to a chair with a white light hanging over me, surrounded by two interrogators. They started to punch me and slap me in the face. They asked me repeatedly, 'When's your friend coming? When's your Israeli friend coming?' All I could say back to them was 'I don't know what you're talking about.' I really didn't know, but they kept punching and hitting and slapping me. They kept me there for two days like that. They wouldn't let me sleep. They told me I was going to jail for being a spy."

Then, pointing at me with hostility in his eyes, he said, "They showed me everything about you. They showed me emails you were sending back and forth to 'some guy' in Israel (no pun intended). They showed me how in the emails you wrote to him not to bring his Israeli passport when he came here. You wrote those emails from my computer. They thought I was in on it with you. That's why they kept asking me when my Israeli friend was coming. They said that when the Israeli came they were going to get him, get you, and get me."

"They also found Israeli coins I brought back from my trip to Egypt and Israel," Jake added. "That also made things pretty bad."

"They've been watching you since you got here," Salim continued. "They had pictures of you from all over campus. In the Student Center, in the hallway, in class. Everywhere."

"So how did you get out of it?" I asked.

"I couldn't answer any of their questions. So, they called some people who work at AUS to check if they knew me. When they said they did, they brought me back here and let me go. They said I should to stop talking to you. They said I don't really know anything about you and that you could be capable of anything."

I smiled at the ridiculousness of the claim. I thought Salim would too because he was my friend. But he didn't.

"Stay away from me. The CID guys are right. I don't know who you are or anything else about you. Whatever you're doing here, leave me out of it. Since I met you all people do is say that I'm a Jew and an enemy of Islam. Just leave me alone. It's a good thing your Israeli friend never came."

He could say that again. Salim's words stung me, but not nearly as much as the realization that had Guy made the trip to Sharjah, we both may have ended up sitting in an Emirati prison cell. I felt like a complete idiot for having tried to convince Guy to come in the first place. Ever since my meeting the third week of the semester with the mysterious bearded man from university security, I'd known that "in Sharjah, the walls have eyes and ears." How could I have been so naïve as to think Guy and I would have gotten away with our operation? I was glad Guy listened to his intuition because mine was clearly off.

The deterioration of my relationship with Salim made me wonder just how fragile my friendships with AUS students were. I began thinking that, apart from Jake and the other Americans, perhaps I hadn't succeeded in developing a single significant friendship the entire semester. No doubt there were numerous people who liked having me around for the sake of entertainment. I was the leading jester of the AUS circus. AUS was nothing more than a cluster of marble white buildings in the middle of one of the hottest deserts on Earth. Day-to-day life there was boring. The only thing I was certain of was that I'd succeeded in bringing some action to campus.

I didn't like being so negative. But I couldn't help it. I didn't discount the fact that I'd given many AUS students food for thought regarding America, Jews, and Israel. I realized how incredible it was that, in the span of four months, I'd become a well-known figure who had shown students the humanity of the Jewish people, a nation so many of them had been taught to vilify. However, I also understood that, in their lifetimes, those same students would be exposed to millions of other voices that would speak out against the very message of Arab-Jewish understanding that I tried to spread. The worst part was I couldn't say which side even those closest to me would take.

During a discussion about personal freedom in the UAE in Dr. Muntassar's class, Muhammad bin Raheem, my honorary Emirati "brother," once raised his hand and said, "In the UAE, the people need more rights. Every time a person wants to launch jihad against Americans in Afghanistan and Iraq, the government comes and stops them. This is not fair. Everyone must have the right to launch jihad against America."

Samira, the Palestinian girl who turned her back on her other friends to build a friendship with me, would occasionally go on angry rants blaming the British, the Americans, the Turks, and anyone else she could think of for the creation of Zionism and all problems the Palestinian people have and would ever face. And Ahmad Jew, my pal from Jerusalem who was as close to a real Jew as I had around me, once conveyed his belief that Osama bin Laden and Al Qaeda were not responsible for the 9/11 attacks. He bought into the conspiracy theory that it was a CIA-Mossad plot used to justify going to war in Iraq.

I acknowledged that Muhammad bin Raheem, Samira, and Ahmad Jew cared about me a great deal. But I questioned whether their feelings would change over time and if our friendships were strong enough to weather future geo-political storms. If Muhammad bin Raheem chose to launch a jihad of some sort against America, would he recall his American friend who used to dress up as a local? If another Arab-Israeli war broke out and the Arab masses damned all Zionists to hell, would Samira acknowledge the Zionist boy she'd flirted with? And, without me around to help him keep his feet on the ground, would I eventually lose Ahmad Jew to the surreal world of Arab conspiracy theorists?

During my final ten days at AUS in the middle of December, I did the unimaginable: I kept to myself. Not completely, of course. Whenever I was in the Student Center, I still hung out with people. But I stopped speaking up in front of large groups and having passing conversations with students I didn't know well. I even refrained from wearing my beloved *kandura* and *ghutrah* to avoid attracting attention. All I really cared about at that point was staying off the radar of the authorities so I could take my final exams, get credit for the semester, and go back to GW.

The day before I flew away for good, I was in my room getting organized and packing my suitcases when I heard my phone ringing. It was Mo. I let the call go to voicemail. I hadn't spoken to him much since my final encounter with his brother Hassan. I assumed his brother had totally convinced him I really was a spy sent to wreak havoc on all nice Palestinian boys in Sharjah.

I wasn't too upset not seeing Mo. I associated him with everything zany and stressful and dangerous that had happened to me during the semester. I was tired of all of it and I was tired of him. He'd had his moments where he'd acted nobly on my behalf, but I still didn't believe he really saw me as anything other than a fountain of gossip and attention.

My phone rang again. And again. And again. When he called for the fourth time, I picked up. I accepted that I wasn't going to be able to leave Sharjah without talking to him one more time.

"Michael, why didn't you answer the phone?" Mo asked.

"I'm sorry, Mo," I said. "I was in the bathroom and I didn't hear it."

"Okay, listen. I really need to talk to you right now in your room. You won't believe what people are saying about you."

"Mo, I don't care what people are saying about me. I'm leaving tomorrow. If you want to come over and say goodbye, you can. But I'm finished hearing all the gossip. When do you want to come over?"

Knock, knock. I hung up the phone. Was that seriously him?

"You didn't answer the phone before so I decided to see if you were around," Mo explained as I let him in.

I pulled up a chair and sat across from him.

"I know you said you don't want to hear what people are saying about you," Mo started. "But I don't care. It's very important. People are saying they don't want you to go back to Palestine."

"Okay," I said, not seeing what the big deal was. "I'm a Jew. Of course people don't want me to going to Palestine. None of you want Jews there."

"No, you don't understand. People say they don't want you going back to Palestine because they don't want anything bad to happen to you. They don't want you to get killed by the resistance."

"I'm confused."

"No, everyone at AUS is confused. No one is sure if you're a spy or not. But people are saying they don't really care. People are saying they really like you and will miss you. They say that you're the good Jew and they asked me to tell you this."

"Who are these people, Mo?"

"I can't say."

"Why not?"

"Because you might be a spy."

I started laughing. Mo laughed too.

"It's nice to know that people really care. But do you and everyone else really think that I'm the only good Jew out there?"

Mo paused for a second.

"What do you mean?" he asked.

"Do you really think that I'm the *only* good Jew in the world? What about my mother, my father, my brother, and the rest of my friends and family? There are more good Jews out there, Mo."

"Maybe. But we don't know them. We know you. There are many people at AUS who don't want you to die. Promise that you won't go back to Palestine! It's dangerous there for Jews. The Palestinians there don't know you. They might kill you. Just promise you won't go there. Don't go back to Palestine."

It touched me that Mo and other AUS students genuinely cared about my safety. But it disturbed me that they viewed me as the only Jew worth saving. They didn't see it as wrong that Palestinian terror organizations deliberately sought to murder Jewish civilians. On the contrary, they still believed Israel should be destroyed by any means necessary and that any Jew around was a legitimate target. Unless, of course, it was their friend Michael, who they happened to know on a personal level.

Clearly, I was seen by most Arabs, both well-educated and not, as part and parcel of the Jewish state. In their lexicon, the words "Jew" and "Israeli" meant the same thing. A Jew is an Israeli and an Israeli is a Jew. It wasn't important that not all Jews had Israeli citizenship. Holding an Israeli passport was considered a mere technicality.

After arriving back in the US and continuing my studies at GW, I felt that I'd changed. I'd lost nearly all my original idealism that lasting progress on the Middle East peace front could happen in the short term.

My experiences traveling and studying in the Arab world taught me that the demonization of Israel and the Jewish people in Arab society was not about to change anytime soon. Too many Arabs were still being taught to seek the destruction of Israel and to view Jews as their mortal enemies, no matter where they were from.

I still believed in a peaceful future between Jews and Arabs and Israel and the Arab world, but I realized that the path to getting there might not be what some might expect. I'd always cared about creating change on the ground. I soon arrived at the conclusion that if I wanted to improve relations between Arabs and Jews in the Middle East, then I had to be in the Middle East to do it. When I graduated from GW, while most of my friends were looking for jobs or about to start graduate school, I made other plans. In August 2008, nearly a year and eight months after concluding study abroad experience in Sharjah, I immigrated to Israel, also known as making *aliyah,* and joined the Israel Defense Forces (IDF). I reasoned it was the single best way for me to continue my fight for peace in the Middle East.

Chapter 15
An Arabic-Speaking James Bond

Israel
August 2008–June 2009

EVER SINCE ISRAEL'S INDEPENDENCE IN 1948, IT HAS HAD TO live by the sword to keep its citizens, as well as Jews elsewhere, safe from harm.

Believing that Israel was dedicated to a peaceful future, I saw the idea of joining the Israel Defense Forces as an opportunity to defend Israel and the Jewish people from enemies I knew on an intimate level. I understood that only by ensuring Israel's strength and survival could true peace between Arabs and Jews ever take hold.

I moved to Israel with a program called Garin Tzabar, which provided a support system for Jews living in the Jewish Diaspora to come to Israel and become soldiers in the IDF for at least two years. In Hebrew, *garin* means "seed" or "core" and is used to describe a group of people who move to Israel together. *Tzabar*, which literally translates to "cactus fruit," refers to a native-born Israeli.

Under the auspices of Garin Tzabar, participants are split into separate groups, or *garinim*. Every *garin* arrives in Israel in August the year they enlist and is placed on a kibbutz, a collective community primarily based on agriculture, which serves as home base for the participants during their service. Since such soldiers typically have no immediate family in Israel, they are designated as "lone soldiers." For three months prior to induction into basic training in November, *garin* members go through a crash-course in Hebrew language and complete all pre-draft logistical requirements, such as physical and psychological examinations, aptitude tests, and interviews.

My *garin* of eighteen people, made up of eleven guys and seven girls, arrived in Israel in mid-August 2008 and were placed on Kibbutz Sde Eliahu, a religious kibbutz near Beit She'an, along the Jordanian border in northern Israel.

The girls in our group seemed to have an endless array of options of where they might get a chance to serve. They could have joined mixed male-female combat units or the education corps, or worked in foreign relations, or as weapons instructors.

The guys, on the other hand, were all being prepared to do one thing: fight. It was viewed as a given that if a guy didn't have any outstanding back or knee problems, he would join an IDF combat unit because it was said that fighters were what the army needed most.

Ironic as it may sound, my desire to join the IDF didn't necessarily mean I intended to become a combat soldier. What did interest me was going into a role where I'd get the chance to make a contribution that only I could make.

"With your knowledge of Arabic and experience in the countries surrounding us, I'm sure you're going to have some very exciting offers from different intelligence units," Doobi, my *garin* coordinator on Sde Eliahu, told me. A Canadian of Eastern European extraction, he'd made *aliyah* to Israel and moved to the kibbutz nearly forty years before, and was so dark from his years of working in Sde Eliahu's fields that he was affectionately known on the kibbutz as "the burnt match." "When you go to your first call up and they ask you about yourself, tell them everything."

So that's what I did. When we all headed over to the regional draft board office in Tiberias to get registered, poked, prodded, and grabbed by the balls (during the medical examination at least), I made sure to tell the eighteen-year-old female soldier interviewing me all about my experiences in the Arab world. I talked about the Hezbollah protests in Lebanon, how a five-dollar bribe got me into Syria, sneaking into mosques, and the Iranian sex party in Dubai. While I described my experiences to the soldier, she had a look of sheer bewilderment on her face. I was sure she'd never met a new inductee like me before.

In the weeks that followed, I was confident her report would be sent to the right people and that I'd receive quite a few interesting invitations. Was I about to begin training to become a spy? Was I going to be asked to become exactly what my enemies in Sharjah had feared I'd been all along?

I wasn't. I didn't have a single interview with any intelligence unit. Other Garin Tzabar participants were. My roommate on Sde Eliahu, Eliram, a cynical but humorous child of Israelis who'd grown up in Connecticut, had numerous interviews in secret locations for a special intelligence combat unit.

After every meeting with his contacts for the unit, Eliram expressed a mix of excitement and anxiety. He felt the way you do when a tremendous opportunity is presented and you know you're being tested every step of the way. I didn't say so, but I was a jealous of Eliram. I was someone who could be dropped into Beirut or Damascus without batting an eyelash. Did Israel have someone else who had navigated relationships with the elites of Emirati society and spoken to crowds at mosques? I wanted to be a spy. Why wasn't anyone calling me?

"Because you're a security threat," Yaniv, a friend I'd met while backpacking and a former captain in a combat engineering special forces unit, said when I spent a weekend at his house. "You have no chance of getting a security clearance, which means you have no chance of getting into intelligence. You have too many contacts in the Arab world. The army doesn't know if it can trust you. How does the army know you're not working with an Arab terrorist group? What if you've been sent to infiltrate the Israeli army?"

The idea that I was suspected of being an Arab spy was frustrating. But the desire to serve in intelligence convinced me I wanted a combat role that would use my Arabic language skills and Middle East experience.

In practical terms that meant finding a unit that operated primarily amongst the Palestinian population in the West Bank, Israel's main battleground during the previous decade.

Israel's presence in the West Bank had always been controversial in the international community, but I'd always believed that the Israeli army did its best to be humane under very difficult circumstances. Now it was time to find out if that was true.

A week before I and the other members of my *garin* were required to state our draft preferences, we were brought to the Tel HaShomer military base, one of the largest bases in the country near Ramat Gan, to hear presentations made by representatives of various units.

One of the spokesmen we heard from was a tall, muscular officer who carried himself with an air of unshakeable confidence. Wearing a camouflage beret on his left shoulder, he introduced himself as Tomer and said he was eager to tell us why the guys among us should come to Kfir, the newest infantry brigade in the IDF.

"Kfir was established in 2005 with the sole purpose of fighting Palestinian terror in Judea and Samaria (the West Bank)," he declared in Hebrew. "As serious as the threats are that surround the state of Israel, the most dangerous threat is one that comes from within. The six battalions that make up Kfir rotate between the six major Palestinian population centers and ensure that terror on Israeli civilians is stopped once and for all. All soldiers in the Kfir Brigade undergo an intense course in urban warfare and house-to-house combat. If you're looking for an interesting and meaningful service where you'll get a real grasp of Israel's situation with the Palestinians, come to Kfir."

With those words, I was sold. I put Kfir down as my top choice on my draft preferences form. When I was accepted into the unit a few weeks later, I was elated. But when Israeli friends expressed concern about my choice I started to worry.

"Kfir does the army's black work," an Ethiopian-Israeli girl named Geula told me in Hebrew while we sat on the beach in Tel Aviv one afternoon. "Kfir does the dirty work against the Palestinians that the rest of the infantry doesn't want to deal with. The guys in Kfir aren't just stopping terrorists. They're teaching the rest of the Palestinians why it's a bad idea to mess with Israel. If there are soldiers in the IDF that know how to give an Arab a beating, it's the soldiers in Kfir."

Yaniv also had doubts whether Kfir was really the right place for me.

"Soldiers in Kfir don't come out the same as everyone else," he said in Hebrew when we spoke on the phone to discuss my options. "Their lives are tense because they're always fighting Palestinians. You've spent a lot of time with Arabs, Michael. You have a lot of Arab friends. What would they think if they knew what you were about to do?"

You didn't have to be an expert in Middle East social dynamics to guess the answer to that one. It had been nearly two years since my semester in Sharjah. The truth was that I wasn't in touch with most people I had known at AUS. In the months after I returned to the US from Sharjah, I'd get phone calls from people here and there. They dwindled over time. At that point, my relationships with Mo, Muhammad bin Raheem, and others were distant memories. There was no reason to update them about my life decisions. It would only upset them.

Before I moved to Israel, I had four Arab friends I felt I had to inform about what the next two years of my life would entail: Joe, my Palestinian-American friend from high school, Ahmad Jew and Ahmad Greasy from Jerusalem, and Samira. It wasn't easy telling Joe and the Ahmads, but I did so well before arriving in Israel without fretting about it too much. Joe had known Guy and me for long enough to understand that our desire to help Israel did not imply any wish to harm Palestinians. Jerusalem-born Ahmad Jew and Ahmad Greasy interacted with Jews regularly at home and had a more sobering grasp than other Arabs of what service in the IDF involved. I can't say they were thrilled to hear about my decision, but they assured me it wouldn't affect our friendships.

Telling Samira truly terrified me and I avoided doing so for months. Whenever she sent me an email asking me for an update on life, I'd write back something vague. Though she'd proved herself to be a solid friend of mine in Sharjah, she lacked the nuanced perspective on the Israeli-Palestinian conflict that I believed Joe and the Ahmads shared. I worried she'd accuse me of betraying her, of deliberately becoming her enemy. I was going to lose Samira once and for all because I'd willfully immigrated to the Zionist entity and volunteered to serve in its butchering military.

Not long before my draft date, I wrote Samira a lengthy email letting her know that I was in Israel and about to begin service in the Israeli army, and why. If this was going to destroy our friendship, then I might as well get it over with, I thought. By steering clear of the topic, I was turning our friendship into a farce. I anxiously awaited a reply from her even though I wasn't certain she'd send one at all.

Samira did write me back an extremely touching email almost immediately that assuaged my fears. She wrote, "I will never stop being your friend. You have the right to choose your own path in life, and I have no right to judge you for it. I may not agree, I may think it's a waste of time and energy, I may even think it's no use because nothing will make peace between us and the Israelis, but the fact that you're willing to try just means you're way more optimistic than I am, and I commend you for that.

"I mean, I don't think I agree with the whole Israeli thing. And no matter how much I try, I can't and probably will never be kind to Israelis in any way. I was raised to believe that the Palestinians are the victims and Israelis are the attackers, the 'bad people' so to speak. I was also raised to believe I should never be friends with one.

"However, that doesn't mean I will stop being your friend. I think that at this point it would be impossible to simply stop being your friend because I met you, got to know you, and I truly think you're a good person. I can't turn my back on you. So, be assured, we will remain friends. I should also say that I am proud of you, and proud that you're strong enough to take this step in your life and to 'walk the walk.'

"I just hope you never do anything that would violate your morals. My only fear is that you're going to find yourself doing awful things to people. I'm scared you're going to lose yourself in this Israeli-Palestinian mess."

Relieved that I'd received Samira's blessing, I reported to basic training and was siphoned off to the Nachshon battalion a couple of days later. Determined to be a fair and just soldier to everyone, Jew and Arab alike, I hoped I could use my knowledge of Arabic language and culture to be a positive force on the ground during Israeli military involvement with the Palestinians.

During my first week of basic training at Peles, a base along the Jordanian border in the West Bank, I was called into personal meetings with each of my officers, so they could get to know me better and discover how I could best contribute to my battalion, Nachshon.

In each meeting, I repeated numerous times that I spoke Arabic well and thought I could be of use to the unit in an Arabic-speaking capacity. Neither my company commander nor my platoon commander took me seriously. Both responded as if I were a two-year-old telling tall tales.

Ohad, my dark black wavy-haired company commander throughout my seven months of basic and advanced training, assumed I'd misspoken.

"I'm very happy to know you are motivated to learn Arabic. You will be an excellent soldier for Nachshon," he assured me.

"Company Commander, I said I *already* speak Arabic," I replied.

"Yes, soldier. I know you want to learn Arabic."

"No, Company Commander. *Ana bahki arabi.* I speak Arabic."

"I didn't catch that last sentence. You should work on your Hebrew."

Yarden, my light-skinned half-Hungarian half-Yemenite platoon commander, accused me of lying.

"Soldier, I understand you're excited to be in the army," he said. "But if you're going to be in my platoon, I'm going to need you to be honest and direct with me at all times. I can't have a soldier lying to me."

"Platoon Commander, I wouldn't lie to you. What do you think I'm lying about?"

"Just stay honest and you'll be fine. You are dismissed."

I understood their skepticism to an extent. Though my Hebrew was decent for a foreigner, by no means did I speak like a native Israeli. To contend that I also knew some Arabic, a far harsher language requiring greater use of one's throat, seemed ludicrous. My goofy American accent and light skin didn't help matters. Who did I think I was, Michael of Arabia?

Luck struck when I finally found an opportunity to prove my Arabic skills. On a rainy day during the second week of basic training, the ninety soldiers in my company jammed into a tiny classroom to receive a lesson about Islam. Enough seats were provided for only half the company. I was stuck sitting in the back, on the floor, squished against Nir, a chubby, red-cheeked behemoth of a soldier who was determined to use the lesson as an opportunity to nap . . . on me.

"Michael, do me a favor," Nir said. "Let me put my head on your shoulder for a bit until a commander walks over."

"No way," I refused. "What am I, your boyfriend? Don't you want to learn about Islam?"

"Some friend you are. Who wants to learn about Islam? I need to sleep."

The squad commanders walked around presenting each soldier with a little Arabic phrasebook and ordered everyone to be quiet. In hobbled a man grasping a cane. He wore makeup to make himself look much older and dressed in a red-checkered *keffiyeh* and a white *jalabiya*. He introduced himself as Eli, an Arabic instructor on the base, and explained that having a basic comprehension and awareness of Islam could prevent avoidable misunderstandings with Palestinians during service in West Bank cities. But, instead of merely spouting out facts, Eli chose to test what we already knew.

"Where is the holiest place in all of Islam?" he started. A softball question, I thought. A few hands went up, but mine was not among them. I knew the answer, but didn't want to come off as a know-it-all. I also felt less than confident speaking Hebrew publicly. Every time I opened my mouth those first few weeks, incessant laughter erupted thanks to my thick American accent. Eli called on a soldier seated in the front row.

"Mooca!" he proclaimed confidently.

"Not quite," Eli replied. Another soldier sitting with his legs crossed in the middle hesitantly raised his hand.

"Mecca, right?"

"Very good," Eli confirmed. The crowd went wild and the whole room filled with boisterous jubilation.

"Okay, let me give you a difficult one. Name and state the oath Muslims state to declare their belief in God."

A few seconds passed. Silence filled the room and the area above everyone's heads remained devoid of anyone's bravely extended limb. Of course I knew the answer, but I was worried I might mix up a word or two. I'd blabbed so much about my professed Arabic skills, so I was nervous about discrediting myself if I gave less than a perfect answer. However, maybe this was the proof I needed to be taken seriously.

I nervously raised my arm. Eli's eyes immediately took notice of my daring. He smiled and told me to go ahead.

The sound of giggling bounced off the classroom walls before I uttered a word. I laughed off the chuckles to calm myself and began to speak.

"The oath Muslims state is called the *shahada*. It goes like this: *lâ ilâha illallâh, Muhammad rasûlu-llâh.*" There is no God but Allah, and Muhammad is his messenger.

Thud! Eli's cane dropped to the floor and his mouth hung wide open. Everyone in the company gasped and turned towards me, wide-eyed with astonishment and suspicion. In ten seconds, surrounded by the unusual silence of rambunctious Israeli teenagers, I'd gone from hapless American to suspected double agent, an Arabic-speaking James Bond sent to discover the keys to Israeli military strategy.

"Michael, where did you learn that?" Eli asked.

"From the mosque," I replied with a smirk. All eyes opened even wider and loud whispers passed throughout the room. I guessed the moment had arrived to provide some clarification, so I wouldn't be court-martialed by the Israeli army for espionage. But, feeling strangely confident and enjoying a jolt of adrenaline, I decided to show off a little first.

"*Ana yehudi. Laakin ba'araf nas al-arab kuwayis,*" I said. I am a Jew. But I know Arabs well.

"*Min wayn?*" Eli replied. From where?

"*Min al-jazeera.*" From Al-Jazeera. Eli's eyes widened. Most people know Al-Jazeera as the popular cable-news television network. However, the term technically refers to the actual Arabian Peninsula. I chose to leave it at that.

Eli took his gaze away from me while everyone else's eyes stayed put. Nir tapped me on the shoulder.

"Michael," he somberly said. "Are you an Arab?"

"No, Nir," I replied.

"You sure?"

"Pretty sure."

"Nachshon!" Eli shouted, quickly grabbing everyone's attention. "It seems one of your fellow soldiers already has a solid background in Arabic. Ask him for help. He knows more than you think."

After the lesson, Eli took me outside the classroom into the pouring rain and we stood for about five minutes conversing in Arabic so he could gauge how much I knew. Immediately afterwards, he informed my commanders my Arabic was more than passable. All my commanders promised that, after our seven months of training were up, a course for combat Arabic translators would open up to which I'd promptly be sent.

"Eli was very impressed by you," Yarden told me later that night. "He told us to use you. We will use you for everything."

And through the end of training, used I was, over and over again, usually to provide entertainment.

To break the boredom of a mock night-time ambush or the routine of a long march in the middle of the day, Yarden frequently called on me to serve as the tool to boost platoon morale. Smack dab in the middle of the thorny wilderness one bright day in the spring of 2009, when the most painful thorn-covered plants were also the most beautiful, we'd just completed an all-night exercise that began with a twenty-kilometer march and ended with an excruciating uphill battle against seventy cardboard terrorists.

After we laid our paper targets to recyclable waste, we lined up in two rows, bent down on one knee, and waited for instructions. Everyone stared at the ground dead from exhaustion, drenched with sweat, and silent with fear that the worst was not yet over. The sun we so anxiously awaited while exposed in the cold before dawn now radiated such burning heat our sweat glued us to our uniforms, making it extremely tough to pick out the thorns stuck in our underwear poking against our pricks.

"Michael! Get over here quick and get down next to me!" Yarden barked. I rose abruptly, clutched my M-4 semi-automatic assault rifle with two hands, and rushed over as fast as my tired bones would allow.

"Confirm that you identify the Bedouin on the slow donkey!" he commanded. A middle-aged, slightly obese Bedouin man rode atop an ass so large it was no wonder it moved at a snail's pace.

"I identify the donkey and the Bedouin, platoon commander."

"Throw out words to him."

"Throw out words to him?"

"What? Are you a parrot? Don't be in shock. Throw out words to him in Arabic." Yarden's pale face was always serious and his tone remained belittling as ever. It was impossible to tell if and when he was trying to be funny. "*Nu*, get on with it."

I sipped some water from the water sack I wore underneath my gear and yelled at the Bedouin to stop. He turned the donkey to face me and looked over. We exchanged greetings, and shortly after, the Bedouin burst out laughing. After I gave him permission to ride off, he pointed in my direction still giggling loudly to himself.

"Michael, what the hell did you say to him?" Yarden asked with a smirk.

"I told him it was going to snow later. I said it would get cold, so he should bring a sheep to bed. Then, I asked if he knew a good restaurant up the hill where I could order a chicken sandwich." The whole platoon started cracking up too.

"What made you to say these things?"

"I don't know. You told me to throw out words. I didn't have anything else to say."

In May, as training wound down to a close, I arranged another time to speak with Ohad to find out when I'd be sent to the Arabic course I'd been promised. I was concerned because no news had arrived and the end of training was imminent. As it turned out, I'd played up my Arabic skills perhaps a bit too well. When I arrived in Ohad's office, I sensed that no news was bad news.

"Michael, I'm going to be straight with you," Ohad began. "You're not going to the Arabic course. You already know more than a six-week course could ever teach you. I don't see a point in wasting a spot on you when I can send someone else who doesn't know any Arabic. If someone else goes, then Nachshon will have two Arabic translators, not one."

My heart sank. That was the only course I'd wanted since the lesson with Eli. I had been counting on it to train me not just to speak Arabic better, but to learn the skills needed to gather critical information. How could I be trusted to effectively serve as the voice of my unit on missions and arrests if I missed out on all proper instruction?

"Company Commander, I think you're making a big mistake," I objected. "I need to be taught the Palestinian dialect. All I know is what I learned from the pocket phrasebook I received in basic training. I need to be taught."

"Michael, relax. Your Arabic is great. Everyone says so. If your Arabic wasn't so good, how could you tell a Bedouin to go screw a sheep?"

"That's not exactly what I said. How'd you hear about that?"

"Michael, I'm pretty sure the Prime Minister heard about that. Listen. The course really isn't what you think. Even if your Arabic isn't what we hope it is, you're still better than everyone else."

"I don't know, Company Commander. I'd still feel better if I went to the course."

"Of course you don't know. You've been in the army for two seconds. Trust me. If a Palestinian is dangerous, he probably speaks Hebrew better than Ben-Gurion."

"But it's not just the language. How am I supposed to know how to handle myself?"

"Michael, stop. These courses are not going to teach you everything you need to know to handle yourself in every situation. That's going to come solely from experience, which your commanders have plenty of. You speak Arabic better than anyone in this battalion. Training's almost over. Soon, you're not going to be using your Arabic just to make people laugh anymore. You'll be using it make people scared. And it's up to you to get yourself ready for that immediately. You are dismissed."

Chapter 16
Palestinians Are Your Grandparents

Jericho, West Bank
May–June 2009

So, who here wants to kill arabs?"
Yarden smiled after he asked the question. Our platoon sat around picnic tables arranged in the shape of a *chet*—a Hebrew letter that resembles an open three-sided square—outside our barracks.

With the May sun beating down on our scalps, Yarden stood at the opening of the *chet* for God knows how long waiting for a response, smiling. He didn't get one. Yarden smiled so infrequently that it terrified all of us when he did. Was his smile genuine and jovial? Was he being deceptive and trying to trick us into saying something we'd regret? None of us knew. None of us ever knew.

Our seven months of training was set to be complete in another two weeks. The commander overseeing all Kfir's new recruits had labeled Nachshon the best battalion in the draft class. His praise came with a special assignment. For those last two weeks of training, rather than suffer through more war-time training exercises in the intense dry summer heat, we were being sent to a base right on the outskirts of Jericho to man the checkpoint at the city's entrance and exit, and patrol the surrounding area in armored Jeeps.

The assignment wasn't particularly sexy or glamorous, but we were eager to take it. We couldn't wait to do something—anything, really. Besides war, taking a tour of duty, called a *kav* in Hebrew, was exactly what our training was preparing us for. Going to Jericho meant we'd finally be dealing with Palestinians, people whom, if it was required of us, we might be forced to kill.

"What happened? Did all of you forget how to speak Hebrew?" Yarden chuckled. "Who here wants to kill Arabs?"

Everyone stared back at Yarden blankly for a few more seconds until a soldier named Ohad proudly thrust his left arm into the air with his trademark goofy smirk. Short but muscular with a mouth full of braces, Ohad came from a family with roots in Libya. Occasionally well-intentioned, he was a totally obnoxious son of a bitch who harbored a great deal of pent-up aggression. He loved picking on people just so he could get into fistfights with them.

During one three-week stretch, early on in basic training, Ohad decided he wanted to fight me. I hadn't done anything to provoke him, but that didn't matter. Ohad decided, and that was that. About three times a day, he'd belligerently grab me by the shirt, scream that I was a faggot, and threaten to fuck me. At first, I tried to be the mature adult and ignored his antics. I was twenty-three years old and Ohad was nineteen. I wasn't going to fight him. I didn't join the Israeli army to fight other Jews.

But one afternoon, right outside our barracks, Ohad tried to knee me in the testicles in addition to his normal routine. I exploded like dynamite.

"You say I'm a faggot? Then I'm going to fuck you!" I screamed with rage. I pushed him to the ground and smacked him in the mouth. We wrestled and jabbed each other in the stomach and head for a couple of moments until we were separated by the other guys. Ohad emerged with blood dripping down his bottom lip and a goofy grin. My cheeks were scratched up and my stomach muscles were bruised. Ohad was satisfied. He'd seen what I was made of. I didn't have another problem with Ohad for the rest of my service, but I never trusted him. When he raised his hand after Yarden asked his question, I wasn't surprised. He'd made disparaging remarks about Arabs before. It made me fearful of what he would do to them when he got the chance.

"Really? Only Ohad?" Yarden asked.

Roy, an easily annoyed Yemenite who had a penchant for screeching like a rabid Chihuahua, lifted his arm as well. No shock there. He was sitting next to Ohad. They were good friends who saw eye-to-eye about the Arabs. I could only imagine the bang-up job they were going to do on *kav* together.

"Okay, now listen carefully. Especially everyone who says they want to kill Arabs," Yarden said. "I had a friend in high school. He was as passionate as you could be about joining the army. He wanted to be in as crazy of a combat unit as there was. He went to the draft board. They asked him why he wanted to do this. He said, 'Because I want to kill Arabs.' You know what happened? The army decided he was crazy and sent him home. They refused to draft him.

"Why? Because in the Israeli army we don't want to kill anyone. We kill only when we must. The reality is that we can and will carry out our duties, no matter what they are, as professionally as possible and while being good people. Anyone who says, 'let's just kill all the Arabs' or 'let's send all the Arabs to Jordan' doesn't live in reality. That person clearly has never been in a combat unit because every fighter who has seen action knows how stupid an idea that is. Welcome to reality. I promise you all there are just as many good Arabs as there are bad Arabs."

"A good Arab is a dead Arab!" Ohad interrupted.

"Shut your mouth, Ohad!" Yarden rebuked. "Don't speak when your platoon commander speaks. And don't speak about Arabs the way the Nazis spoke about the Jews. The truth is it's not my or any other commander's job to care one way or the other what your opinions are. My job is to make sure you act according to the army's rules. And that means one thing: Treat Palestinians like your grandparents."

Excuse me? Did we hear you correctly, commander?

"That's right," Yarden assured us. "From now on, Palestinians are your grandparents. When you get to Jericho and man that checkpoint, you talk to people like you were talking to your grandmother. You don't curse at them. You don't touch them for any reason. If a Palestinian offers you food, jewelry, money, or anything else, you say, 'thank you, but no thank you.' You will take nothing from a Palestinian. When you're inside a Palestinian house doing a sweep, an arrest, or anything, you might find some nice things in there. You'll learn there are quite a few Palestinians with money. You might even think to yourself, 'this guy is a terrorist asshole. No one will care if I take a small bracelet or a necklace.'

"And the truth is your commanders won't check you either. No one's got the time to go through everyone's stuff after every arrest to see if you stole something. You'll also have a gun. Having a gun means you have power. But that doesn't mean you should do it. The second you abuse your authority you become no better than the terrorists trying to hurt our people and destroy what we've built. If you are caught acting against the values of the army in any way, I promise you will pay a heavy price. When you wear the green IDF uniform you behave with honor. You represent something bigger than yourselves. Let's not give the Palestinians any good reasons to hate us."

Ohad and Roy let out giggles.

"Why are you laughing?" Yarden snapped. "You don't think any Palestinians have good reasons to hate Israelis? You think that if you don't steal from a Palestinian or beat a Palestinian senseless, then anything else you do is okay? Wake up! If you're standing at a checkpoint and you see a father and son approaching and you notice that the father's teeth are messed up, you might think it's funny. You might think that guy looks hilarious. You might start laughing uncontrollably. But remember this: That man's son is probably thinking to himself, 'what's so funny? There's no dentist in my village. Even if there was we wouldn't have the money to pay for one.' That man's son is going to grow up with a reason to hate Israelis. And that would be a shame because all we're trying to do is to keep things quiet and peaceful so that everyone, both Israelis and Palestinians, can sleep safely at night. Let's go over some protocol now. Michael, are you listening?"

"Yes, Platoon Commander," I answered anxiously. Though my Hebrew had improved by leaps and bounds since arriving in Israel, I was still a bit nervous speaking publicly when put on the spot.

"Michael, let's say you and I are out and about in a village somewhere. Some Palestinians start throwing rocks at us. I order you to shoot a Palestinian who has no visible weapon. What do you do? Do you follow my order?"

"No, I would refuse."

"Even if I tell you you'll go to jail for disobeying your officer?"

"I would refuse."

"Good. If you shot a Palestinian just because I told you to, both you and I would go to prison for a long time. There is no excuse for following illegal orders. Soldiers are expected to think for themselves and behave morally. We don't shoot first and ask questions later. Roy! You're standing at a checkpoint and a man begins firing at you from fifty meters away. How do you respond?"

"I'd open fire on him," he belted out.

"Correct!" Yarden affirmed. "If your life is in immediate danger, you must fire back. That terrorist has already chosen his fate. But Roy, what if he has an ax in his hand and he's running at you screaming '*Allahu Akbar*' (God is Great)?"

"I'd do the same thing. I'd fire on him."

"Wrong! What's he going to do to you with an ax from fifty meters away? He can't do anything. Only after you shouted at him to stop and shot a bullet sixty degrees in the air to warn him, may you shoot him in the legs to disable him. You may only shoot to kill a terrorist if he has the ability, the intent, and the method to kill you. Nachshon."

"*Kavod!*" the entire platoon chanted in response. Honor.

"When we go to Jericho, we'll carry out our duties with *kavod*. Don't forget. Palestinians are your grandparents."

Only a ten-minute drive from the Dead Sea, Jericho was arguably the oldest city in the world with a history dating back more than ten thousand years. The first Palestinian city in the West Bank to have control handed over to the Palestinian Authority under the Oslo Accords, it enjoyed a tourism boom in the late 1990s. This saw the creation of the five-star Jericho Intercontinental Hotel, which hosted a popular casino that catered to tourists from around the world, including Israel.

However, at the beginning of the second Palestinian intifada in 2000, Jericho became the launching pad of numerous terrorist attacks and a hideout for Palestinian fugitives. Fighting between Palestinian militants and Israeli soldiers around the Jericho Intercontinental forced the successful casino to close its doors. The Israeli government was unable to guarantee the safety of its citizens in Jericho, so it banned Israeli Jews from entering the city. Although the Israeli army nominally re-took Jericho in 2001, it still allowed the Palestinian Authority to control the inside of the city, as the Oslo agreements dictated.

Aside from a brief Israeli incursion in 2006 to capture Palestinians responsible for assassinating former Israeli tourism minister Reha-vam Ze'evi, the cooperation between the Palestinian Authority and Israel over the years had generally been well-received by both sides. Consequently, as a goodwill gesture to the Palestinian Authority, the Israeli government agreed to remove the Jericho checkpoint at the city's entrance in June 2009. My Nachshon draft class was going to be the last IDF unit to regulate who passed in and out of Jericho before the checkpoint was dismantled.

The checkpoint we were set to man was stationed right in the mid-dle of the road. It was a barricade of four-foot-tall cement slabs in a rectangular shape, with poles along the edges holding up a tin roof. Since the checkpoint took up so much space on the road, the pave-ment had been widened to enable cars to pass.

Groups of five soldiers and one squad commander operated the checkpoint in eight-hour shifts. While the squad commander ensured the overall functioning of the checkpoint, two soldiers were assigned to control the entrance and two others the exit. Of each pair, one sol-dier checked Palestinians' IDs and car trunks. The other stood watch from behind one of the concrete slabs with his gun ready in case of trouble. On the left side of the road facing Jericho, the fifth soldier sat atop a guard post with a machine gun to protect the rest of the squad from a possible long-range attack.

Hardly a few minutes after getting off the bus, I was one of the soldiers ordered to take the first shift at the checkpoint. It was two in the afternoon and one hundred degrees outside. Walking to the checkpoint to assume our positions, the other guys cursed the heat.

"How do they expect us to stand for eight hours wearing our ceramic vests and the rest of our gear in this kind of weather?" Yonatan, a short sharp-shooter born in Colombia, complained. "Are we not human beings?"

Everyone let out a grunt of agreement. Everyone but me. Sweat dripped off my brow and I had to take a long swig of water, but I couldn't feel the heat. I barely heard Yonatan. All my brainpower and senses were preoccupied with one powerful emotion: fear. I wasn't thinking about the possibility of getting hurt or killed. I was afraid of the angry, disgruntled expressions of Palestinians whose freedom of movement I was about to obstruct and whose valuable time I was about to waste.

I was disturbed by the idea that Palestinians would view me as merely another enforcer of the occupation even though our stated goal was to keep the peace. I'd spent so much time trying to be friends with Arabs over the years. Now that push came to shove, it pained me that although I was there in an IDF uniform to fight for peace, everyday Palestinians weren't going to understand that right off the bat or ever.

Of course, I didn't believe that Israeli checkpoints were inhumane or unnecessary. On the contrary, checkpoints were one of the most effective means of preventing acts of terror. They'd enabled Israeli soldiers to find explosives and weapons hidden in Palestinian ambulances, on pregnant women, and inside baby carriages underneath crying infants. I also knew that Israeli soldiers didn't want the task of working at checkpoints any more than Palestinians wanted to pass through them. It was a necessary nuisance for innocent people on both sides.

As I approached the checkpoint and gazed at the tan-colored Intercontinental Hotel in the distance, I hoped that Andre, my hulk-sized Russian-born squad commander with a constant stone face, would let me start the shift on the guard tower or by providing cover. Originally from a small village in Siberia, Andre immigrated to Israel with his family at the age of twelve and never lost his thick accent or stern Soviet demeanor. Watching the other soldiers interact with Palestinians first would help me get a grip.

"Bassin, you're up first for checking IDs and trunks," Andre said. "You're the Arabic speaker. Go give it to them."

I did as I was told and stepped forward. I anxiously scanned the road until a beat-up brown Toyota with a green Palestinian Authority license plate came into view. As the car came near, I reminded myself to treat whoever was inside like my grandparents. If I did that, I reasoned, I couldn't hold myself responsible for their attitudes towards me.

When the Toyota ground to a halt, I saw an elderly Palestinian couple inside. I smiled at them. I expected a measure of civility from them as I hoped they did from me. What I did not expect, however, was for them to literally behave like my very own grandparents.

"Hello, our precious soldier," the man in the driver's seat said in Hebrew. "It is so hot out today. Take a bottle of water. Take." His hijab-covered wife sitting beside him fished out a liter-and-a-half bottle of water and handed it to her husband, who tried to shove it my hands along with their ID cards.

"Thank you, but I have enough water. The IDs are enough," I said back in Arabic. "May I look inside your trunk?"

"A soldier who speaks Arabic?" the man asked ecstatically once more in Hebrew as he popped the trunk. "That is truly amazing! You are a very special soldier."

Indeed, I supposed I was. Few infantry soldiers knew any Arabic beyond the basic phrases "show me your ID" and "stop, stop or I'll shoot you." After I verified that their dusty trunk had only dates and a carton of tomatoes inside, I thanked them for their patience and assured them they were free to go on their way.

"Give me something to give the boy to eat," the husband told at his wife in Arabic.

"No thank you. I can't accept anything."

"Nonsense. You must be healthy. Take chocolate for you and your friends. It is good for you, precious soldier."

He then shoved three completely sealed candy bars into my hands. If I hadn't accepted them, they would have fallen to the ground. Andre saw it all happen. He didn't let any of us eat them, but he did let out a rare laugh after the couple drove off.

"Arabs like you," he said. "That's good for us."

That made me happy. I realized that I was not the first Israeli Palestinians have come across. Israelis and Palestinians had been interacting with one another for over forty years by then. Many Palestinians, particularly from older generations, had worked for or with Israelis and spoke Hebrew to some degree. To average Palestinians who knew Israelis and just wanted to live comfortable, stable lives, such as the elderly couple I'd stopped, Israeli soldiers weren't looked on as evil bogeymen who could act with impunity. Rather, they saw Israeli soldiers working at checkpoints for what they were: people doing what they had to in order to make the best of a difficult and dangerous reality.

In the coming days, cars would stop and I'd immediately accost them with cheerful Arabic greetings. Not used to hearing an Israeli soldier speak Arabic with an American accent, some Palestinians asked me to repeat myself to make sure they were hearing correctly and that I was, in fact, speaking their language.

"What's the problem?" I'd reply to these befuddled people in Arabic. "You don't understand Arabic? Don't worry. It's not a hard language to learn. I'm sure you'll pick it up quickly."

They'd typically beam toothy smiles afterwards and engage me in light conversation, which usually involved a lot of compliments directed my way. On a few occasions, after passing inspection, fully covered Palestinian girls even blew kisses at me and waved.

One evening around dusk, a white Ford pickup truck pulled up packed with four Palestinian brothers and their American cousin, who was visiting from San Francisco. All of them had their IDs ready except for one, the youngest brother who suffered from some form of mental retardation. Smile and wave his hands at me as he did, I wasn't authorized to let anyone over the age of fourteen pass who did not carry their Palestinian ID on them. Not even a mentally retarded man.

"But he is our brother," the driver, a seemingly genuine guy in his early twenties wearing a pink V-neck t-shirt promised in Arabic. "We must get him home. We live only a few kilometers from here."

"I believe you, but you know the rules," I said. "Think about it from my side. I don't know who you are. What if he isn't your brother? What if you've taken him away from his family and want to harm him? I don't know. The fact that your brother has a disability is more reason for me not to let you pass. You could be anyone. I can have your brother stay here with someone to watch him while you go home and bring his ID."

The driver, who had been telling the truth, did as I suggested and the issue was resolved. His cousin from America was pleasantly surprised by how civilly the whole ordeal had been handled.

"That's cool that you wanted to protect my cousin from harm," he said with praise. "I wouldn't have expected that from an Israeli soldier. I hope the rest of the soldiers are doing as good of a job as you."

I was pleased to report that that seemed to be the case. Though the rest of the soldiers from Nachshon were not quite as buddy-buddy or gregarious with the Palestinians, they carried out their duties with manners and compassion. I even caught Ohad and Roy making small talk with Palestinians and joking around with them in Hebrew. It filled me with pride that whenever Palestinian school children walked through the checkpoint, my commanders insisted that each of them drink two cups of water from our supply.

Yup, everything was going much better than I'd expected, which was why I was taken aback when Yarden pulled me aside outside the dining hall to express concern over my behavior.

"All the commanders agree that your work in Arabic is incredibly helpful," he began. "They also say you're extremely friendly with the locals, maybe even too friendly with them. Now, I'm not saying that's always a bad thing. But I hope you understand that it's not good to get too friendly with the Palestinians."

"Why not?" I asked. "If I'm doing my job, what's wrong with being friendly?"

"Because they're not your friends. They may laugh with you at the checkpoint, but afterwards they're laughing at you. Not all of them necessarily, but a lot of them are. The friendlier you are, the weaker they perceive you. If they see you as weak, they see all of us as weak. And if that happens, the wrong people might get the idea that now they have a chance to pull off an attack against us."

Yarden's point hit home the next day when I was on a Jeep patrol with Andre. We'd stopped at a popular gas station and tourist rest stop at the Almog junction on the main Jerusalem-Dead Sea highway to fill up on gas and stretch our legs. Israeli-owned but Palestinian-operated, its Palestinian employees gave us soldiers as many free cups of cherry-flavored smoothie and ice coffee as we could handle. I thought they were doing it just to be nice. It didn't occur to me that there was another reason for their generosity.

While our driver filled up the tank and Andre and the other soldier on the patrol were buying pastries and salty snacks for the road, I wandered past all the tourists and Dead Sea skin care products and into the bathroom. When I returned, Andre was livid.

"Michael, where the hell were you?" he screamed at me.

"The bathroom. What's wrong?" I said back to him.

"You have to tell me where you're going at all times. A soldier was attacked in that bathroom in 2008. Two Palestinians followed him in there, stabbed him in the back, and stole his weapon. Do you know why they give soldiers free ice coffee here? It's to keep us coming back. You left yourself unprotected just now. Don't be a fool. Just because you can't see your enemies doesn't mean they're not there. Not everyone who's against us is going to hold up a flag to show us who he is."

But shortly thereafter, someone did. I was once again checking cars traveling into Jericho when Ohad ran up to me and shrieked that he and I had to switch positions.

"Go over to Roy on the other side. He's got an Arab acting like an asshole on his hands," he said. "Go take care of it."

I walked over and saw a yellow Palestinian shared taxi van filled with people at a stop. Flying from a pole connected to the roof was a bright yellow flag waving in the wind.

"Tell the driver to take the flag down!" Roy demanded. "I told him in Hebrew, but he wouldn't listen."

Turning to the driver, a husky middle-aged man with a dense black mustache and a *zebiba* prayer bump on his forehead, Roy yelled in Hebrew, "Do what he says or else."

"What's wrong with the flag on his roof?" I asked Roy dumbfounded.

"Because it's against the law to fly flags."

That wasn't exactly true. Before the signing of the Oslo Accords, it had been forbidden for any Palestinian to fly the Fatah or Palestinian national flags in Israeli-controlled territory. After the peace process began, Palestinians were allowed to fly those two specific flags, but not those of Hamas or any other terrorist group. It was possible that the flag was a sign of support for Hezbollah because of the color yellow, but I wasn't sure, because it didn't have any Hezbollah insignia on it. Whether the driver was permitted to fly his yellow flag really depended on what the flag meant.

"It's just a flag!" the driver said defensively in Arabic. All his passengers remained silent.

"Whose flag is it?" I asked.

"It's my flag."

"I know it's your flag. What does it mean?"

"Nothing. It's just a yellow flag."

"What's it doing with you, then?"

"It's not with me. It's on the roof."

"I can see it's on the roof. Why did you want to put it on the roof?"

"Because I like it."

"Why do you like it?"

"Because I like the flag."

"Michael, is everything under control?" Andre asked from afar.

"I'm trying to get him to tell me what his flag means, so I can see if he needs to take it down or not," I replied.

"If he's giving you problems, then make him take it down."

"*Mashallah!*" the driver mumbled to his passengers. Wow. "These soldiers are dogs."

This guy was acting like a jerk for no reason and it was easy to see he wasn't afraid of disobeying our commands. I didn't care about his silly yellow flag. He could have told me he flew it to show support for a soccer team or something. I would have believed him and sent him and his customers on their way. But he didn't. Now, I was left with no choice.

"Pull off to the side of the road and stand outside with your ID in your right hand!" I barked.

The man scratched his mustache anxiously and did as I said. Once he got out of the taxi van and stepped off to the side, I collected his ID and addressed his passengers.

"All of you might want to come outside too and wait for another taxi," I explained. "Your driver and his taxi might be staying here for a while."

"What's your problem?" he screamed as he pointed his finger at me. "This is my business. Why are you destroying my business?"

I drew my weapon to ready myself if he became violent. Roy pointed his gun at him too. I understood that, as someone who was probably more than twenty years my senior, he didn't like young soldiers like us telling him what to do. But I couldn't allow him to speak like that to me. It would have made all of us look weak and inspired others with dangerous intentions to test us. That would have been extremely irresponsible, so, for the first time in my service, I was forced to publicly humiliate a grown Palestinian man in front of his people.

"Lower your finger!" I yelled. "I didn't tell you to take down your flag. I asked you what your flag meant and why it's on your car. I did not receive answers. You got smart with me instead. Now, go up there and take your flag down!"

"Why? Why?" he protested. I wasn't about to give him an answer. I was finished negotiating.

"You have half a minute. *Yalla!*" The driver stood there defiantly with his arms crossed over his chest. "Are you deaf?" I screamed. "Or just stupid? Take the flag down or I'll keep your ID and we'll impound your vehicle! With no vehicle, you can't work. That, my friend, would be destroying your business."

Grudgingly, he climbed to the roof, untied the flag from the pole, and climbed down. I walked over to him and, as I gave him back his ID, said, "Don't do this again!"

The driver hopped back into his vehicle and drove off muttering to himself.

"Whoa Michael, are you sure you're not going to give him a kiss goodbye too?" Roy joked. "I have no idea what you said, but I know one thing. That Arab's going to curse you for a thousand years."

"Oh Mike, *I'm* ready to kiss you after that," Ohad cried out with his trademark goofy smirk.

What had just happened? I replayed my words and actions from the incident over and over in my head and came away with the same conclusion. Although I could have chosen to use slightly less colorful language, ultimately the driver's behavior forced me to speak to him condescendingly. That realization made my stomach turn. I'd tried hard to remain polite and it still happened.

What was that Palestinian man thinking trying to test me after I'd been standing for hours in the sun, thirsty, and possibly embittered from dealing with other obnoxious people before him? The most frightening part of the ordeal for me, however, was that deep down, I enjoyed the power I held over him. Authority is clearly addictive. After he proved uncooperative, it felt good to talk down to him in front of his customers. This was a side of me I didn't know existed, but that inherently comes with the position of authority I was placed in. It was a side of me I hoped I would be able to keep in check, though that would prove difficult when I was put in situations that weren't so clear.

One of my last days on the Jericho *kav*, I was operating the checkpoint's exit when a flashy black BMW convertible playing loud Arabic pop music came by. Its driver was a Palestinian in his early twenties with a goatee, a polo shirt, and a head of long, wavy hair. When he put the car in park, he looked straight at me with a frown. I yelled at him to turn his music down, but he didn't. Instead, he held his hand up to his ear and mockingly shrugged his shoulders to indicate that he couldn't hear me. Already he'd gotten my blood to boil.

I stood there patiently and vowed to wait until he got the hint. What did I care? I had to stand at the checkpoint either way. It was he who supposedly had somewhere to go. The driver sat in his convertible with the music blaring and stared straight ahead for a good forty-five seconds until he realized he'd be stuck if he didn't lower the volume.

"Turn the music off completely," I said in Arabic. "Please hand me your ID."

"Your Arabic is very, very bad," he said scornfully. "Who taught you Arabic? A donkey?"

Now, my Arabic was certainly nowhere near the level of a native speaker. But I was conversationally sound and I knew how to ask to see someone's ID. Nevertheless, there was no reason for him to insult me.

"Show me your ID and open the trunk," I ordered.

"Just speak to me in English!" he said in fluent English. Clearly, he was not only wealthy, but educated too. "Your Arabic is terrible. Do you speak English? Did you go to school? Do you need me to speak more slow for you?" Well, somewhat educated.

"Slowly!" I corrected his English. "You should have said, 'Do you need me to speak more slowly for you?' Show me your ID. Some cars are about to arrive and I don't want to have you here holding up the line."

"So, let me go."

"Show me your ID and I will."

"Why should I show you my ID? You are not from the Palestinian army. I don't have to follow the rules of an occupying racist force."

"I'm not here to argue politics with you. Show me your ID."

The car's trunk popped open suddenly.

"My ID is in the trunk. Go get it if you want to see it bad enough."

And just like that, I snapped. I smiled, walked over to the trunk, picked up his ID, made sure it was him in the photo, and told him to park his car on the side of the road and wait.

"Wait? Why?" he protested. "You can see it's me in the photo. I have to be in Ramallah in twenty minutes."

"It's my job to protect Israel from all threats. You've been hostile towards me from the moment you drove up. So, I feel I must investigate you with the Shin Bet (the Israeli equivalent of the FBI) to see if you're a fugitive or not. It's for the safety of my country, I assure you."

Like all soldiers, I certainly had the right to stop a driver at random to make such an inquiry if I felt it was necessary. The truth was I knew that this arrogant rich kid posed little, if any, threat. Wanted Palestinian fugitives didn't flaunt flashy sports cars or insult soldiers so readily. But, since he'd actively disrespected me, I couldn't let him get off so easily. If a basic sense of respect wasn't upheld time and time again, a much more dangerous reality would eventually ensue.

After he parked his convertible and stood where I could see him, I handed his ID over to Andre, who called all the relevant contacts while I checked other Palestinian cars. The entire process of conducting a thorough background check only took five minutes. When it was over, I was ready to give him back his ID. But when I walked over to him to do just that, he started up again with more shenanigans.

"Soldier, you are a *sharmoota!*" he yelled, calling me a whore. "I'm not like you. I'm better than you. I don't need to be here. I have somewhere better to be right now! You give me back my ID now! Now!"

Immediately, I stopped walking towards him. Once again, I needed to see that he could treat me with a basic level of respect, the same respect that I had intended to show him when he drove his car up to my area of the checkpoint.

"I'm afraid I can't do that now," I said again. "The inspection will take longer. Be patient."

He responded by screaming out curses in Arabic. I put the man's ID in my pocket and returned to my post for another thirty minutes before giving it back and letting him drive off. Though I hadn't done anything explicitly illegal, I understand how it could be argued that I'd held him up and wasted his time for reasons that did not pertain to Israel's direct security.

But if I'd let him get away with walking all over me, who knew where it would end? I began to realize that even though I truly wanted to treat Palestinians in a respectful and humane manner, it wasn't always possible. It was the Palestinians who often dictated the response they received from Israeli soldiers. Especially when things got violent.

Chapter 17
A Patrol of Fear

Tarqumiya, West Bank
August–November 2009

THE FIRST TIME A PALESTINIAN TRIED TO KILL ME, I SHOULD have been asleep. My Nachshon draft class and I were in our second week on the *kav* outside Tarqumiyah, a Palestinian town near Hebron in the southwestern area of the West Bank. We were exhausted. After completing an intense two-month, battalion-wide training session in the summer of 2009, we were thrust onto the *kav* by ourselves, with too many responsibilities and too few soldiers to carry them out.

At all hours of the day we were being called up to do guard duty, kitchen duty, Jeep patrols, makeshift checkpoints, foot patrols, twenty-four hour ambushes, and two-day long shifts inside a pillbox.

A pillbox is a thirty-foot-tall multi-story fortified tower with a panoramic view, surrounded by a small outdoor area and protected by a sealed-off circle of tall concrete slabs. These towers are usually stationed near major Palestinian traffic arteries where soldiers take shifts monitoring the scene below. When Andre told me I was going up to the pillbox for a stint with him, Yonatan, and Giddy, a giant of a soldier who happened to be the gentlest guy in the platoon, I was elated.

To civilians, the thought of being locked away inside a tower for forty-eight consecutive hours must sound like torture; but to me and the rest of the soldiers who'd been functioning on as little as three to four hours of sleep per day, operating the pillbox was almost as good as a beach vacation. For every four hours of monitoring, a soldier was allotted twelve hours of down time afterwards to sleep, eat, or do just about anything else he wished.

We entered the pillbox just before six in the evening. Determined to seize the opportunity for a good night's sleep, I volunteered for the first four-hour shift. Time flew by. The other guys sat and chatted with me during most of the shift and together we enjoyed an extended meal of chicken cutlets and rice. By the time Giddy replaced me at ten o'clock on the dot, I was so drowsy from the meal that I passed out immediately on the thin mattress I'd hauled from base for what I hoped would be one of the longest slumbers of my army service.

Shortly after midnight, I woke up to faint shouts from outside. I yelled up at Giddy to look around the perimeter and see what was going on. When Giddy didn't answer, I knew there was a problem. I raced up to the top of the pillbox to find big Giddy dozing off in his chair right in the middle of his shift.

"Open your eyes!" I ordered as I shook his shoulders violently.

Giddy sat up slowly, rubbed his eyes underneath his glasses, and yawned.

"I was sleeping," he told me.

"Thanks for updating me," I said sarcastically. "I heard shouting from outside. Check out who's shouting and why."

I gave Giddy a pat on the back and trudged down the steps.

"Michael, go open the door quick!" Giddy yelled an instant before I could lie back down on my mattress. "Wake up, Andre. It's Ohr outside. Shit. What's he trying to pull now?"

To the sorrow of most of my platoon, Ohr, fresh out of officers' school, was our new platoon commander. He'd replaced Yarden, who was moved to a more veteran platoon in the middle of the summer training session. Shorter than average with beefy arms and a chest that was too muscular for his frame, Ohr walked and talked like Buzz Lightyear in olive green fatigues. People joked that the radio set he wore on his back over his gear functioned as his jet pack.

Like many newly minted commanders taking over a new group of soldiers, Ohr tried to establish himself as our leader by acting like a tough-as-nails, anal bastard. Even though we were out of training, he maintained psychological distance and berated us for the slightest infraction. He constantly pestered us to keep all our equipment perfectly in order at all times and go out of his way to catch soldiers he suspected were likely to break guard duty. Unfortunately, Giddy was one such soldier. For some reason, Giddy was incapable of focusing solely on guarding for any significant period. If it was reported that someone was caught reading a newspaper, playing with their cell phone, or sleeping on duty, eight times out of ten Giddy was the soldier in question.

While Andre sat up from his mattress and composed himself, I stepped out of the tower, unlocked the entrance to the pillbox, admitted our unpopular platoon commander, and prayed that he hadn't come just to test us.

"Everybody up right now!" Ohr demanded. "Get your gear, put your helmets on, and get to the *ze'ev.*" In Hebrew, a *ze'ev* is a wolf. In the IDF though, it refers to the Wolf Armored Vehicle, an Israeli-made heavily armored crew carrier that seats up to twelve and looks like a Ford F-550 on steroids. "I already have six other soldiers in there. We're waiting for all of you. Now move!"

"Who's replacing us here in the pillbox?" Andre asked.

"Nobody right now! We have something more urgent to deal with. There's been an incident. I'll explain in the *ze'ev.* Just tell me why the hell it took all of you so long to open the door. Who was sleeping when they were supposed to be watching for terrorists?"

"I was," Giddy confessed as he came down the stairs.

"Congratulations Giddy. You're staying on base for Shabbat."

"*Zayin!*" Penis! In army slang, belting out the word "penis" is akin to saying "shit."

"Let's move!"

To infinity and beyond, I half-expected him to say. Once we piled into the *ze'ev* and joined the other soldiers from our platoon, Ohr explained that Israeli Jews from a nearby settlement had reported the theft of three pickup trucks and a tractor.

Local police radioed all military Jeep patrols in the region to keep watch for the stolen vehicles. Approximately thirty minutes before Ohr showed up at the pillbox, one of our company's Jeeps caught sight of them and launched a full speed chase. The tractor managed to break down the entrance to one of the internal security fences that separated Israeli and Palestinian-controlled territory in the West Bank to get away. That fence was located inside the area Nachshon was responsible for protecting.

All the trucks followed the tractor. The pursuing Jeep requested permission to continue the hunt into Palestinian territory. Permission was granted, but the Jeep was forced to wait for backup. Along with another Jeep ferrying Ohad, the company commander, and his personal three-man squad, we were the backup.

Our *ze'ev* met up with the two Jeeps at the broken fence. The fence was wide open and the lock to its access point was destroyed. Four soldiers were rushed over from our base to keep watch over the site, so that intruders wouldn't be able cross through. The location would have to be guarded around the clock, which meant one more task to carry out by our already thinly stretched company. Daniel, a fast-talking Russian who'd been in the Jeep tracking the culprits, was furious his patrol hadn't been allowed to keep up the chase.

"We could have caught them by now!" he insisted. "We were right behind them. When they broke through the fence we could see their taillights and the dust being kicked up from their tires. Now they're long gone."

Not so fast, fast-talking Daniel. The West Bank is laden with thousands of tiny cameras that enable the IDF to keep track of most movement in the territory.

After just a few short minutes at the site of the break-in, our commanders were notified that the tractor and trucks had been spotted heading towards a Palestinian town called Beit Awwa. Immediately, we shut the doors to the *ze'ev* and followed the two Jeeps in pursuit of the thieves.

Located right on the Green Line, the border separating the West Bank from Israel proper, Beit Awwa was a place where Israelis were despised. Destroyed by the Israeli army during the 1967 war, Beit Awwa was rebuilt by residents who came to be avid supporters of Hamas and who sent a fair share of their boys to serve in the Izz ad-Din al-Qassam Brigades, the Hamas military wing.

The Israeli army avoided incursions unless it had an urgent need to enter the town. Stolen property that successfully made its way into Palestinian towns and cities would never be seen again. Palestinians wouldn't cooperate with Israeli investigators to track down the crooks nor could the Palestinian police be relied on to carry out a serious search. Thousands of Israeli vehicles were stolen by Palestinians each year and taken to chop shops just over the Green Line. If we didn't find those stolen vehicles that night, no one ever would.

We took bumpy, unpaved back roads and got to Beit Awwa in less than ten minutes. Sitting in the last row of the *ze'ev*, I couldn't see much of the town out the tiny, barred window to my side. But I could hear everything. Ramadan had begun a few days before and Beit Awwa's residents were clearly having a rowdy all-night celebration. Fireworks were going off, Arabic music boomed from speakers, and hundreds of people packed the streets cheering and dancing.

Some people stopped and watched us pass as we sped down the street. overall, the townspeople kept on celebrating and appeared determined to ignore us. That was good, I thought. We didn't come looking for trouble. We had a clear purpose and no desire to interfere with anyone's festivities. However, I was about to learn once more that in the Middle East appearances can be deceiving.

After slowly advancing for another half minute, we began hearing dozens of rocks hitting the armor of the *ze'ev*. They sounded like pebbles harmlessly bouncing off the sides. Then, about ten Palestinian men crowded around us and banged on our doors with clubs and sledgehammers. Two Palestinians stared at me through my tiny window and grinned as they took turns smashing the surface right below it with a metal club. Thwack, thwack! Because I was in the *ze'ev*, there was virtually no chance they could have hurt me, but that didn't stop my heart from racing. The men scattered when heavy cinderblocks and bricks rained down on us from the buildings next to the street.

"Make sure your heads don't touch the ceiling," Ohr commanded from the front passenger's seat. "Not even your helm—" He stopped speaking when a cinderblock crashed into the front windshield right in front of his face. Luckily, the windshield was made from shatterproof plexiglass, so the cinderblock didn't break through and crush him. Still, the impact made most of the windshield impossible to see through and forced our driver to completely stop.

The two Jeeps ahead of us stopped as well. Through the small section of unbroken plexiglass, we could see a glass bottle smash into the corner of the roof and side of Ohad's Jeep and burst into a ball of flame. For a few seconds, we watched in awe as parts of the roof and side were lit ablaze. Thankfully, the fire fizzled out on its own after only a couple of seconds.

"We've been hit by a Molotov cocktail!" we heard Ohad stammer over the radio. A Molotov cocktail is a breakable glass bottle holding a flammable substance, such as gasoline or kerosene, with a wick held in place by the bottle's stopper. When the wick is lit and the bottle is broken, a raging fire erupts while the remainder of the fuel is consumed. "Another one exploded next to us. A crowd of Palestinians is blocking the road. They refuse to move."

Trapped. I didn't have the faintest idea how we were going to get out of there without running over Palestinians with reckless abandon. While Ohr conversed with Ohad over the radio, rocks continued to bounce off the *ze'ev*'s armor and the Palestinian men with the heavy tools went right back to bludgeoning our exterior. I closed my eyes and thanked God we were safe from the mob trying to lynch us. Our doors were locked and there was no way anyone was getting in.

"Open up the back doors!" Ohr ordered.

"What?" someone yelled.

"Have you gone crazy?" another screamed.

"I need someone in the back to get out of the *ze'ev* and end this party!" Ohr said. "Michael's back there, right? Michael, get out of the *ze'ev* and throw a few stun and gas grenades in different directions. Yonatan, you get out too and give Michael some cover."

"They're going to kill us if we go outside!" Yonatan objected. "What if someone has a gun?"

"You have a gun. If they have guns, shoot them! Get out now!"

Gulp. I rose from my seat and hunched beneath the ceiling while Yonatan opened the doors. I felt so nervous that I couldn't speak. We were not trained to fight two-on-ten or a hundred or two hundred or however many Palestinians were out there. Nevertheless, when Yonatan jumped out with his gun pointed straight ahead, I did the same without hesitating.

As soon as our feet hit the pavement, we cocked our assault rifles. All the Palestinians with sledgehammers and clubs moved away, as if they were unsure what their next move should be. But, the rocks kept coming and we had to constantly watch for bricks and cinder-blocks. Another soldier from inside the *ze'ev* pushed the box of grenades towards me. Yonatan aimed his gun at whoever was in his sight while I fished for a grenade.

I grabbed a gas grenade and moved around the back door on the right side and looked at all the people who up until a few minutes before had been having a party. A part of me felt bad. None of those people had planned for any of this. They couldn't have known that Nachshon was about to roll into town. They were just celebrating Ramadan. But then I saw four young men trying to light more Molotov cocktails. I wasn't sure if they could throw them far enough to hit me, but I wasn't willing to take the chance. The people around us might not have anticipated our arrival, but they had obviously been more than ready to unleash surprises of their own.

I pulled the pin, hurled the gas grenade across the street as hard as I could, and watched the people run for cover. People covered their eyes and noses with their shirts as they ran from the scene. Others barricaded themselves inside the homes and businesses along the street, and shut all the windows. I took a stun grenade and tossed it at the men who'd been pummeling the *ze'ev*. They too sprinted away, but a few slowed down and one man fell to the ground when the grenade went off. I tossed two more stun grenades in various directions and watched the crowd scatter. In a strange sort of way, the experience was exhilarating. It made it easy to understand how, in the fog of battle, soldiers can end up getting carried away.

"Alright. Ohad's soldiers successfully neutralized the blockade in front of us," Ohr said. "Yonatan and Michael, get back in the *ze'ev*."

Yonatan was hopping up into the vehicle when I noticed a masked man running towards us from about thirty feet away with a lit Molotov cocktail in his hand. According to the army's code of conduct, I was authorized to shoot him in the legs to disable him. However, I blanked over whether I had enough time to properly warn him.

A gas grenade already in my right hand, I decided to use that instead. I pulled the pin and underhand tossed it in the man's direction. The gas started spewing after a few short seconds and the man immediately stopped. He threw his weapon of choice directly at me before dashing away. The Molotov cocktail was in the air for probably just over a second, but it was enough time for me to fill my mind with plenty of unpleasant thoughts.

I'm going to burn to death. My fellow soldiers are going to have a catastrophe on their hands. I should have shot the bastard when I had the chance.

Fortunately, the Molotov cocktail crashed and exploded about ten feet in front of me with just a few shards of glass slicing into my clothes. Shaken, I stared at the fire for a moment, then jumped back into the *ze'ev*, and closed the doors. Due to our damaged windshield, we returned to base instead of continuing the search for the stolen trucks and tractor. We lost them.

I went to bed that night replaying the image of the Molotov cocktail flying at me. Overjoyed to be safe and healthy, I promised myself I wouldn't endanger my life like that again. I decided that the next time someone tried to kill me, I wouldn't be afraid to put a bullet in him.

I got the chance to test that readiness a few weeks later. Nachshon's failure to find the stolen trucks and tractor apparently gave other local Palestinians the idea that they could pull off similar feats. Every couple of days, reports trickled in about Palestinians destroying parts of the internal security fence under Nachshon's jurisdiction to steal scrap metal or to smuggle through people, drugs, or bomb-making material. These repeated incidents compelled Nachshon's battalion commander to authorize Jeep patrols to tour Palestinian-controlled territory close to the fence.

I was on a Jeep patrol with Andre and Alexey, a sharp shooter originally from Uzbekistan who was Jewish on his father's side, one pitch-black evening on the Palestinian side of the internal security fence when the driver, Taher, a heavy-set Bedouin from the Galilee, suddenly switched off the motor and declared that he was hungry.

"Everybody out now!" he instructed. "Someone grab the food. We're eating dinner on the hood of the Jeep. I can't hold out any longer."

I took out the food with Alexey, and we set it up on the hood of the Jeep. We started to chow down on couscous, tomato and cucumber salad, and hard-boiled eggs, when Taher brought up the same topics of conversation with me he always did when we were on a Jeep patrol together.

"Michael, you are a spy?" he asked me in Arabic with a wink.

"Maybe. If I was would I tell you?" I asked in response.

"Who are you with, the Mossad or the *mukhabarat*?"

"You don't want the answer."

As expected, Taher laughed uproariously and informed Andre that I was now the one in charge.

"Michael is the commander, not you, Andre," Taher announced in Hebrew. "Michael, tell me. When you were in Egypt, you fucked Arab chicks?"

"Maybe. Maybe not," I said.

"Michael, you must tell me."

I couldn't decide if the idea of me having sex with Arab women bothered him or not. I opted not to tell him, partially because I didn't think I owed him an answer, but mostly because it was fun to drive him nuts from not knowing.

Soon into the meal, we heard slow footsteps in an olive orchard nearby. Instantly, we all put our hands on our guns.

"Stop. Identify yourself!" I commanded in Arabic. "Remove your ID and hold it in your right hand. Then, raise your hands in the air."

The man did as I said. Andre shined the flashlight on his gun at him, so I could inspect his ID. The guy looked like an Arab stereotype from forty years ago. He was about thirty years old, balding, sported a dark black mustache, and wore khaki pants and a plaid shirt of various shades of brown. He said he lived up the road and was just on a walk. He didn't have a weapon or tools on him, so we accepted his story.

We were about to let him go when Taher asked if he could see the man's mobile phone. A tad confused, the man complied and handed it over. Taher skimmed through all the songs on it. He even found a few pictures of some naked women the guy had downloaded from the Internet and passed it around for us to see. We all giggled and, although he was clearly embarrassed by what we'd found, the Palestinian man did too. Taher told him a few jokes in Arabic that I didn't understand and, after another couple of minutes, the man continued on his way.

"That man was a *sharmoota*," Taher proclaimed after the man was out of earshot.

"What makes you say that?" I asked. "You seemed to get along well with him."

"Michael, don't be so naïve. All these Palestinians, they're all liars and cheats. They won't stop until they've screwed over everyone who's ever worn an IDF uniform."

"What are you saying all this for? You just looked at the man's phone."

"Yeah, yeah. He was nice and friendly to me. They all are. They act that way because they respect me. But why do they respect me? Because I have two hundred friends (bullets) that can all run faster than they can. Deep down, I know they hate me. How can they not? These people are taught to hate us. They want all Israelis dead. They hate you, Michael. They hate you because you're a Jew. But they hate me more. I'm an Arab working with Jews. They see me as the Jewish lap dog."

"So, what would you tell a Palestinian if he called you out on that and said you were a traitor for working with the Jews?"

"I'd say 'Fuck you, what the hell is a Palestinian? You think my Bedouin grandmother was a Palestinian before the Jews took over this land?' Hell, the people who call themselves Palestinian treated the Bedouin like shit. I have nothing in common with Palestinians. If I had to pick, I'd be a Jew through and through over being a Palestinian. They say my identity is messed up? Their identity is messed up. I like my life, I do my job, and I support who supports me. And that's Israel. They say I'm a traitor? They can go to hell."

"Then why did you take that guy's phone and tell him jokes?"

"To show him that I'm a human being. That it's possible to be an Arab, a Muslim, and serve in the same army as the Jews. The Jews are the people fighting for peace and stability in this country. Being here in the Israeli army, I feel like I'm defending my tribe from people who want to harm us. Even if that guy curses me afterwards, at least he'll have that idea stuck in his head. Maybe deep down he'll be more open-minded."

I was interested in continuing our heart-to-heart about Arab-Jewish coexistence, but was forced to stop when a rusty old pickup truck drove down a nearby hill at top speed heading straight towards us. We stood there in shock wondering what the driver was thinking. He was traveling in the direction of the fence alright, but he clearly didn't see us standing in his way.

He finally did, roughly sixty feet before reaching us, slamming on his brakes and swerving left to avoid us. His two left wheels were lifted into the air, the truck nearly flipping over. When the wheels landed back on the ground, the truck's motor died and the vehicle came to a complete stop. Without flinching, Alexey, Andre, and I dropped our food, put on our helmets, cocked our rifles, and ran towards the truck screaming, "*Waakef, waakef!*" Stop, stop!

"Get out of the truck!" I yelled in Arabic. "Out of the truck now!"

The driver refused to heed my order. I was about to repeat myself when the man unleashed a handgun and fired. Due to the angle he fired at, there was no real chance he was going to hit us. Nevertheless, all three of us dropped to the ground.

"Shoot him in the head!" I heard Taher yell from the Jeep. "Shoot the asshole in the head."

The driver fired two more inaccurate bullets before re-starting his engine and stepping on the gas.

"I give you permission to fire on the vehicle!" Andre said. "Shoot to kill the driver."

I crouched down on one knee, aimed my gun at the upper left windshield near the driver's head, and pulled the trigger three times. The noise from the gunshots was deafening. During target practice, soldiers always shoot with earplugs to protect them from potential hearing loss. In real-life combat, this is impossible because soldiers must be able to hear everything around them at all times. Andre and Alexey fired on the windshield as well. One of them aimed for the tires too and may have blown one out, but I wasn't certain. The driver swerved when his windshield shattered, but didn't stop. He stuck his gun out the window one last time and fired another misguided round before speeding away.

Although we failed to kill or capture the assailant, we did prevent a potentially calamitous assault on the internal security fence that might have resulted in an untold number of deaths if we hadn't been there at the right time. What truly amazed me was how completely unfazed I was by it during and afterwards. I didn't feel emotion of any kind, only the surge of adrenaline that put my survival instincts in overdrive. I had tried to kill another human being and it didn't bother me. It seemed natural. He'd made himself my enemy and therefore, he deserved to die.

Army intelligence deduced that our enemy, along with most of the other Palestinians who'd taken a crack at vandalizing the fence, hailed from the close-by town of Idhna. Situated thirteen kilometers west of Hebron and one kilometer east of the Green Line, it had been inhabited for thousands of years by Jews, Arabs, Byzantines, and others. Since attacks on the fence and intrusions into Israeli territory had not ceased, only one tactic might make Idhna's residents stop.

"Causing them fear," Ohr stated coolly while he briefed our platoon a week later. "Today I'm taking five soldiers out on a patrol of fear. We'll be going to the outskirts of Idhna to intimidate people in any way we can. It's the only way these people are going to stay away from the fence. They must know that there will be consequences if they choose to mess with us. If we disrupt these people's lives, maybe they'll actively discourage their friends and family from coming near the fence. There are 19,000 people who live in Idhna. I want every one of them to know that the army won't put up with any more of their antics."

"What are you saying? We're going to beat Arabs?" Alexey asked.

"We're not going to beat anyone. We're just going to scare them. It's called psychological pressure."

"How are we going to do that?"

"It's simple. We'll use Michael."

The way Ohr explained it to me before we set off on the twelve-hour patrol was that I was going to walk alongside him in front of the four other soldiers and basically annoy and scream at any Palestinian we came across. The Israeli army was known far more for its improvisation than for its detailed planning, but this specific mission seemed particularly not well thought out. I didn't know how I should go about "intimidating" local villagers and what the line was in terms of humane and inhumane treatment. Ohr said there was a fine line and that we would do our best not to cross it. I wasn't sure we'd succeed.

A *ze'ev* dropped us at the access point of the internal security fence nearest Idhna around ten in the morning. After Ohr opened the entrance with his key, he let us all through and locked it behind us. Although the area was technically Palestinian-controlled, Israeli combat units could enter when high-level commanders gave them clearance to do so. We began to march through fields that were totally devoid of people. Only after a half-hour of walking did we spot our first Palestinian far off in the distance, riding a brown donkey. I couldn't tell with my naked eye whether the Palestinian in question was a man or a woman. It mattered because we were constantly being warned by our superiors not to speak with Palestinian women unless absolutely necessary.

"Call out to the Palestinian!" Ohr roared. "And tell him something he'll never forget."

Getting myself fired up and into the role of being a complete jerk, I screamed in Arabic, "Hey you! Come over here. I want to speak with you now." The Palestinian stared back at me in silence. "What's the problem? I told you to come over here. Do as I say or else." The Palestinian kicked the donkey and the donkey began to run. "Hey, stop that donkey."

"Enough talk!" Ohr said. "Everyone after the donkey. *Yalla!*"

There we were, six Israeli soldiers carrying heavy equipment on our backs running in vain after a Palestinian on a strong, fast donkey. We ran after the Palestinian on the donkey until we were completely out of breath. Ironically, when we stopped the chase, the Palestinian made the donkey slow down as well. Ohr cocked his rifle and fired a bullet in the air. The Palestinian on the donkey looked at us unflinchingly as we re-grouped. Suddenly, an elderly man carrying a cane and dressed in a discolored bluish *jalabiyya* hurried over to us from a different field screaming. I recognized fully that my belligerent behavior had thus far not yielded any positive results. But still, I was disgruntled from having been disobeyed. It made me want to get into character even more.

"What do you want with my wife?" the old man yelled. "That is my wife on the donkey."

"You stop right there. You don't ask me questions. I ask the questions!" I snapped. "Do you understand?" The man stopped talking, closed his eyes for a moment, and crossed his arms. "Okay, now. I wanted to speak to your wife about her permit for being in this area. She did not respond to my calls to stop her. Tell her to come over here immediately. And show me your permit for being here too."

Palestinians were required to obtain special permits if they had to tend to crops very close to the internal security fence.

"Why do you yell at her? Leave her. She is my wife! I am responsible. I don't have the permit with me. It is with Captain Hamoudi (the local Druze IDF officer in charge of the civil administration of the region). I am waiting for an extension."

"Why should I believe you? I come here and what happens? Your wife disobeys me. You don't have your permits with you? Do I need to take you both to jail for trespassing?"

"I am very sorry I don't have my permit with me. It's with Captain Hamoudi. I am waiting for a new one. This is my land. I have a right to be here. Please, I can't go to jail. My heart can't take it."

The man lowered his head trembling while his wife on the donkey frowned at us. Why was I behaving this way? I was humiliating an old man who almost certainly bore no responsibility for the disturbances in the area. Feeling extremely silly, I relaxed my tone of voice and told him he didn't have to worry about anything, but that he and his wife should walk around with their permits.

"Thank you, thank you," the man responded. I felt bad because it seemed that the only reason he was thanking me was because he knew I was not about to humiliate him further or cause him any more strain. "Please, may I get some tea for you and the rest of the soldiers?"

I declined his offer on behalf of the squad and we continued with our patrol.

"I liked your aggression, but we should really be focusing on younger men," Ohr said. "They're the ones we're really after."

We found two such younger men just standing around a bit farther up the path. Looking to be in their mid-twenties, their hair was gelled and their white t-shirts were dirty with mud and hay. When they noticed us walking towards them, they smiled. I scowled. I ordered them to hand me over their IDs. After they did, I spent a good minute glancing over their pictures, reading through all their personal information, and conferring with Ohr. I wanted them to think that I had reason to be suspicious of them and that we were specifically out searching for people that matched their description.

"Is there a problem?" the taller of the two asked.

"Yes, there is," I answered. "We're looking for people who like to make trouble near the fence. Do you like to make trouble?"

"No, no. I do not make trouble," he said nervously.

"Tell me where you work," I said coolly. He paused. "Where do you work?"

"I work in the . . . the . . . chicken coop," he stuttered.

"Where is this chicken coop?"

"Over there."

"Does your friend work there too?" He nodded his head. "How long has he worked there? How long have you worked there?"

"Uh . . . uh . . . five years and three years."

"Who's worked there five and who's worked there three? Tell me now!"

"I have worked there for five years and he's been there for three years."

"Why do you work there? Why of all the jobs in Idhna did you choose to work there?"

"It belongs to my fa . . . fa . . . mily."

"How many eggs do you eat a day?"

"*Shoo?*" What?

"I said how many eggs do you eat a day? Tell me!"

"Uh, about three or four."

"No, no, no, no, no!" I yelled disapprovingly.

"What no? What no?" he asked frantically. His face reflected so much angst I wondered if he'd wet his pants.

"That's terrible for your health. You know what cholesterol is? You should only eat one egg per day. Got it?"

"Ah, yes sir. One egg is much better."

"Now, why do you like to make trouble near the fence? Why?"

"I don't make trouble near the fence!" he howled in clear desperation.

He seemed like he was telling the truth, so I asked Ohr for approval to let them go. It was granted and the two went back to work. As we walked away, I acknowledged to myself that I'd probably just ruined that guy's day. I'd publicly demeaned him and visibly shaken him up. He had to have hated me for that. After his encounter with me, he might have become more likely to join a terrorist group or to support attacks against the fence. Or he might have understood that the only reason I'd come after him on his turf was because people from his town had come after my unit and me on our turf. If there were no assaults on Israeli property or people, there would be no intrusions into his village. It was difficult to figure out what kind of effect my actions were really having and if there was a way to be effective without being overly aggressive.

We eventually headed into a narrow, rocky valley that signaled the start of Idhna proper. On top of both sides of the valley stood large, multi-story homes made of marble and concrete. Each house had a large balcony where families had congregated to spend a lovely afternoon together. As we encroached further into the valley, nearly all the people within sight leaned over the edge of their balconies and began to shout at us. At first, it was hard to make out what they were saying. But, as we climbed the left side of the valley and approached an upward path leading to the town, the message was loud and clear.

"*Itbach al-yahud! Itbach al-yahud!*" Slaughter the Jews! Slaughter the Jews!

Rocks started to hail down on us as people continued to chant. Ohr shot three bullets straight in the air to startle our attackers. It worked. The people ducked away onto their balconies for enough time for us to get to the top of the valley and onto the main road. Once there, we spotted a group of about ten people bent over picking up stones.

"Stop right there!" I shrieked in Arabic. "Everyone stand up straight with your hands up and come near me slowly. Do you all understand?"

They acted as if they did not. Instead of doing as I asked, they fled up a steep hill towards Idhna. Every one of them ran as fast as their legs could take them. We chased after them briefly before Ohr ordered each of us to fire two bullets in the air. The shots startled the fugitives and all of them stopped in mid-sprint. All of them except for one bold, overweight man wearing a navy-blue sweatshirt who clumsily maintained his stride.

"Get that man in the blue shirt over here now!" I yelled at the crowd of Palestinians facing me.

"What man?" a middle-aged woman wearing a green hijab asked. "There is no man in a blue shirt or a yellow shirt or a red shirt."

"We don't understand," a tall bearded man carrying a construction hat reiterated.

"Are you all blind?" I screamed flabbergasted. None of the people made eye contact with me. They were clearly trying to protect this man for some reason. Maybe he was armed and dangerous. Maybe he was a wanted terrorist they knew would be locked up if caught. "There is a man in a blue shirt running away!" I reiterated. "Get him to come here now or else we will catch him. If we have to catch him, we will arrest him and all of you."

The woman in the green hijab gave in. She immediately turned around and called out to the man.

"Walid!" she screeched. "Come back! Stop running! Please come here now!"

The man in the navy-blue sweatshirt, apparently known as Walid, slowed down and came to standstill about a hundred feet away from us. He stood with his back towards our position for a few moments while he recovered his breath. Then, he gradually turned around and looked straight at us. I couldn't see his facial expression, but I imagined it expressed disappointment, anger, and hatred. Walid wasn't going to get away today. He was going to have to deal with some very annoyed Israeli soldiers who wanted to know why he had run from us and what he had to hide.

"Walid, come down here!" I said in Arabic. "I want to talk to you. Come to me right now!"

Walid came alright, but not how I expected him to. Without any advanced warning, he raced towards us as quickly as he could. As he got closer, I ordered him to slow down and to put his hands up in the air. He didn't listen. He kept on running straight at us.

"Walid, I need you to slow down!" I shouted. "Slow down now."

"Nachshon, the man might be armed!" Ohr warned us in Hebrew. "Keep your sights on the people. If he comes after us I will be the one to fire."

"No, no! Please don't shoot him!" the woman begged. "Don't shoot him, please."

Ohr ignored her plea and pointed his gun right at him. However, as Walid came closer and closer, I noticed he didn't look normal. His eyes were small and upturned, his face was incredibly round, and his mouth was hanging wide open. Clearly, Walid had Down syndrome.

"Ohr, put your gun down," I implored in Hebrew. "Walid is retarded. Walid is retarded."

I understood that Down syndrome and mental retardation were not one and the same. Yet, I didn't know how to say Down syndrome correctly in Hebrew, and I didn't want the guy to get shot because of my inability to translate. Ohr lowered his weapon and Walid's run slowed into a brisk walk. He didn't stop until he stood two feet in front of me with a smile of total innocence plastered across his face.

"Hi, I'm Walid. You want to talk?" he slurred as he extended his hand out for me to shake.

Some of the Palestinians began to smile. So did a few of the soldiers who had their guns pointed at the people. I removed my right hand from my assault rifle and took his hand in mine. Walid then drew even closer and gave me the only hug I ever received from a Palestinian during my service in the IDF. "I am Walid," he repeated. "What's your name? Will you be my friend?"

Not knowing what else to do in that situation, I wrapped my arms around Walid and hugged him back.

"Walid, my name is Michael," I replied in Arabic. "I would be happy to be your friend."

All the Palestinians who'd previously screamed "slaughter the Jews" and all the Israeli soldiers who were ready to kill the Arabs started to laugh. For a moment, it felt like everyone there, Jew and Arab like, appreciated each other's common humanity.

Chapter 18
The Law Isn't Always the Law

Beit Jala, West Bank
April–July 2010

IRONICALLY, THERE WERE OTHER TIMES WHEN JEWS AND ARABS found a common enemy: me.

My platoon eventually joined one of the three veteran companies that made up Nachshon. In May 2010, we were deployed to Beit Jala for a *kav* overseeing a handful of Palestinian towns in the Bethlehem Governorate and Jewish settlements in the Gush Etzion settlement bloc. The Bethlehem Governorate, with its roughly 180,000 Palestinian citizens, and the Gush Etzion settlement bloc, with its 70,000 Israeli Jewish settlers, were literally two names for the same territory. In this region, Palestinian towns and Jewish settlements surrounded each other in all directions. Identifying your location depended on your nationality and/or political opinion.

Weeks after my company arrived in the area, a gang of young Palestinian men was suspected of hurling white plastic bags from their vehicles onto a road just past the entrance to Al-Khader, the last Palestinian town before the Jewish settlement of Efrat. Sometimes these plastic bags contained fruit, vegetables, or empty cans. Other times they contained nothing at all.

Sounds harmless, right? That's exactly what conspiring Palestinians hoped Israelis living in Efrat would think when they carelessly drove their cars over these bags while heading to or from home. Eventually, however, one of these harmless little white plastic bags might have ended up concealing an Improvised Explosive Device (IED), which would detonate if a car drove over it and killed or injured anyone inside.

My commanders didn't believe that the perpetrators were residents of Al-Khader. It seemed more likely that they were Palestinians from a village or clan in dispute with folks from Al-Khader and chose to get back at their adversaries by framing them for a future crime.

To stem the possible placement of IEDs, my company sent squads of four soldiers to Al-Khader's entrance to operate check posts, search car trunks for white plastic bags, and generally keep tabs on the area. Jewish settlers and Palestinians alike behaved as though they genuinely appreciated the reasoning behind Nachshon's presence there. Jewish settlers from Efrat saw us as defending them from potential terrorists and Palestinians living in Al-Khader viewed our being there as preventing their rivals from further harming their interests. Both Jewish settlers and Palestinians rewarded our efforts with food.

"Thank you for protecting the nation of Israel from harm," a young married Orthodox Jewish woman said in Hebrew as she dropped off a pizza for the other soldiers and I to enjoy one night. "You are doing God's work in the land of Israel."

"I thank Allah for every day the army is here in Palestine," an old Palestinian man told me in Arabic right after dawn one morning as he set down a bag of pitas and a bottle of Coca Cola next to my feet. He'd walked all the way from his home inside Al-Khader to drop off his offering. "You do more here today than Fatah ever has."

"Sir, we cannot accept this food from you," I replied to him.

"I don't care. I refuse your refusal!"

So, eat and drink we did, even though it violated army protocol. Thankfully, the pitas and cola weren't laced with poison. If anything, the food gave us more resolve to continue with our mundane mission. We all felt as if we were among friends, and it was difficult to fathom a sudden change in our relationships with either people. Until it happened.

It was a blistering hot afternoon and I was operating the check post with Giddy, Yonatan, and a new squad commander named Ben, a tall Yemenite with dark brown skin and a quiet, cool demeanor. A white

Mazda 3 sedan with a yellow Israeli license plate pulled off the road coming from Efrat and turned onto the narrow path leading to Al-Khader. Inside was a muscular but pot-bellied middle-aged Israeli man with a large knitted kippah covering his head. In Israeli society, wearing a knitted kippah usually indicated support of right-wing politics and of the growth of Jewish settlements in the West Bank. As the driver approached our position, he rolled down his window and greeted us.

"Shalom, soldiers!" he said with a wave and a smile. "Thank you, thank you for being here. I'll see you when I come out."

"Come out of where?" I asked confused.

"Al-Khader! Where else?"

This was unexpected. Despite the warm reception we'd received from Palestinians living in Al-Khader, we couldn't allow an Israeli to enter the town. Territory in the West Bank was divided into Areas A, B, and C. Area A was under the sole jurisdiction of the Palestinian Authority; Area B was ruled by both the Palestinian Authority and Israel; and, Area C was completely controlled by Israel. In late 2000, the IDF officially banned Israelis from entering Area A after several Israelis were kidnapped and murdered there.

Al-Khader was part of Area A and that meant there was no way this kippah-wearing Israeli was getting in. There was even a large red sign warning Israelis in Hebrew, Arabic, and English that, by entering Al-Khader without written permission from Israeli authorities, they were knowingly breaking the law.

"Who cares about the law?" the Israeli man growled. "I need to get my car fixed. My battery's about to die. There's a guy named Mustafa who always takes care of my car. I've been seeing him for more than ten years in Al-Khader."

"Why can't you take your car to an Israeli mechanic?" Ben posed.

"Do you want me to get robbed? The Palestinians will take better care of my car for a better price. You can't go wrong with them."

"And what am I supposed to tell my officer if you go into Al-Khader right now and someone murders you?"

"That won't happen. I have a gun on me. I was a colonel in the IDF for God's sake. Let me in!"

Our new settler friend shifted gears and his car began to slowly inch forward.

"Back your car up now!" Ben commanded.

The man backed up, but he didn't drive off. He turned off the car, stepped outside, got on his cell phone, and made a few calls. Within five minutes, two more Jewish settlers wearing kippahs arrived, as did five Palestinian men who hurried over from Al-Khader. Predictably, they all began talking at once.

"Everyone in Efrat comes to Mustafa in Al-Khader to get their car fixed. What our friend is trying to do isn't unusual!" one of the other settlers, who also carried a handgun, tried to emphasize.

"Without these Jews, I don't have any business. No Jews, no money. I can't work. Please, let me work!" the great Mustafa pleaded with us in Hebrew.

"We will make sure the Jews will be safe in Al-Khader. Nothing will happen to them if we are with them," a younger Palestinian man tried to assure us.

"Could Mustafa fix your car right here so that you don't have to actually go into Al-Khader?" I suggested.

"Impossible! That's totally impossible!" the Israeli with the Mazda 3 in question retorted. "All his tools are in Al-Khader."

"Could you just wait here while he takes your car into Al-Khader?"

"You're telling me I'm supposed to wait outside Al-Khader like a lost donkey? Absolutely not."

Ben walked away to speak about something else over the radio with Nir, our new platoon commander, who'd recently replaced Ohr.

"I am very sorry for the trouble," I told Mustafa in Arabic. Suddenly, his eyes lit up.

"You speak Arabic!" he said joyously to me in Arabic. Everyone there became silent. "And you speak Hebrew. But you have a funny accent in both."

"I'm an American. What can I do?"

"What you can do is help me convince your commander to let us do business. Palestinians and settlers have been working together for years. It's the only way anyone can make any money around here!

Without the Jews, there are no jobs for Palestinians. We need Israeli customers. It is good for business. It is good for peace."

"I understand your situation, but there's nothing I can do. The law is the law," I said. Mustafa threw his hands up in the air and told his Jewish customers what I'd said in Arabic.

"Soldier, you understand the Arabs. Look at me. My name is Moti," the Jewish settler with the car trouble said to me. "It's nice to meet you. I am an Israeli, I am a Jew, I live in a settlement, and I wear a kippah. Do you really think I would be going into Al-Khader if it was really all that dangerous? Surely, you can talk to your commander. Tell him how things really are between settlers and Palestinians around here. We know there's a law. But, in Israel, the law isn't always the law. The law is more of a guideline."

"I can't help you. We have to follow the law."

"Oy!" he lashed out. "You came all the way from America just to make everyone's lives miserable, didn't you? You know Hebrew, you know Arabic, and yet you are the biggest obstacle to peace between Jews and Arabs I've ever met. There will only be peace in this land when Jews and Arabs can get to know each other and do business. Good work, soldier. Because of you, Arabs and Jews will fight for another hundred years."

With that, Moti jumped into his car in a fury and sped off. His two friends from Efrat followed his lead.

"Now I have no business!" Mustafa shouted at me in Hebrew as he trudged back towards Al-Khader with the other four Palestinians. "You are bad for Israel. You are bad for Palestine. You are bad for everybody."

Although I was disappointed to have served as a roadblock to Israeli-Palestinian economic cooperation, it pleased me to see that such relationships between Jewish settlers and Palestinians did exist. Unfortunately, most interaction between Israelis and Palestinians in our region of responsibility were less than friendly.

Rachel's Tomb lies on the outskirts of Bethlehem less than fifteen hundred feet from the edge of municipal Jerusalem. The burial spot of the biblical matriarch Rachel, the site had been venerated as a holy place by Jews, Christians, and Muslims alike for more than 1700 years. Jews come to the grave to pray for fertility, since Rachel was believed to be barren before she gave birth to Joseph and Benjamin. Likewise, Muslims regard Rachel as an Islamic saint. Throughout the nineteenth and early twentieth centuries, the land around Rachel's Tomb was used as a Muslim cemetery in accordance with the belief that being buried near a saint will increase a person's rewards in heaven.

Starting in the mid-1990s, however, Palestinians began launching violent attacks on Jewish worshippers at Rachel's Tomb with stones, Molotov cocktails, and gunfire. In a sharp break from traditional Muslim theology, Palestinian Muslim religious authorities began arguing that Rachel's Tomb was not the grave of Rachel the matriarch, but the burial site of Bilal ibn Rabah, an early follower of Muhammad the Prophet who became Islam's first *muezzin,* the person in charge of calling Muslims to prayer. Subsequently, Rachel's Tomb went from serving as a place of joint Jewish-Muslim spirituality to one of pure contention and conflict. Israel responded by fortifying the area with a twelve-foot-thick concrete barrier and a guard post. Nevertheless, Palestinians continued to assault visitors to Rachel's Tomb as well as Rachel's Tomb itself.

Intelligence reports stated that three of these Palestinians were nineteen-year-old men from the Al-Arroub refugee camp fifteen kilometers south of Bethlehem. Friends who lived in the same neighborhood, they struck their targets as a team.

For example, when a bus full of Jewish worshippers would come to the turnoff point to Rachel's Tomb, one of the three would jump out onto the road to get the vehicle to slow down, swerve, or topple over. The second assailant would then hurl stones at the driver's side window, while the third would throw a Molotov cocktail or two at various parts of the bus before the whole team would flee the scene. None of their attacks resulted in any deaths, but they did manage to knock two bus drivers unconscious, cause considerable damage to the buses themselves, and inflict severe psychological trauma on passengers.

On a dry July night, this neighborhood posse launched its last offensive. Around eight o'clock in the evening, the three threw a hail of Molotov cocktails at the guard post inside Rachel's Tomb before dashing away. As soon as the episode was reported over the radio, Nir barged into my room.

"*Hakpatzah! Hakpatzah!*" he yelled at the top of his lungs as he hit the door with his fist. In the Israeli army, a *hakpatzah* is an emergency call to duty. In this case, it was directed at all members of the rapid response unit, which I and five other soldiers were a part of that night. "Get to the *ze'ev* fast! We had to be at Rachel's Tomb five minutes ago."

When we showed up at the fortified shrine, the attackers were long gone. Protocol meant we weren't allowed to make that assessment until we'd performed a search of the area on foot, even though, at the time of the incident, their identities were still unknown. After our scan yielded no results, Nir ordered our *ze'ev* to travel beyond the West Bank security barrier into Bethlehem with the idea that the culprits might still be running away on foot or searching for public transportation to get home. Regrettably, the only thing of interest we found was an upscale Chinese restaurant with dragon banners covering the outside walls. We returned to our base in Beit Jala empty-handed.

Three hours later everything changed. Nir called the entire platoon into the war room. Every one of us piled in and took seats as fast we could.

"By now, you all know about the event at Rachel's Tomb this evening," he said as he adjusted his eyeglasses. "We may have failed to capture the terrorists responsible at the scene, but army intelligence managed to capture their identities. It was three men from the Al-Arroub refugee camp. They've been wanted by the IDF for a number of attacks. Their names are Ali, Mahmoud, and Ibrahim. We have their photographs and their home addresses. They all live on the same street. We'll be arresting all three of them tonight. We don't have much time. Be ready immediately."

Before exiting the room, every soldier was issued a blindfold, handcuffs, and a fragmentation grenade to keep inside their vests. The entire platoon left for Al-Arroub in two *ze'evs* at a little after one in the morning. Arrests were almost always conducted under the shield of night. It was the easiest time to slip into a Palestinian refugee camp unnoticed, and when a wanted Palestinian was most likely at home.

For most arrests, the platoon split into three groups. One group, commanded directly by the platoon commander, would lead the operation by heading straight for the front door to confront the wanted

Palestinian directly and give him/her a chance to come out peacefully. The two others were led by squad commanders and stationed around the perimeter to seal off any potential escape routes.

As the Arabic speaker, I was nearly always attached to the first group. I was also charged with carrying a special pack containing a sledge hammer, wire cutters, and a crowbar that I would use to open the front door if they refused to let us in.

Joining me and the platoon commander were usually a sharp-shooter who also functioned as a medic, and another soldier who was equipped with a grenade launcher on his M-4 rifle, and about twelve grenades in special pouches wrapped around his legs.

For our triple arrest in Al-Arroub, Nir assigned me to the first group with Alexey and Roman, another Russian-born grenade-shooting specialist. Although he left Russia at the age of one and lived in Israel for nineteen years, Roman still spoke Hebrew with a thick, defiant Russian accent, making him the most culturally Russian person I knew who had grown up in Israel. On the other hand, Alexey, a sharp shooter, left his native Uzbekistan for Israel at the age of ten, spoke flawless Hebrew, but made glaring mistakes in Russian.

When our *ze'ev* reached the outskirts of the refugee camp, we all donned black face masks before putting on our helmets. Our masks were made from wool, which made our heads sweat profusely. Discomfort notwithstanding, the masks kept our identities safe and disoriented the enemy.

We jumped out of the *ze'ev* fifteen hundred feet from the home of our first target, Ali. Jogging in line behind Nir, Yevgeny, and Roman, I was always surprised that towns like Al-Arroub were referred to as refugee camps. When I think of refugee camps, what comes to mind are tin shack shanty towns, tent cities, garbage heaps, and penniless exiles wandering around at all hours searching for a scrap of food and a flicker of hope. I never saw a tent in a Palestinian refugee camp. All the camps I'd been in had paved roads, running water, and reliable electricity. Like all urban environments, the houses and buildings were packed together, but generally in good condition. Most of the buildings had multiple satellite dishes on their roofs and quite a few luxury cars parked out front.

Nir, Yevgeny, Roman, and I advanced up the five steps leading to the white front door of Ali's house. Nir knocked on it five times, while the rest of the platoon remained silent. Nir was told over the radio that a light in a room one story up was switched on. Two little girls were hoisted by adults out the window and managed to spot a few of our soldiers surrounding the building. The girls were pulled back inside and the light went off again. They knew we were there. Nir knocked on the door five more times. No answer. He then gave me the signal to do what I did best: scream.

"Open the door!" I shrieked in Arabic. "Army! Army! Open the door! We know you're inside. Let us in." A woman inside let out a squeal and we heard other people moving around. "I repeat. Open the door. Open the door or we will enter with force!"

They ignored the order, so we were left with no choice but to go in on our terms. Roman pulled out the sledgehammer and handed it to me. Nir, Yevgeny, and Roman moved to my left to give me room to operate. They had their guns ready in case someone inside unleashed a weapon through a crack in the door. I swung the sledgehammer back and smashed it right below the doorknob as hard as I could. The door didn't budge. I swung the sledgehammer again, but this time brought it forward more slowly to get an exact hit on the correct spot. The door slowly creaked open.

A moment later Nir and Yevgeny entered the house, immediately aimed their guns to the sides, and gave Roman and me the signal to follow. All the lights were off, which scared me half to death. Going into a strange house to make an arrest is unnerving enough when you don't know what threat lies behind every corner. Doing so in the dark is worse.

Using the flashlights on our rifles, we checked the first floor for any signs of life. We didn't find any, but we did notice that the living room and kitchen could have come out of any luxury home in any Western country. The leather couches, big screen television, multiple video game consoles, paintings, and state-of-the-art kitchen appliances made the house I'd grown up in America pale in comparison.

Nir and Yevgeny led us up the narrow staircase to the second floor. Before they arrived at the top, a crying woman in a blue hijab hurled a glass picture frame at Nir. It bounced off him and smashed on the concrete floor.

"*Ithaboo illa al-jaheem!*" she screeched as she retreated to a bedroom. Go to hell!

Nir waved me over to reason with her, but before I uttered a word, a light turned on and a man with gray hair wearing a white *jalabiyya* emerged with his hands in front of his face.

"*Ani chaf mi pesha!*" he said calmly in fluent Hebrew. I am innocent. "What do you want from us?"

"Why didn't you answer the door?" Nir snarled. "Where's Ali?"

"We were all asleep. We did not hear you."

"Liar! Where's Ali?"

"Ali is not here. He is in Ramallah with a cousin. Why do you want him?"

"Liar. Get the IDs of everyone in your family and take them all downstairs to the living room."

The man complied. After collecting all the IDs, he, his wife, a different teenage son, and his two younger daughters were escorted by Roman downstairs. His wife continued muttering under her breath in Arabic that we should all go to hell.

The lights were out in every room on the second floor except for the hallway. I asked Ali to come out peacefully in Arabic, but received no answer in response. We swept the parents' bedroom and bathroom first, opening the shower doors, rummaging through the closet, and checking underneath the bed. We then moved on to the younger girls' bedroom and quickly located Ali huddled up inside a laundry basket with a Barney the Purple Dinosaur blanket on top of him. Nir and Yevgeny aimed their guns at him while I provided cover from behind. Shaking with a nervous frown on his face, Ali rose from the laundry basket voluntarily. He was wearing only a white wife-beater shirt and striped gray boxer shorts. I located a bathrobe and slippers in his parents' room to wrap himself in and to protect his feet.

We waited to handcuff and blindfold him until we were out of the house away from his family's view. Nevertheless, as we escorted Ali outside, his mother burst into tears and grabbed him by the shoulders before falling to the ground. One of his younger sisters tugged on the bathrobe

Ali wore with a blank expression on her face, as if she didn't understand what was happening or how she should feel. She glanced up at me with big brown eyes that demanded answers. I had none to offer her.

Once outside, Ali quivered with fright as Roman handcuffed and blindfolded him. I honestly thought the guy was going to vomit. We reunited with our platoon, dumped Ali off to Giddy, and braced ourselves for what lay three doors down at the home of Mahmoud, our second target.

All the commotion from the first arrest woke up the neighbors. As we came towards Mahmoud's front door, people on the roofs began throwing glass bottles and rocks. Two bottles landed right next to my feet before one finally hit my helmet and shattered. The initial sound paralyzed me for a second. I saw a gash on my right forearm with blood staining my uniform, but I couldn't feel a thing due to all the adrenaline. Roman fired a gas grenade at the roof of the building the bottles were coming from. Ali, our blindfolded prisoner, didn't need to see to understand what was going on. Knowing that he had his neighborhood supporting him, he actively encouraged the commotion.

"Wake up, Al-Arroub!" he yelled in Arabic. "The Jews are here. Come out of your houses. Kill the Jews!" He repeated this a couple of times and only stopped when normally gentle Giddy threatened to tape his mouth shut.

While we waited for someone in Mahmoud's house to open the door, I looked up and saw four little kids peeking at us from a window. They laughed and waved as they watched us under assault. One of them gave me the finger. As I stared back at them, I truly wished there was something I could have done to scare them and get them to turn away. But there wasn't. Even children knew that no soldier would shoot them indiscriminately or lay a hand on them because of a little disrespect and provocation.

Mahmoud's parents answered the door appearing just as upset as Ali's. His mother, who did not cover her hair, narrowed her eyes at us as we entered their home with our weapons ready for anything. His distressed-looking father popped a cigarette into his mouth, lit it, and took a seat on a cloth armchair. Pacing around the main foyer and living room were another three worried women, who I took to be

Mahmoud's sisters, and an older man who must have been Mahmoud's grandfather. Mahmoud presented himself shortly after in baggy jeans and a blue Tommy Hilfiger t-shirt. He asked politely if he could return to his room to grab a jacket. Nir gave the okay as long as Roman and I went with him.

We followed him around the corner to his bedroom in total silence with our guns pointed at his back. He turned on the light and fished through his closet. While I faced him, I couldn't stop thinking about the fact that standing only feet away from me was a young man who'd voluntarily chosen to spend his time harming innocent people. On the surface, he seemed nice and normal enough. He lived in a pleasant home, had a supportive extended family, and was clearly well-dressed and well-fed.

What kind of indoctrination could have gotten him to throw away his entire life to go sit in an Israeli jail? Worse, I started to wonder how long he'd be in Israeli jail, what kinds of innovative terrorist techniques he'd learn from other Palestinians in there, and if and when he'd strike again.

We led Mahmoud out the door, handcuffed and blindfolded him, and dumped him onto Yonatan to handle. While we were in the house, other people in the neighborhood came out of their homes and tossed more rocks, bottles, and even a few bricks at the remaining soldiers in the platoon, who responded by having soldiers with grenade launchers on their guns fire more gas and stun grenades at the residents. We regrouped once more and, amid a hail of projectiles, hurried towards the home of Ibrahim, our last target of the night, who lived five hundred feet further down the street.

Personally, I was skeptical we'd catch Ibrahim. Ibrahim must have heard by then that the army had picked up his two buddies and was now on the hunt for him. He'd probably fled to a friend's or different family member's house somewhere. The last thing I expected was for a wide-eyed Ibrahim to willingly open the door to his home and eagerly surrender himself to us. But that's what happened.

Right as Nir, Yevgeny, Roman, and I walked up to his address, a man matching Ibrahim's description opened the door, closed it behind him, and called out to us.

"I am Ibrahim," he said in Hebrew. "I have been waiting for you. Please be quiet. My family is trying to sleep." He put his hands above his head and turned in a circle to show us he was unarmed. Stunned by his behavior, we moved towards him slowly to make sure he wasn't tricking us somehow. "I could not allow my friends to go to prison without me."

Technically, soldiers aren't supposed to converse with their captives. The logic is that no one wants to give a Palestinian any legitimate reason to claim he was physically or verbally abused in custody. But this Ibrahim character, with his fluent Hebrew and enthusiastic demeanor, confounded the soldiers in my platoon. Riding in the *ze'ev* with him on the way to a detention center, Roy asked him where he learned his Hebrew.

"Every Palestinian who's ever worked a day knows Hebrew," Ibrahim responded. "I worked at a gas station."

"You act like you're happy about going to jail. Why?"

"I'll get to learn from the other prisoners how to kill more Jews." The way he said it was so matter-of-fact it was frightening. I knew Roy was aching to sock the guy in the face. We all were. "Hit me if you want to. I can take it. I'd love to tell the judge about it at my tribunal. One day I'm going to find a way to kill you all. I'm not like you. I'm not afraid to die. I'll blow you up the second I get the chance."

Just as with Ali, Giddy ordered Ibrahim to shut his mouth or he'd tape it shut.

"I have one more question for you before we hand you over, Ibrahim," Roy said. "If I add you on Facebook, will you accept me as a friend?"

Ibrahim couldn't help but smile. Every soldier in our *ze'ev* practically gagged from laughter. It was all we could do.

On August 31, 2010, Hamas gunmen shot and killed four Jewish settlers traveling in a car near Hebron. Three of the victims lived in Beit Haggai, a settlement in the Hebron hills. The fourth victim was a young schoolteacher and mother from Efrat, where Nachshon had been operating regularly. Tragically, her husband was one of the first paramedics to arrive at the scene.

That day was a Thursday, the last day of the workweek in Israel, and our platoon had been slated to get the weekend off. After the attack, however, our leave and that of every other combat soldier in the West

Bank was cancelled. We were told we had to remain on duty to provide manpower for an array of other tasks intended to boost security in case of copycats.

One of those tasks was to go into Bethlehem that Friday morning to help the local Israel Border Police unit manage the checkpoint next to the West Bank security barrier that ran along the city's northern border. Although ninety percent of the barrier was a fence, the portion surrounding Bethlehem was a twenty-five-foot concrete wall.

Fridays at the checkpoint were always maddening because thousands of Palestinians tried to get to the Al-Aqsa mosque in time for Friday prayers. Palestinians who successfully passed through the checkpoint and the barrier between four in the morning and noon had permission to travel to Jerusalem, where the mosque was located.

Men and women were split up into separate long lines, with male border police checking the men and female border police checking the women. Due to the terrorist attack the day before, Palestinian men between the ages of fifteen and fifty were banned from crossing.

Since it wasn't always easy to tell how old someone was, and border policemen were inevitably going to make mistakes when verifying the birth years of male Palestinians, five soldiers from my platoon were selected to supply extra sets of eyes. Four of them were called up with a squad commander to guard the area outside the security barrier and check Palestinians before they sought ground transportation.

I was the fifth soldier brought to Bethlehem that day, but I was given a different responsibility. As the Arabic speaker, I was slated to manage a special humanitarian line with Yarden, who had since become my deputy company commander. This humanitarian line allowed Palestinians who were extremely old or in need of immediate medical attention to bypass the checkpoint altogether and head straight for a hospital or doctor's office by taxi. Those Palestinians were supposed to be thoroughly inspected by members of the Palestinian police before being sent to me for a final evaluation. If I deemed a Palestinian ill enough to be let through, I'd give Yarden my recommendation and he would then make the final call.

Very few of the people sent by the Palestinian police deserved to be admitted to the humanitarian line. Some merely walked with a cane, a few complained of dehydration, and one guy thought he was entitled to get through because of a sprained wrist he had in a splint. I turned these people back without hesitation and ordered them to go to the end of the line. If they tried arguing with me, I told them to take it up with the Palestinian police officer who'd let them through in the first place. I wasn't even supposed to let people through with chronic health problems.

"Soldier, please. I really need to go through the barrier right now. I can't go through the checkpoint because I have asthma," an older Palestinian woman in a black hijab explained in Arabic. I was unmoved.

"Are you having an asthma attack right this second?" I asked her without emotion.

"No, but it might come later. I don't feel very well right now."

"Do you need an ambulance?"

"No."

"Do you have a doctor's appointment?"

"No."

"Do you want to see a doctor? I can get you a doctor right now if you would like."

"No, no. No doctor, thank you. That is unnecessary."

"Ma'am, if you don't need an ambulance, you don't have a doctor's appointment, and you don't want to see a doctor, I cannot let you through. Go back, please."

Yarden and I suspected that the Palestinian police deliberately sent us Palestinians they knew had no chance of getting through. It was like a PR stunt to make the Israeli army look bad. Throughout the checkpoint foreign journalists, cameramen, and pro-Palestinian activists from Western countries wandered around waiting to pounce on any morsel of controversy or misconduct by a soldier.

Mass murder was occurring all over Africa, China continued suppressing minorities, and a Sunni-Shia insurgency was engulfing Yemen, and all these foreigners wanted to do was interrogate me for not being more empathetic to Palestinians with bad cases of the hiccups. They seemed to be convinced that *something* was going to happen if they waited long enough for it. When nothing did, they often chose to invent their own controversies.

"This is the humanitarian line? You must be joking!" a tall, blond, male pro-Palestinian activist from some northern European country accused me angrily in English after the woman with asthma left the line. "According to international law, there must be a humanitarian line here. If you do not create a humanitarian line, I will write up a press release of this incident."

"I am the humanitarian line," I said back to him. "Humanitarian cases come through when the Palestinian police let them through. Now, please move off to the side away from the checkpoint."

"I will move from the checkpoint only when I see you giving ailing Palestinians their rights."

Four muscular border policemen who looked ready for some action walked up to us and asked if Yarden and I needed any assistance in dealing with our new friend.

"Move off to the side or these men here will force you off," I told him.

"I will move when I see movement here!" he said.

Alright, I thought. He'd chosen his fate. Lights. Camera. Action. The four border policemen surrounded the man, handcuffed him, and escorted him to the side where he was handed off to other border police-men and taken away from the checkpoint. Two vigilant camera crews filmed the whole incident and followed the blond freedom fighter away.

Even without the pesky foreigners running around, their presence radiated. The section of the security barrier near where Yarden and I stood was covered in political graffiti that was most likely not the work of Palestinian artists.

"Poland 1942. South Africa 1991. Palestine 2007."

"Portugal For Palestine."

"Repression Must End."

Another piece of graffiti read "Palestinian Tiger" and had a cute picture of a tiger's head drawn next to it. Palestinian children pointed it out and giggled. Nobody there seemed to know what it meant or why it had been painted.

Towards the end of the morning, a gaunt elderly woman in a wheel-chair was pushed up to us by her teenage grandson. The woman was covered in blankets and held used tissue papers in her hands. She couldn't even speak. She just looked up at us dazed. Her grandson, a tan young man with a frown on his face, handed me her ID card. This would be a no-brainer. Of course, we would let them through.

"Please let me see your ID as well and then you can go through," I said to the boy in Arabic.

"I don't have it," he responded casually.

"Well then, she can pass but you can't."

This was a standard rule. Every Palestinian, except for small children, was required to present proper identification if they wanted to leave official Palestinian Authority–controlled territory. I also had to verify he was below the age of fifteen.

"My grandmother is sick. I need to take her to Hebron to see a doctor."

"She's allowed to pass. It's you who can't pass until I see your ID."

The grandson stood there silently with whimpering eyes. However, after seeing how unfazed I was by his facial expression, he switched tactics and turned into a pit bull.

"How can you do this?" he screamed at me. "I have to go with her."

"Go back to your house and get your ID! Would you go to the airport without a passport? Get serious. Don't be a fool."

The boy continued to pout when two blonde pro-Palestinian German girls came over.

"Step back and don't interfere!" I said in English before they could get out a word. Then, looking back at the woman's grandson, I said, "Your grandmother can stay here. We'll have people watching over her and we'll give her water and shade. She'll be fine for a half-hour while you run home."

"I live too far away."

"Then how did you bring your grandmother here?"

The grandson stared at me with hostile eyes. I wouldn't budge and he hated me for it. A Palestinian taxi driver standing nearby approached us during our standoff and suggested a solution.

"The woman looks very ill," he began. "I can drive her to Hebron. I can take her to the doctor and bring her back here. Is that good?"

I thought it was. The teenager standing behind his grandmother's wheelchair did not. He scowled at me and, without saying a word, wheeled his grandmother away back towards Bethlehem. The sick old woman dropped tissue paper on the ground as she gazed confusedly all around her. The two German women glared at me in disgust. So did dozens of Palestinians waiting in line.

What the hell did I do? I wanted to shout out to everyone there that I'd just offered to let the old lady pass. Her grandson was the reason she'd turned back. And, if he wasn't to blame, it was the Palestinian police who were at fault. It was they who let the boy through when he failed to show proper ID. It was like all the Palestinians and pro-Palestinian activists there cared more about how they felt about a situation than about what made sense.

While men and women were being checked by border police in their respective lines, a large swath of space between them was left wide open. Shortly before the checkpoint closed for the day, a Palestinian man in his mid-fifties walked right through that area straight towards me. The Palestinian man didn't look like anyone official. His hair and beard were completely gray, and he wore a long-sleeved, button-down shirt and brown khaki pants. But, he walked with a sense of confidence I rarely saw among Palestinian men at checkpoints. It was as if he knew exactly where he was going. And I was in his way.

"Sir, stop right there!" I roared at him in Arabic. "Please move to the side."

The man nodded his head quickly at me as if he knew what I was going to say and immediately started talking.

"Soldier, I am the commander," he declared.

"The commander of what?"

"I am the commander of the Palestinian police in Bethlehem."

"Okay. Then show me your ID."

"I don't have it on me."

"Then I can't let you go past me."

After I told him that, his eyes just about jumped out of his head.

"Soldier, move aside. I have permission to be here."

"How am I supposed to know that? Would you drive a car without any ID? Why should I believe you?"

My obstinate attitude frustrated him. He bit his bottom lip, clenched his left hand into a fist, and nervously wiped the sweat off his brow with his right. Seemingly out of nowhere, the same four muscular border policemen who dragged the blond guy away showed up.

"What's the problem here?" one of them said in Hebrew. Before I had a chance to explain, the other three grabbed the Palestinian and handcuffed him.

"Take your hands off me," he protested in Arabic. "I'm the Palestinian commander."

"Do you have ID?" the one border policeman not holding him down asked in Hebrew.

"I don't have any ID on me."

"Why don't you answer me?" the border policemen asked in Hebrew.

"I did answer you. Now let me talk to that soldier over there. The one that speaks Arabic!" the Palestinian said in Arabic.

This was weird. The Palestinian understood the border policeman's Hebrew and knew full well that the border policemen didn't speak a word of Arabic. Yet he refused to utter any Hebrew. In response, the border policemen hauled the defiant Palestinian off to their commander as he screamed and unsuccessfully attempted to wriggle away from them.

Later, I learned that the Palestinian man had, in fact, been the commander of the Palestinian police in Bethlehem. A man who was supposed to be an example to the Palestinian people arrogantly believed he was above the law and threw a childish hissy fit when he didn't get his way. He could have explained the situation to everyone calmly in Hebrew, gone off to get his ID, and been granted access to anything he pleased.

But no, that was impossible. Instead, he had to wage a battle for pride. His attitude made me cynical about prospects for cooperation between Israelis and Palestinians because his behavior showed that many of the reasons for misunderstanding in the Middle East were trivial and stupid.

Chapter 19
A Final Resolution

Beit Jala, West Bank
July–September 2010

OFTENTIMES, THESE MISUNDERSTANDINGS WERE EXACER-
bated and encouraged by journalists and pro-Palestinian activists from abroad, who deliberately incited dangerous confrontations
between soldiers and Palestinians.

During the summer of 2010 pro-Palestinian activists converged
just hundreds of feet away from our base in Beit Jala to disrupt the
construction of the security barrier Israel began building in 2002.
Although ninety percent of the barrier was a fence, the portion surrounding Bethlehem was a twenty-five-foot concrete wall. The construction workers were almost all Palestinian and the protesters
themselves claimed they were merely invoking their Israeli govern-
ment-protected right to protest. Still, these "peaceful" demonstrations
rarely proved peaceful.

To provide the Palestinian construction workers with a safe work
environment and ensure that no dangerous incidents occurred, Nachshon was required to send twelve to fifteen soldiers to seal off all access
points to the barrier and declare the territory a closed military zone.

Each week, our commanders handpicked soldiers to wake up early,
sit through a briefing, don riot gear and ceramic vests, and confront
the merciless taunting of self-described "peace activists" with nothing
better to do on a Sunday morning.

The day of one such protest in July 2010, Ohad, who was doing a
shift as the daily assignment scheduler, banged on the door to my

room at 6:15 in the morning. Lucky for my three roommates and me, the door to our dilapidated living quarters was missing an outside handle and could only be opened from within. Whenever someone other than a senior commander needed something from one of us they had to ask nicely or else we'd refuse to open.

"Bassin!" Ohad shouted. "Get up. You listening? Wake up."

I did my best not to pay attention. I'd finally fallen into bed at 6:05 am after an eight-hour all-night Jeep patrol. Not one soldier had enjoyed an iota of sleep because Akram, our Druze driver, spent the whole night bickering in Arabic with his fiancée about napkin covers for their wedding.

Druze hold a national pact with the Jewish people, binding males to perform military service just like their Jewish Israeli counterparts. As much as I enjoyed the chance to practice Arabic with Akram, I preferred to avoid the night-time Jeep patrol and didn't feel like hearing arguments about a wedding I would not be able to attend.

I was finally asleep and didn't care if Jesus Christ was coming back to Bethlehem because I'd just spent the whole night making sure the streets were safe even for a Jew like him.

At 6:27 Ohad banged louder. I wanted to hit him again just like I had in basic training.

"Bassin! I will beat you if you don't get up. You have a briefing in thirteen minutes for the protest in Beit Jala. Be in the briefing room on time. *Kibalta?*" You got it?

"*Kibalti.*" I got it. I rose and began to prepare myself for Sunday's circus.

If there was one soldier from my platoon who was scheduled to go to Beit Jala that day, it was the most proficient Arabic speaker, and that was me.

At 6:39 I trudged up the stairs towards the briefing room.

I stepped inside and saw Roman and Alexey already there, leaning against the wall half-asleep, their guns strewn next to them.

Yarden walked in looking noticeably irritated. After every soldier arrived and sat down, a composed, but pissed-off Yarden stood up and commanded everyone's attention.

"I don't know who you ladies think you are," he said. "But I asked everyone to be here at 6:40 sharp. We're starting five minutes late. That means I have five minutes less to brief, you have five minutes less to organize your equipment, and we may be five minutes late getting to the protest."

I didn't quite understand the math and how we lost so many minutes so fast, but I didn't interrupt.

"Time is holy," he went on. "Be here when I tell you to be here. Our task today is clear. We're going to Beit Jala to defend the construction of the security barrier against people who don't understand that good borders make good neighbors."

Yarden was giving the briefing because Hashai, our short, bearded company commander, had already left to pick out points for our perimeter positions. After assigning soldiers to those stations, I waited for personal instructions. Andre nodded in my direction.

"Michael, Alexey, and Roman, listen up," Yarden said. "You three and Andre will confront the protest itself on the main road towards the construction site. You'll place barbed wire blocking off traffic, separating yourselves from any physical contact with the protesters. If they try to push past you, use your riot gear shields to keep them back."

I found it discomfiting that in facing off against angry demonstrators, I'd be carrying an assault rifle but forced to rely on a plastic, armored shield to protect myself.

"There will be absolutely no live fire. You will not discharge your weapons for anything. Even if someone in the crowd has a gun, by no means are you authorized to return fire. We want these protesters to go home pretending they're heroes, not in body bags."

The last thing Israel needed was live video coverage showing Israeli soldiers stupidly drawn into accidentally shooting civilians.

"That being said," Yarden proceeded, "the only person authorized to speak on the megaphone or say anything else is Michael."

All eyes peered at me.

"Get some phone numbers from some ladies!" someone shouted.

"Shut it until I'm finished!" Yarden screamed. "Michael is the voice of Nachshon in Arabic and English. You'll use the megaphone when

Hashai tells you to. No one else says a thing. We're going to do our job and keep the peace. Meeting adjourned. Be ready to leave at 9:00 am sharp."

We departed for the protest on time, which according to Yarden's logic, meant we saved at least five minutes somewhere, I think. We stood on the partially paved road near the protest site, the sun reflecting harshly off the unfinished white buildings. Palestinians gathered on their roof-tops and outside their homes awaiting that day's showdown. I held one end of the string of barbed wire while as Alexey pulled the other end across the road, temporarily blocking off all local traffic. Inconvenienced drivers stopped their cars and turned around long before reaching our location.

Children from the group of houses just beyond us tested their bravery by striding confidently in our direction against their mothers' orders. Their friends peered in disbelief wondering how close their buddies could get to us seemingly vicious soldiers without being shot. These kids believed soldiers took pleasure from shooting small children. It was the national sport for the Zionists, the older ones told them.

The ringleader of the group, a swaggering boy with gelled hair wearing a red polo shirt, stopped a couple of meters in front of me. He was an innocent, defenseless Arab child pitted against me, a heavily-armed monster ready to terrorize the neighborhood. The boy stared at me coldly for a few seconds before running back to his friends to receive a hero's welcome. Where were the cameramen to photograph our standoff and put us on the cover of *Time*?

Ninety minutes later, camera crews arrived and reporters jumped from moving vans. The real photo op was about to begin. The media personnel ran for the hilly, rocky expanse on the left side of the street and quickly assembled their equipment.

"Get into position!" Andre called out from the right. "The crowd is on the move." The four of us stood in formation, backed up by two female Israel Border Police officers in case female activists became unruly.

Just up the street, roughly thirty screaming marchers headed straight for us, a sea of faces looking ready for a confrontation. Hashai paced around flanked by a radioman and a medic. Four other soldiers were positioned to our left in case more demonstrators came from unexpected directions.

I gulped, looked around, and calculated that if the crowd stampeded us, my riot gear shield-wielding left arm would have to push back at least a half a dozen people since my right hand held a gun I wasn't authorized to use.

The group approached our position with a sign that read "Beit Jala Protest Against the Apartheid Wall" in English and Arabic. Hashai pulled me aside and shoved a megaphone into the ceramic vest covering my chest and stomach.

"Handle them," he ordered. I raised the megaphone to my mouth and calmly addressed the group first in Arabic, then in English, and finally in Hebrew.

"Stop where you are. This is a closed military zone. Peaceful protest is permitted. For your own safety, please stay back. Do not touch the soldiers. I repeat, stay back." Inaudible shouts in Arabic drowned out my words. My modest requests seemed to incense the crowd. When I finished speaking, the protesters only chanted louder and crept closer towards us until their shouting mouths were less than a foot away from our faces.

A Palestinian teenage boy taunted me, waving his hands right in front of my face over the barbed wire. He stood next to a brown-haired British female journalist from the Ma'an news agency, a wire service based Bethlehem, and her cameraman. The boy seemed to know the journalist and her cameraman well and glanced at her for approval every few seconds while he screamed epithets at me, trying to get me to snap. The journalist's cameraman recorded us like we were on a movie set.

"Hit me in the face, you stupid soldier. Hit me for the camera. Please, please!" the Palestinian teenager yelled in Arabic trying to create a media spectacle for that evening's news. He smiled and pointed to his journalist friends. "Hit my hand! Hit my finger. Come on! Do as I say, you Jewish dog."

I stared at him blankly while he screamed. Flickers of spit struck my cheeks. He wasn't scared of me. He knew my gun and ammunition amounted to little more than stage props. A younger boy standing next to him waved a sign in my face. A picture, obviously doctored using Photoshop, displayed images of dead bodies strewn along the security barrier. The caption above the photo read "Apartheid Wall Kills Little Childs Again." Clearly, it had not been put together by a native English speaker.

I looked to my left and saw protesters attempting to push past Roman at the edge of the barbed wire and shove the border police-women out of the way. Three Palestinian men and two European women moved at once to blow past our forces and provoke a reaction from us. An older Palestinian man disrespectfully tapped Roman's helmet to divert his attention, pushing his head backwards and yelling at him in English. "You should die!" he shouted. "Leave this place, you evil soldier."

"You'll be sorry if you touch that soldier again!" I threatened in English.

The border police-women intercepted the two European women, warning them to stay back. One of them, an Irish brunette with thick black glasses, walked directly into the police-women's path. Before making physical contact with her, the bespectacled brunette purposely fell backwards, as if she were trying to snag a Best Actress award.

She wailed, "The occupation oppresses me too! Today I also stand with Palestine." Actually, she was sitting for Palestine, I thought. Hashai tapped my shoulder and grabbed the megaphone from me.

"These people are getting out of control," he said. "Help Roman block the opening next to the barbed wire and stand by for my response."

I ran towards Roman just as a militia of angry demonstrators prepared to stampede him. Seven men, including several Europeans, dodged photographers to get around the barbed wire and hurled themselves at Roman and me. I bent myself forward slightly as one man lunged at my riot gear shield. He knocked me back a little before punching the upper part of the shield with his fist.

Three stones whizzed at me from the far side of the road, two striking my ceramic vest and another directly hitting my helmet. I glanced over at Alexey and Andre and saw they were also targets of these peaceful rock-throwing vigilantes. A European man with dreadlocks wearing a t-shirt that read "Anarchists for Palestine" called out at us.

"I hope every stone hits you in the face," he blurted out. Two Palestinian teenagers he was standing next to were preparing to throw more stones our way. I'm sure they appreciated his encouragement.

Reasoning with these people was less than effective. A different response, one that didn't need a megaphone translation, was needed to prevent this scene from devolving into a full-fledged riot.

Hashai lobbed a stun grenade at the feet of the seven-man mob next to Roman and me. The activists scrambled backwards before the non-lethal weapon detonated with a bright flash and a loud bang. The intent of a stun grenade is to disorient a person with light and sound. It can blind someone for up to five seconds and disturb the fluid in their inner ear to the point where they can't walk properly. Hashai threw another grenade at the rock throwers, sending four masked men wearing red-checkered *keffiyehs* sprinting to a safe point behind the other protesters.

For a few moments, everything stopped. The chanting ceased and all the hecklers went quiet. I thought maybe the jolt of our crowd-control grenades had shocked the protesters into quitting their antics and coaxed them into behaving like the peace seekers they professed to be.

But then, like meteors falling from the sky, more stones shot from behind the crowd. A few missed our positions while others bounced off the shields we held up to protect ourselves. Hashai's radioman fired a tear gas grenade from the grenade launcher attached to his M-4 that landed directly behind the rock throwers' point of origin. Hazy gas spewed out of the canister sending dozens of people fleeing, desperately trying to escape the effects.

"You're acting like Nazis. You're acting like Nazis!" the Irish brunette alleged, still seated firmly on the ground as if she were too oppressed to move.

"If we were acting like Nazis, you wouldn't have the guts to talk back," I snapped.

Hashai calmly walked towards me, glanced at the mayhem, and pulled out a hand-held tear gas grenade to quell the stoning once and for all. This would teach them to heed my calls for peaceful protest, I thought. The grenade firmly in his right hand, he twisted the pin clockwise with his left, and flicked the grenade at the ground where the remaining protesters stood. Soon enough, it would all be over.

Still, a hand-tossed gas grenade generates far less fear to intercept than a hot projectile shot from a gun. The second the canister smacked the ground, a mustachioed, balding Italian photographer with arm pit stains the size of pitas became a hero. He picked up the grenade with his right hand, tossed it up in the air, and in a failed attempt to drop kick the device, managed to knock it just a few inches with his shin so it became entangled in the barbed wire. Women screamed, the mustachioed dunce moaned woefully, and I took a deep breath and saw something they didn't. The canister's opening was pointed directly at Alexey and me.

In basic training, commanders force new recruits to do twenty pushups and sing the Israeli national anthem inside a tent filled with tear gas to get them used to the feeling if they're ever exposed. But I learned in those first moments that singing about the longing for Zion in an enclosed environment is nothing compared to a full canister's compressed contents spraying mightily at your face.

We stood in place because we had no permission to leave. Demonstrators could have run through our blockade if we'd fled. So, Alexey and I planted ourselves together, confident we'd overcome the uncomfortable effects and show the world Israeli soldiers never falter. We were the ultimate fearless warriors laying our lungs on the line for our country. That brave idealism lasted all of seven seconds.

I lost track of time and the world became a haze. I couldn't help but cry in front of the cameras. Four cameramen excitedly zoomed in on my panicked face as if what had happened at the protest was something important and newsworthy. My vision blurry, I could barely make out the figures standing only a few feet away. It was difficult to focus on my media image as I knelt on the gravel road, gasping for breath, feeling like I was about to die.

I loosened the strap of my helmet and dropped my riot gear shield. Although nothing of consequence had ensued at the protest site, television crews from around the world took photographs that presented me as the gun toting, mucus spouting, occupation enforcing, disheveled Israeli soldier I appeared to be.

I rubbed my eyes with my hands, but that only intensified the burning. I seized and twitched from stress. I stared up at the July sun beating down and felt completely vulnerable despite the M-4 semi-automatic assault rifle still dangling around my neck.

To my right I could vaguely make out my brother-in-arms, Alexey, suffering a similar reaction, coughing and crying incessantly. Roman stood assertively off to the left. He had managed to avoid the brunt of the blast and now made sure no activists came near his wounded comrades.

"*Eto piz`dets*," Roman yelled in Russian. This is fucked up.

Cheers erupted meters away. The cackles of adolescent Palestinian boys and the female European "peace activists" they wanted to screw filled my ears.

"The occupation has collapsed. The occupation has fallen!" a blonde-haired European woman yelled as she pointed her index finger straight at me. A Palestinian man in his twenties translated it into Arabic. Before I knew it, a few dozen people were laughing at my pain.

When my eyes stopped tearing and I mustered the strength to rise to my feet, my lungs still burned, but I saw a much emptier scene. Most protesters had run for the hills, probably due to the fear of eventually feeling how I looked, but the British woman and her cameraman from Ma'an stood just a few feet away from me with the Palestinian teenage boy who'd taunted me earlier. My face was still flowing with mucus and tears and I continued to cough.

"I'm ready for my close-up," I joked snidely in English before I coughed again. The British woman laughed.

"Why do you speak English and Arabic so well?" the British woman asked as her cameraman videotaped our conversation.

"I'm originally American and I've spent a lot of time in the Arab world."

"You've been to the Arab world?" she asked incredulously.

"Yeah, all over really. Egypt, the UAE, Lebanon. But that was before I was in the army."

"So then why do you hate Arabs so much?"

"Why do you assume I hate Arabs? I don't hate Arabs."

"Then why are you participating in the crimes against the Palestinians we filmed here today?"

"What are you talking about?"

"Today you and the other soldiers used lethal force against peaceful protesters."

"What are you talking about? This was nothing more than a movie set. We were standing here when the protesters got violent and started throwing stones at us while you videotaped. We fired tear gas back at them to keep everything under control."

"Your commander fired tear gas on innocent people. Tear gas can cause an allergic reaction that can cause sudden death. The footage we have shows everything. When it goes up, people are going to know what happened here."

"I'm the one who ate all that tear gas, not the protesters. And video footage can tell whatever story a narrator wants them to tell. Even lies like the ones you're spewing."

The cameraman immediately lowered his camera.

"I'm no liar!" she yelled back at me.

"Well, you're certainly no journalist. The scary thing about you is that it sounds like you believe your own lies. Or maybe you're just paid to."

"Call our coverage lies all you want. The world will believe our lies."

Unfortunately, I had to agree with her. I'd long known that when it came to the conflict between Israel and the Palestinians, the facts themselves didn't matter much to the rest of the world.

During my last few weeks in the IDF, I contemplated all that I'd seen and experienced in the various places and situations I'd put myself in throughout the Middle East. It bothered me deeply that from the time I first took an interested in the Arab-Israeli conflict when I was four-teen years old, it looked no closer to being brought to a final resolution. In my lifetime, peace never seemed further away. This made it difficult for me to remain hopeful or to feel like any of my actions made the slightest difference.

The day before I was supposed to return my equipment and sign my release forms, Nir found me in the lounge on base watching a movie, and told me he was sending me on one final assignment.

"They're tearing down the checkpoint inside Bethlehem next to the security barrier and building a new one that's more efficient," he stated. "You and Ben are going to stand in front of the construction site in the city and make sure cars and people don't get near it. You'll be there for eight hours."

"So, for eight hours we'll just be standing in the sun wearing ceramic vests and helmets?" I asked.

"Glamorous for your last day, isn't it?" he joked. Very funny, I thought.

The next morning on our way to Bethlehem, we stopped at a gas station to buy some snacks. Ben and I split eight *burekasim*, a Middle Eastern pastry with a cheese, potato, spinach, or pizza filling. Once we moved past the construction site and stood firmly in front of Bethlehem's maze of human and automobile traffic, we chowed down.

After my third *burekas*, I could eat no more. Not wanting to let my final *burekas* go to waste, I glanced at a young Palestinian boy with black hair, smooth tanned skin, and a bored look on his face. He was lounging with his backpack in a lawn chair next to a place called the Christmas Tree Restaurant, an eatery for tourists with Christmas decorations up year-round.

I called out to the boy in Arabic and asked him if he was hungry. Nonchalantly, he rose from his chair, walked up to me, and I handed him the bag. He looked inside, picked out a *burekas*, and put it in his mouth. He stepped back a few feet away from Ben and me and stood there silently. Something about his demeanor suggested he was comfortable with us. After he finished off the *burekas*, he stared at my rifle.

"It's an M-4. Would you like to hold it?" I asked him.

His eyes lit up and he nodded his head up and down.

"Can I really?" he asked excitedly.

"No," I said as I swayed my head back and forth. "You can't. I was joking. For that you'd have to be in the Israeli army. Would you like to join the Israeli army?"

My words may have been ridiculous, but I was just having a little fun. Besides, the boy seemed to get my sense of humor.

"I'll think about it," he replied sarcastically. He told me his name was Ahmad and that he was eleven years old. I told him I had a bunch of friends named Ahmad. He seemed puzzled by this. "You are a funny soldier," he said to me. That I was.

My new friend Ahmad couldn't just stand around and schmooze with me all day. He had to work. Despite being a Muslim, in his backpack were hundreds of postcards with pictures of Bethlehem on them and key chains painted with Christian symbols. Every time a tourist walked past, he and a few younger boys would run after them and pitch their merchandise.

"Mister! Mister!" they'd shout out in English at their much taller potential customers. "How are you? I am fine. Good morning. Buy! Buy!"

Their sales strategy was ineffective. When the boys shouted, "Buy! Buy!" the tourists thought they were saying "Bye! Bye!" and waved at them as they walked away. After watching this happen a couple of times, I called the boys over and gave them some tips on salesmanship.

"When you talk to these tourists, don't shout. They won't like it," I said. "Try saying in English, 'Excuse me. I have very pretty things. Very cheap. Thank you.'"

I predicted that they'd completely mangle the English. But if they were polite enough, I figured, tourists might warm up to them and buy something. Before Ahmad and his little friends went back out to try again, they all gave me high fives.

Around lunchtime, the owner of the Christmas Tree Restaurant approached Ben and me and asked us for permission to let a tour bus full of American Evangelical Christians park down the road near the building. The area he asked for was technically a little too close to the construction site, but he promised it would be parked there for only an hour. Ben and I didn't object.

When the tour bus pulled up and the tourists emerged, I pushed Ahmad and company to introduce themselves and offer up their souvenirs. I said hello to the tourists as well and assured them that Ahmad and his friends' merchandise was the best they'd find in town. The tourists happily bought up postcards and key chains before sitting down to eat. This made Ahmad's day profitable. The owner of the restaurant grabbed my arm and cheered heartily to all the tourists in English, "You see. There is peace in the Holy Land."

Later in the day, as Palestinians returned to Bethlehem after working outside the city, Palestinian taxi drivers jammed the streets in hopes of shuttling them home. Gradually, they came closer and closer to the no parking area Ben and I were guarding. When we ordered drivers to turn around and park somewhere else, they agreed only after an irritating amount of arguing.

"I just want to park my car here for five minutes while I drink coffee," one driver insisted.

"I need my car here for the shade!" another reasoned.

"I don't care what you need!" I'd shout back. "Move your car now or I'll get a bulldozer here to move it for you."

Having to nag people began to frustrate Ben and me. Luckily, some friends of ours came to help us out. Spread out across the street, Ahmad and his companions voluntarily waved at cars to turn around and actively blocked them from parking in forbidden spots. The kids yelled vehemently at drivers who refused to listen. All in all, the boys seemed to enjoy being our little assistants. It was probably the first time in their lives they'd ever tasted any kind of authority. While I certainly thought the scene was entertaining, not everyone was amused.

"Hey!" a dusty-blonde woman with a British accent called out in English as she watched from her spot near the Christmas Tree Restaurant. "You leave those children alone. How dare you use them to enforce the occupation? What kind of people are you? You're turning Palestinian children against their own people."

"Shut up. Shut up!" the owner of the restaurant cried out in English at her. "Leave the soldiers alone. You don't know what you are saying. These are good soldiers."

"They are forcing children to work for them!" the woman argued.

"No! The children are their friends. You don't understand nothing. Go back to your country. Don't come here to make more problems for Israel and Palestine! Now shut up!"

The woman muttered under her breath and trotted off.

At five o'clock on the dot, I told Ahmad that I had to leave Bethlehem and go back to my army base. If he wanted, I offered, he could walk Ben and me over to the security barrier and see us off. He shrugged his shoulders and marched along with us.

"Michael, next time you are in Bethlehem, will you come in normal clothes or will you still be in the army?" he asked.

"Normal clothes. I'll be done with the army tomorrow," I told him.

"So, you'll come back soon?"

"I don't know. I don't know if it's safe for me to come back here."

"Because you are a Jew?"

"Because I am a Jew."

It seemed Ahmad appreciated the tragedy of the situation and accepted it. I was wrong.

"Michael, if I come visit you in Israel, will you keep me safe?" he asked.

"Of course, I will," I said. "You are my friend."

"Then, if you come visit me in Palestine, I'll keep you safe. You are my friend."

Touched, a feeling of relief passed over me that I hadn't felt in a long time, and I couldn't help but smile. Ahmad's simple offer of friendship showed me that whatever differences in nationality or religion we may have had, two people recognizing each other's common humanity can break down any barrier.

I shook Ahmad's hand one last time and slipped through the partition of the security barrier. Shortly thereafter, someone flipped the switch closing the barrier shut. Ahmad waved his hand at me smiling until we couldn't see each other anymore. I looked at the concrete wall separating Israelis from Palestinians and me from Ahmad, and I thought to myself that maybe there is hope for peace in the Middle East after all.

Terms/Glossary

Abaya—(Arabic) A loose, ankle-length black robe worn by Arab women in the Persian Gulf. Worn with a shayla.

Adhan—(Arabic) Muslim call to prayer.

Al-Hamdu-Lilaah—(Arabic) Praise God.

Allah—(Arabic) God.

AUC—American University in Cairo.

AUS—American University of Sharjah.

Baksheesh—(Arabic) Tip, bribe.

Burekas—(Hebrew) A Middle Eastern breakfast pastry.

CID—Criminal Investigation Department. UAE secret police.

Dabka—(Arabic) Traditional line dance popular in the Arab world.

Dirham—(Arabic) Currency of the United Arab Emirates.

Diwali—(Sanskrit) A Hindu festival known as the "Festival of Lights."

Eid al-Fitr—(Arabic) The three day festival at the end of Ramadan that marks the cessation of fasting. Commonly known as just "Eid."

Fuṣḥā—(Arabic) Modern Standard Arabic, literary Arabic.

Garin—(Hebrew) Seed. May refer to a collective group.

Ghutrah—(Arabic) White headdress that accompanies the kandura.

GW—George Washington University.

Halal—(Arabic) Permissible according to Islam. Similar to kosher.

Haram—(Arabic) Forbidden.

Hijab—(Arabic) Traditional head covering Muslim women wear to cover their hair in front of heterosexual men.

IDF—Israel Defense Forces.

IED—Improvised Explosive Device.

Iftar—(Arabic) The evening meal marking the end of each fast day during Ramadan.

Inshallah—(Arabic) God willing.

Intifada—(Arabic) Uprising.

Isha prayer service—(Arabic) The fifth daily Musli prayer service.

Jalabiyya—(Arabic) A loose-fitting, ankle-length, long-sleeved robe worn by men predominantly in Egypt, Sudan, and surrounding countries.

Jinn—(Arabic) Supernatural creatures mentioned in the Qur'an that occupy a parallel world to that of mankind.

Kandura—(Arabic) A white, ankle-length, long-sleeved robe worn by men in the UAE. Accompanied by the ghutrah.

Kav—(Hebrew) Line. Refers to a military tour of duty.

Keffiyeh—(Arabic) Traditional male Arab headdress.

Kippah—(Hebrew) A skullcap worn by Jewish men.

Maghreb prayer service—(Arabic) The fourth Muslim prayer service of the day.

MSA—Modern Standard Arabic. Known as fuṣḥā in Arabic.

Mukhabarat—(Arabic) Secret police.

Nu—(Hebrew) Slang for "get on with it."

Qur'an—(Arabic) The central religious text of Islam.

PCC—Palestinian Cultural Club of the American University of Sharjah.

PLO—Palestine Liberation Organization.

Ramadan—(Arabic) Holy month in Islam. Muslims fast during sun up.

Rosh Hashanah—(Hebrew) Jewish holiday celebrating the Jewish new year.

Sayeret—(Hebrew) General term for special forces unit in the IDF.

Shahada—(Arabic) The oath converts to Islam take declaring their faith God and in Muhammad, his messenger.

Shahid—(Arabic) Martyr.

Shayla—(Arabic) Black headdress worn by Arab women in the Persian Gulf. Worn with an abaya.

Shaytan—(Arabic) Satan.

Shikara—(Kashmiri) A small wooden boat paddle-boat used in northern India.

Souq—(Arabic) Market.

Sura—(Arabic) Term for chapter in the Qur'an.

Taqiyah—(Arabic) Skull cap popular in the Arab world.

UAE—United Arab Emirates.

Wahhabism—(Arabic) Staunchly conservative Islamic sect prominent in Saudi Arabia.

Wahhabi—(Arabic) A follower of Wahhabism.

Walla—(Arabic) By God.

Yalla—(Arabic and Hebrew) Let's go.

Ze'ev—(Hebrew) Wolf. Refers to the Wolf Armored Vehicle, an Israeli-made heavily armored crew carrier that seated up to twelve.

Zebiba—(Arabic) Raisin. Refers to the prayer bump, a clump of calloused skin, on the foreheads of some Muslim men.

Acknowledgments

GETTING *I AM NOT A SPY* WRITTEN AND OUT TO THE WORLD would not have been possible without the immense support and assistance of numerous people.

First and foremost, I would like to thank my parents, Jeff and Gayna Bassin, and my brother, Eddie Bassin, for providing me with so much support and encouragement throughout this entire process. Your faith in me really gave me the confidence that writing *I Am Not a Spy* was important and that I could do it.

I would like to thank Barbara Selya, my first editor, who always believed in my writing, asked me the best questions, and helped me think through my process; Leah Scheier and Justus Weiner, who dedicated much of their time to reading all my new chapters as I wrote them and who provided me with constant positive and constructive feedback; the late Dr. Barry Rubin and Haim Watzman, for giving me valuable insights into the business aspects of being an author; Bea Opengart, who critically edited my manuscript line-by-line to make it ready to present to people outside my initial circle; Rachel Schneider, who designed my book cover; and to Allie Maldonado, Bruce and Karen Gowen, Liesel Jones, and the rest of the WiDo Publishing team for making the publication of this book a reality.

The moral support and companionship I received throughout this process from the following people was truly invaluable. Thank you so much Guy Wiener, Joe Barkawi, Gregg Roman, David Bratslavsky, Eliram Nof, David Maze, Andrea Nadel, Jamie Dalin, Aaron Hoffman, Jacob Bourgeois, Sasha Appatova, Nili Gubin, Jeremy Gubin, Isaac Selya, Pinchas and Nomi Landis, Amy Frankel, Aaron Frankel, Ilana

Frankel, Talia Schmidt, Edan Razinovsky, Nathaniel Rabkin, Ariel Steinberg, Dan Schwartz, and Avi Egron. You are all amazing friends!

Lastly, I'd like to thank all the people I met and interacted with during my experiences in the Arab world and serving in the Israeli army. Thanks for all the material, as well as for the good times and the bad.

About the Author

MICHAEL BASSIN HAS TRAVERSED THE MIDDLE EAST AS A STUdent, soldier, journalist, businessman, and adventurer. His Middle
East expertise has made him a
frequent speaker and consultant to organizations, corporations, and politicians with
an interest in the region. A
graduate of The George Washington University, Bassin is a
partner in a Tel Aviv-based
technology company and also
provides regular commentary
to news outlets on the Middle
East. He has been featured on
Public Radio International,
the BBC, the *Times of Israel,*
and the *Jerusalem Post.* He
lives in Ramat Gan, Israel.

CPSIA information can be obtained
at www.ICGtesting.com
Printed in the USA
FFOW05n0029250917